More Praise for *Enough Is Enough*

"If you think there must be a better way forward than more of the same, *Enough Is Enough* is the book for you. It tackles our affluenza, our growth fetish, and our wildly unfair social order head-on and points the way to a better place. I highly recommend it."
—**James Gustave Speth, former Dean, Yale School of Forestry and Environmental Studies; cofounder, Natural Resources Defense Council; and author of *America the Possible***

"Walking in the steps of E. F. Schumacher, Ivan Illich, Thich Nhat Hanh, and of course the great religions, perhaps best represented by the Taoists and Buddhists for their ethics of simplicity and not grasping always for more, Rob Dietz and Dan O'Neill bring the modern dilemma of growth and the dogma of 'more is better' into the contemporary reality. *Enough Is Enough* offers important new thinking on how to address the planet's most urgent crises and establish an economy that achieves true biological sustainability and shared wealth for all."
—**Doug Tompkins, founder, The North Face; cofounder, Esprit; and President, Conservation Land Trust**

"In *Enough Is Enough*, Dietz and O'Neill have accomplished something special. They offer a hopeful and practical plan for righting the economic and environmental ship, and they do it in a very engaging way. I hope my colleagues in Parliament are paying close attention to the ideas in this book—I know I am."
—**Caroline Lucas, Member of the UK Parliament and former leader of the Green Party of England and Wales**

"*Enough Is Enough* is the most accessible and well-argued case for a sustainable economy I've ever read. With stories, examples, and plenty of data, but without the tedium of academic writing, Dietz and O'Neill dismantle the most persistent of all economic myths—that economies must grow without limit to provide full employment and improve the conditions of the poor. They explain how a different economic model can meet our needs without irreversible damage to the life-support systems of our planet. I can't recommend a book more highly."
—**John de Graaf, coauthor of *Affluenza* and *What's the Economy for, Anyway?***

"Rob Dietz and Dan O'Neill have written the most readable description of the fundamental problems with the 'growth at all costs' economic paradigm and how focusing on 'enough' material consumption can make room for all the other things that contribute to human well-being. If you've had enough of the crazy economics of growth for the 1 percent at the expense of well-being for the 99 percent and the planet, then this is the book for you."
—**Robert Costanza, Professor of Sustainability, Portland State University, and Editor-in-Chief, *Solutions* magazine**

"What scope is there for moving beyond today's increasingly desperate pursuit of conventional economic growth? For politicians to carve out some real space in that territory, they need to immerse themselves in the 'beyond growth' debate, and there is no better way of doing that than familiarizing themselves with the ideas and insights in *Enough Is Enough*."

—**Jonathon Porritt, founder and Director, Forum for the Future, and author of *Capitalism as If the World Matters***

"This is the book we've all been waiting for as we watch the growth economy collide catastrophically with the constraints of a finite Earth. It's a clear, informed, practical, honorable, and witty guide to where we are, where we need to go, and how to get there. If you are one of so many of us who are bewildered or despairing about the fate of the future, this is the book that will give you an energized sense of purpose and reason-based hope."

—**Kathleen Dean Moore, Professor of Philosophy, Oregon State University; author of *The Pine Island Paradox*; and coeditor of *Moral Ground***

"Two qualities that allegedly distinguish humans from other species are high intelligence and the capacity for forward planning. At no time in history has there been a greater need for these qualities or less evidence of their existence—the global human enterprise is on a trajectory toward social and ecological collapse. But clear-thinking, forward-looking people can take heart. *Enough Is Enough* provides both the unassailable rationale and the visionary plan the world needs to live well, more equitably, and sustainably within the means of nature."

—**William Rees, Professor of Public Policy and Ecological Economics, University of British Columbia, and cocreator of the ecological footprint**

"*Enough Is Enough* should be required reading for every economics student as an antidote to the wacky assumption that a finite planet can support infinite growth. Dietz and O'Neill show the importance of growing long-neglected human capacities for creativity and compassion rather than obsolete economic indicators like GDP. Whether or not you agree with all their proposals, this highly readable and provocative book will profoundly expand your thinking about what's possible."

—**Michael Shuman, author of *Local Dollars, Local Sense* and *The Small-Mart Revolution***

"Saying 'Enough!' is heresy in our growth-based economy, in which more, bigger, and faster are the only permissible goals. The authors not only offer specific policy proposals for an economy of sufficiency but argue persuasively that we could all be happier by exiting the growth treadmill. This is a book that every American should read."

—**Richard Heinberg, Senior Fellow, Post Carbon Institute, and author of ten books, including *The End of Growth***

"In an age where economic orthodoxy remains all too fixated on growth, *Enough Is Enough* offers a thoughtful contribution to creating an ecologically sound economic system that meets human rather than financial needs."
—**Gar Alperovitz, Professor of Political Economy, University of Maryland, and author of *America Beyond Capitalism***

"*Enough Is Enough* is a fine addition to the growing literature on how society might change its ways and actually avoid catastrophic collapse. Everyone should read it and become more aware of the scale of the human predicament, the economic insanity that is largely responsible for it, and the desperate need for dramatic change."
—**Paul Ehrlich, Professor of Population Studies, Stanford University; President, Center for Conservation Biology; and coauthor of *The Dominant Animal***

"In the sixth century BCE, Lao Tzu wisely wrote that the person who knows that enough is enough will always have enough. It has taken us twenty-six centuries of apparent progress to forget that, and it is high time to relearn it. Rob Dietz and Dan O'Neill provide a compelling case for us to do just that. As well as an accessible guide to the growth-and-greed economy, they offer a series of simple and achievable steps to replacing it with something sustainable and infinitely more satisfying."
—**Molly Scott Cato, Professor of Strategy and Sustainability, Roehampton University, and author of *Environment and Economy***

"The notion that economic growth is the enemy and not our salvation still has about it more than a whiff of heresy. Not after this admirably lucid book, though. Dietz and O'Neill argue persuasively that adopting a governing axiom of 'enough' rather than 'more' will help make our politics more democratic, our economy more egalitarian, and our society more creative—and then they show how to bring it about. How bad is that?"
—**Marq de Villiers, journalist and author of thirteen books, including *Our Way Out***

"*Enough Is Enough* is an extremely important and timely work. Herman Daly and his many colleagues have masterfully articulated the importance of creating a new economy that can enhance rather than destroy our natural resources and, at the same time, improve our quality of life. Now, in *Enough Is Enough*, Rob Dietz and Dan O'Neill have laid out a pragmatic scenario that describes, in great detail, how we can all become involved in making that economy a reality in the communities and on the planet in which we live. This is a must-read for all those interested in their own welfare and that of their children and grandchildren."
—**Frederick Kirschenmann, Professor of Philosophy, Iowa State University, and author of *Cultivating an Ecological Conscience***

"Rob Dietz and Dan O'Neill are leaders in the new generation of thinkers and doers on the steady-state economy. In *Enough Is Enough* they present a compelling case for why 'enough' should replace 'more' as the goal of a successful economy, and they provide information, arguments, and examples to show how our lives would be much improved by such a fundamental change."

—**Peter Victor, Professor of Environmental Studies, York University, and author of** *Managing Without Growth*

"This wonderful book focuses on the heart of the matter: our world is being destroyed because, as a society and an economy, we have become oblivious to limits of every kind—limits of resources on a finite earth, limits of planetary carrying capacity, and most of all limits to human material aspirations. This book is a great primer for systematically unpeeling the dominant insanity of our time and then waking up and doing something to change it. It should be required reading for every high school and college class devoted to the economics of sanity—and every government official as well."

—**Jerry Mander, author of** *In the Absence of the Sacred* **and** *The Capitalism Papers*

"*Enough Is Enough* provides a preview of the new world we must inevitably enter. Although Dietz and O'Neill pay careful attention to real-world limits to growth, these two visionaries show us how we can lead happy lives by embracing an economy of enough."

—**Richard Lamm, former Governor, Colorado**

ENOUGH IS ENOUGH

ENOUGH IS ENOUGH

BUILDING A SUSTAINABLE ECONOMY
IN A WORLD OF FINITE RESOURCES

Rob Dietz and Dan O'Neill

Berrett–Koehler Publishers, Inc.
San Francisco
a BK Currents book

Berrett-Koehler Publishers, Inc.
235 Montgomery Street, Suite 650
San Francisco, CA 94104-2916
Tel: (415) 288-0260   Fax: (415) 362-2512   www.bkconnection.com

Ordering Information
Quantity sales. Special discounts are available on quantity purchases by corporations, associations, and others. For details, contact the "Special Sales Department" at the Berrett-Koehler address above.
Individual sales. Berrett-Koehler publications are available through most bookstores. They can also be ordered directly from Berrett-Koehler: Tel: (800) 929-2929; Fax: (802) 864-7626; www.bkconnection.com
Orders for college textbook/course adoption use. Please contact Berrett-Koehler: Tel: (800) 929-2929; Fax: (802) 864-7626.
Orders by U.S. trade bookstores and wholesalers. Please contact Ingram Publisher Services, Tel: (800) 509-4887; Fax: (800) 838-1149; E-mail: customer.service@ingrampublisherservices .com; or visit www.ingrampublisherservices.com/Ordering for details about electronic ordering.

Berrett-Koehler and the BK logo are registered trademarks of Berrett-Koehler Publishers, Inc.

Printed in the United States of America

Berrett-Koehler books are printed on long-lasting acid-free paper. When it is available, we choose paper that has been manufactured by environmentally responsible processes. These may include using trees grown in sustainable forests, incorporating recycled paper, minimizing chlorine in bleaching, or recycling the energy produced at the paper mill.

Library of Congress Cataloging-in-Publication Data
Dietz, Rob.
  Enough is enough : building a sustainable economy in a world of finite resources / Rob Dietz and Dan O'Neill. — First Edition.
    pages cm
  Includes bibliographical references and index.
  ISBN 978-1-60994-805-4 (pbk.)
  1. Sustainable development.   2. Consumption (Economics)—Environmental aspects.
  3. Economic development—Social aspects.   4. Economic development—Political aspects.
  I. O'Neill, Daniel W., 1977–   II. Title.
  HC79.E5D547 2012
  338.9′27—dc23   2012039714

ISBN: 978-1-60994-805-4

First Edition
18   17   16   15   14   13   10 9 8 7 6 5 4 3 2

Cover design by Cassandra Chu   Cover art from Veer, © Szasz-Fabian Jozsef
Cartoons: Polyp (polyp.org.uk)   Figure 15.1 © Alexander A. Sobolev/Shutterstock.com

Produced by Wilsted & Taylor Publishing Services
Copyediting: Nancy Evans   Design: Yvonne Tsang
Proofreading: Melody Lacina   Indexing: Andrew Joron

CONTENTS

PART III: ADVANCING THE ECONOMY OF ENOUGH

FOREWORD

I have long wanted to write a book on the subject of "enough" but never did. Now I don't have to because Rob Dietz and Dan O'Neill have done it in a clearer and more accessible way than I could have. Therefore it is a special pleasure for me to write a foreword calling attention to their important contribution.

Enough should be the central concept in economics. *Enough* means "sufficient for a good life." This raises the perennial philosophical question, "What is a good life?" That is not easy to answer, but at a minimum we can say that the current answer of "having ever more" is wrong. It is worth working hard and sacrificing some things to have enough; but it is stupid to work even harder to have more than enough. And to get more than enough not by hard work, but by exploitation of others, is immoral. Living on enough is closely related to sharing, a virtue that today is often referred to as "class warfare." Real class warfare, however, will result not from sharing, but from the greed of elites who promote growth because they capture nearly all of the benefits from it, while "sharing" only the costs.

Enough is the theme of the story of God's gift of manna to the ancient Hebrews in the wilderness. Food in the form of manna arrived like dew on the grass every morning and was enough for the day. If people tried to gather more than enough and accumulate it, it would spoil and go to waste. So God's gift was wrapped up in the condition of enough—sufficiency and sharing—an idea later amplified in the Lord's Prayer, "give us this day our daily bread." Not bread for the rest of our lives or excess bread with which to buy whatever luxuries we may covet, but enough bread to sustain and enjoy fully the gift of life itself.

This story from Exodus has parallels in the thoughts of the pioneer ecological economist and Nobel Prize–winning chemist Frederick

Soddy. Soddy observed that humanity lives off the revenue of current sunshine that is gathered each day by plants with the aid of soil and water. Unlike manna, some of the sunshine was accumulated and stored by geologic processes, and we have consumed it lavishly with mixed results. Today we also try to accumulate surplus solar income and exchange it for a permanent lien on future solar income. We then expect this surplus, converted into debt in the bank, to grow at compound interest. But the future solar-based revenue, against which the debt is a lien, cannot keep up with the mathematics of exponential growth, giving rise to debt repudiation and economic depression.

For the Hebrews in the wilderness the manna economy was designed with "enough" as a built-in feature. Our economy does not have that automatic regulation. We have to recognize the value of enough and build it into our economic institutions and culture. Thanks to Dietz and O'Neill for helping us do that.

HERMAN DALY
Professor Emeritus
School of Public Policy
University of Maryland

PREFACE

The numbers are telling us something:

- 7 billion people on earth, with 2.7 billion scraping by on less than $2 per day.
- 394 parts per million of carbon dioxide in the atmosphere, threatening to destabilize the global climate.
- $15 trillion of public debt in the United States, an unfathomable sum of money to be paid back by the next generation.
- 2 percent of adults owning more than half of all household wealth in the world.
- 400 ocean zones devoid of life, with the dead zone in the Gulf of Mexico estimated to cover almost as much area as the U.S. state of New Jersey.

Hidden in these numbers are stories of real people and real places in real trouble. And perhaps the most important number of all is *one*—one single blue-green planet with finite resources that we all must share.

But how do we share this one planet and provide a high quality of life for all? The economic orthodoxy in use around the world is not up to the challenge. The core of this orthodoxy is a strategy that has ensnared all nations, from China to Chile, from the United States to the United Arab Emirates, from Switzerland to Swaziland. That strategy, the pursuit of never-ending economic growth, has become dysfunctional. With each passing day, we are witnessing more and more *uneconomic* growth—growth that costs more than it is worth. An economy that chases perpetually increasing production and consumption, always in search of *more*, stands no chance of achieving a lasting prosperity. The 7 billion of us have to do better, and we'd better do better soon.

We need to find ways to reverse the climate change we've set in motion and halt the extinction crisis. At the same time we have to eradicate poverty and erase the divide between the haves and the have-nots. Now is the time to change the goal from the madness of *more* to the ethic of *enough*, to accept the limits to growth and build an economy that meets our needs without undermining the life-support systems of the planet. The good news is that ideas for creating an ecologically sound economy are emerging from all corners of the world. In fact, the desire to assemble a cohesive set of such ideas formed the motivation for this book.

Enough Is Enough was conceived as a collection of policy proposals for achieving a prosperous, but nongrowing economy (also known as a steady-state economy). The book sketches a plan for solving the sorts of social and environmental problems described by the numbers above. Such a plan cannot flow from one or two minds. Indeed, much of the information on these pages stems from workshops, presentations, and discussions that took place at a remarkable conference held in Leeds, U.K., during the summer of 2010. Participants at the Steady State Economy Conference offered a wealth of ideas, and these ideas form the core of this book. The conference concentrated on tough questions about how to build a better economy and tasked the attendees with generating viable answers.

It's a hopeful assignment, this business of figuring out how to change the economic paradigm from *more* to *enough*. If we can successfully harness our know-how for the job of remaking our economic institutions, we'll commence a process of healing—healing degraded ecological systems, healing relationships with our neighbors, and healing the lives of people who have been left behind by the current economic system. Historians will mark the effort as a turning point, a singular and triumphant achievement shared by all.

ROB DIETZ, *Corvallis, Oregon, United States*
DAN O'NEILL, *Leeds, United Kingdom*

Note to the reader: This book is a collaborative work, but sometimes you will encounter the pronoun "I" in the text. In such cases, the "I" refers to Rob Dietz. The purpose of these first-person accounts is to help describe concepts in an accessible way.

[PART I]
QUESTIONS OF ENOUGH

[CHAPTER 1]
HAVE YOU HAD ENOUGH?

A person who knows that enough is enough will always have enough.

LAO TZU (SIXTH CENTURY B.C.E.)

A game of checkers offers very little insight into how to solve the world's intertwined environmental and social problems, or so I thought. In one particular game, my opponent opened with a series of reckless moves, placing checker after checker in harm's way. When I jumped the first one and swiped it off the board, I briefly wondered if I was being lured into a trap. But it was just a fleeting thought. After all, my opponent was only five years old.

I was playing against my daughter. She had just gotten home from her kindergarten class, and I was giving her a few strategy pointers from my limited bag of tricks. Her moves showed some modest improvement, but after a while, we both lost interest in the game. Besides, there are other fun things you can do with checkers, like seeing how high a tower you can build. At first, we were fast and free with our stacking—we even plopped down two or three checkers at a time. But as the tower grew, we changed our approach. With the light touch and steady hands of a surgical team, we took turns adding checkers one by one to the top of the stack. By this point, our formerly straight tower had taken on a disconcerting lean. On our final attempt to increase its height, the mighty checker tower reached the inevitable tipping point and came crashing down to earth. Like a reporter interpreting the scene, my daughter remarked, "Sometimes when things get too big, they fall."

I sat back amid the pile of checkers scattered on the floor and smiled. With a simple observation and eight words, she had managed to sum up the root cause of humanity's most pressing environmental and social problems. Even a partial list of these problems sounds grim:

- Greenhouse gas emissions are destabilizing the global climate.
- Billions of people are living in poverty, engaged in a daily struggle to meet their basic needs.
- The health of forests, grasslands, marshes, oceans, and other wild places is declining, to the point that the planet is experiencing a species extinction crisis.
- National governments are drowning in debt, while the global financial system teeters on the verge of ruin.

People desperately want to solve these problems, but most of us are overlooking the underlying cause: our economy has grown too large. Our economic tower is threatening to collapse under its own weight, and beyond that, it's threatening the integrity of the checkerboard and the well-being of the players. The economy is simply too big for the broader social and ecological systems that contain it.

That's a strong indictment against economic growth, but (as we'll see in the next chapter) this indictment is backed up by scientific studies of environmental and social systems. The evidence shows that the pursuit of a bigger economy is undermining the life-support systems of the planet *and* failing to make us better off—a grave situation, to be sure. But what makes the situation even more serious is the lack of a viable response. The plan being transmitted from classrooms, boardrooms, and pressrooms is to keep adding more checkers to the stack.

The model of *more* is failing both environmentally and socially, and practically everyone is still cheering it on . . . it almost makes you want to climb to the top of the highest building and shout, "ENOUGH!"

Crying out in such a way expresses intense frustration at the seemingly intractable environmental and social problems we face, but it also carries the basic solution to these problems. By stopping at *enough* when it comes to production and consumption in the economy, instead of constantly chasing *more*, we can restore environmental health and achieve widespread well-being. That's an incredibly hopeful message, but it opens up all sorts of questions. What would this economy look like? What new institutions would we need? How would we secure jobs? This book attempts to answer these and related questions by providing a blueprint for an economy of *enough*, with detailed policies and strategies for making the transition away from *more*.

Before diving into the science (Chapter 2) that clarifies why *enough* is preferable to *more*, it's worth thinking about it from a commonsense perspective—perhaps even incorporating the wisdom of a checker-stacking kindergartner. More is certainly a good thing when you don't have enough. For instance, if you can't find enough to eat, then more food is better. If the alarm wakes you up before you've gotten enough sleep, hitting the snooze button and resting for a few more minutes feels great. If you didn't study enough to pass an exam, then spending more time hitting the books would have been useful. But what about times when you do have enough? Eating more food leads to obesity. Sleeping too much could be classified as a medical condition. Studying more could mean missing out on other things in life. More, then, may be either helpful or harmful, depending on the situation, but enough is the amount that's just right.

People often overlook this relationship between *more* and *enough*, especially in economic affairs. It took me a long time, a lot of dot-connecting, and even some soul-searching to get it. My path to understanding began years ago in an improbable place.

When I was a kid living in the sprawling suburbs of Atlanta, Georgia, I had a poster taped to the wall of my bedroom. In the background of the poster, a gaudy mansion sits on a seaside cliff. The light at dusk bathes the scene in a soft, orange glow. A walkway curves down from the mansion to a huge garage that takes up the whole foreground. The taillights of five luxury cars (a Porsche, a Ferrari, a Mercedes, a BMW, and some other fancy ride that I can't recall) stick out from the arched openings of the garage. Scrawled across the top of the poster is the title: "Justification for Higher Education."

The strangest thing about this poster was that I didn't find it strange at all. The culture—my culture—is largely about owning things, and the more the better. The prospect of owning a big house and an expensive car or two seemed like a valid reason for attending college. My cluttered closet, which sat right next to the poster, provided further illustration of the culture. The entire closet floor was covered with Rubik's Cube–style puzzles, Star Wars action figures, and other plastic ghosts of Christmas past. Like a fish that pays no attention to the fact that it's swimming in water, I was swimming in a consumer culture and had no idea of its existence. This culture, which values owning and consuming over doing, being, and connecting, goes hand-in-hand with an economy that pursues *more*.

One day, having resolved to clean my room, I stared at the mess in my closet, and something clicked into place. I realized that I received precious little joy from all these things. Their novelty had long since worn off, and now I was just spending time shuffling them around when I could be doing something else—anything else! When I finally took the sensible step of giving the stuff away, I felt lighter and freer. I felt as though I had enough.

A few years later when I went to college, I majored in environmental studies. But, worried that I wouldn't be able to find a high-paying job to "justify my higher education," I also majored in economics. In truth, I was hoping to combine lessons from the two fields—to use the tools of economics to fix environmental problems. And what problems they were! Climate change, degraded water and air quality, persistent toxic substances, loss of soil productivity. These are what E. F. Schumacher called "divergent problems,"[1] meaning (among other things) that you couldn't solve them overnight with a couple of tweaks to the system.

In contrast, the economics program seemed to gloss over the problems. Environmental issues barely figured in the discussion, and social problems, such as poverty and inequality, received only slightly more attention. The problems that we did study, such as how to forecast future prices and smooth out business cycles, mostly came with stepwise prescriptions. You supposedly could solve these problems with a few tweaks to the system (as well as some nearly incomprehensible mathematics).

I had a tough time trying to apply economic methods to environmental problems, both inside and outside of academia. Admittedly some of the fault lay with the practitioner, but I found economics (at least the economics I was learning) to be ill-equipped to deal with the divergent problems of the day. I don't mean to be overly harsh. The discipline definitely contributes some useful tools and helpful ways to analyze worldly matters, but I mostly failed when I tried to apply its lessons.

When faced with failure, it's helpful to get a fresh perspective. Author, farmer, and activist Wendell Berry offers an outstanding piece of advice for how to do that. He maintains that you're unlikely to solve big problems by talking about them remotely. You have to see them for yourself. He says, "[I]t is in the presence of the problems that their solutions will be found."[2] Later, when I was working for the U.S. Fish and Wildlife Service, I got a chance to follow Berry's advice. That's when the landscape taught me something important about *enough*.

Bosque del Apache, a wildlife refuge in central New Mexico, is an enchanting place. On winter mornings, as the desert sun rises over the San Pascual Mountains and illuminates the marshlands along the Rio Grande River, tens of thousands of waterfowl take to the skies. The immense flocks of snow geese and sandhill cranes are quite a sight, and so are the flocks of binocular-toting bird enthusiasts. These visitors are able to encounter wildlife on a scale that's become rare these days.

It can be a magical experience for visitors, but in a way they're deceived. The birds are present, so the food and other resources they need must also be present. But the refuge provides adequate resources only through careful management by a dedicated staff. The natural functioning of the Rio Grande River, which forms the backbone of the refuge, is long gone, taken by dams and diversions for irrigation. Floods, the major driver of the ecosystems that provide for the birds, no longer occur at their historical scale and frequency. Refuge managers, biologists, and other staff find ways to work the land and water to provide enough resources. In some cases, they try to mimic conditions that would have occurred naturally. For example, they use pumps and diversion channels to flood fields and create temporary wetlands. In other cases, they grow corn and other crops to supply bird food. Without these interventions, the flocks would be much smaller, and might not even spend the winter at Bosque del Apache.

The problem is that the modern landscape lacks a set of interconnected, highly functional conservation areas, mostly because society has appropriated so much land and wildlife habitat for economic purposes. Intensive refuge management may be the best option for conserving wildlife under such circumstances, but this approach amounts to triage. We have chosen to apply bandages (i.e., intensively managed refuges) on the landscape to stop the bleeding (i.e., habitat conversion, species extinctions, and declining ecosystem function). However, as any good doctor knows, preventing disease or trauma is much more effective than treating symptoms after the damage has been done. Preventive medicine in this case calls for balancing the amount of economic activity with the amount of wilderness preservation—a clear example of the principle of *enough*.

I've learned a lot by roaming places like Bosque del Apache, and I wish I had the powers of observation to unlock more of their wisdom. But most of my progress toward the destination of *enough* has come from people as opposed to places. I met one such person, Brian Czech, while I was still working at the Fish and Wildlife Service. Brian is an avid "wildlifer" and an even more avid "enougher." He takes issue with economic growth—well, at least the continuous pursuit of economic growth. When you first meet him, he's quick to ask what you think about "the economic growth issue."

In the work leading to his doctorate, he analyzed the causes of species endangerment. It turned out that the causes were, as he puts it, a *Who's Who* of the American economy. Agriculture, mining, urbanization, logging, tourism, and other sectors of the economy were the culprits behind habitat loss and exotic species invasions that were wiping out native species. Once Brian understood this, he began researching the conflict between growing the economy and protecting the environment. This research led him to another teacher.

Herman Daly is an economist who is known around the world for his analyses and writings on economic growth and human development. His intellectual curiosity and tenacity have turned him into something of a salmon, swimming against the mainstream economic current. Despite many years fighting the misguided pursuit of economic growth, he's managed to avoid cynicism. In person and in prose, he conveys a heartfelt desire to create an economy that cares for both people and the planet.

I first met Herman at an academic conference where I acquired his book (new at the time), *Ecological Economics: Principles and Applications*,[3] which he co-wrote with Joshua Farley. I proceeded to read it from cover to cover. I'm well aware that reading an economics textbook for enjoyment constitutes bizarre behavior. But it was a revelation. I kept asking myself, "Where was this information when I was in college?" Brian opened the door to a new world where I questioned my economic assumptions, and Herman filled that new world with a vision of a sustainable and fair economy—what he called a "steady-state economy." I wanted to be a part of developing and promoting that vision.

Soon after, I agreed to help Brian run an organization he had established, and I became the director of the Center for the Advancement of the Steady State Economy. Thankfully, its name is usually abbreviated to CASSE (rhymes with classy). CASSE's purpose is to help people understand why continuous economic growth is impossible and undesirable, and to promote the steady-state economy as a positive alternative.

Since you can already read Herman's books or visit CASSE's website to find out more about the concept of a steady-state economy, what's the purpose of this book? To answer that question, I need to introduce one more character. Dan O'Neill, my coauthor and good friend, is an ecological economist working at the University of Leeds in England. Early in my tenure with CASSE, he became the director of our European operations.

In June 2010, Dan and I found ourselves sitting side-by-side in his office at the university. Tired and grouchy from being trapped under the fluorescent lights on a delightful day, we were trying to sketch an outline for a report to transmit the wealth of information in front of us. The day before, we had achieved a great success. In partnership with Economic Justice for All, a discussion forum of scholars and activists based in Leeds, we had organized and run the first-ever Steady State Economy Conference. The conference brought together academics, business leaders, politicians, activists, the media,.and the general public to explore the steady-state economy as an ecologically and socially responsible alternative to economic growth.

Both Dan and I were already admirers of Herman Daly's work, but we had been asking ourselves for some time how a steady-state economy would work in practice. Herman had previously identified the main problems with pursuing continuous economic growth, and he had described a broad vision of an alternative economic system. But we were hungry for more details—specifically, the policies and transition strategies that would turn his vision into a reality. That's why we had decided to work together on the conference and report. We hoped to understand for ourselves, and help others understand, what a steady-state economy would mean in practice.

Months later, with too many late nights to recount, with plenty of arguments over content, and with outstanding contributions from numerous scholars, we released our report.[4] The information collected at the conference and compiled in the report provides the backbone of this book.

You probably have some of the same concerns as we do about the environment and the economy. We're not pessimists, but with all the disturbing facts that confront us, it's hard to avoid feeling worried about the future we face. Yet there is still hope in the midst of such worries. Once we put aside our obsession with growth, we can focus on the task of building a better economy. At the Steady State Economy Conference, Tim Jackson (the author of a brilliant book entitled *Prosperity without Growth*[5]) provided a much-needed rallying call. He said:

> Here is a point in time where our institutions are wrong. Our economics is not fit for purpose. The outcomes of this economic system are perverse. But this is not an anthem of despair. It's not a place where we should give up hope. It's not an impossibility theorem. The impossibility lives in believing we have a set of principles that works for us. Once we let go of that assumption anything is possible.[6]

This book tries to provide a new set of principles that *can* work for us. We don't want to mislead you into thinking we have a precise set of directions for fixing everything that's wrong with the world—after all, the economy and the ecological systems that contain it are highly complex. We do, however, have an economic plan that can help move humanity toward a better future where sustainable and equitable human well-being is the goal, not economic growth. Successful implementation of this plan rests on three requirements:

1. **Widespread recognition that our planet is finite.** Humanity (along with all the other species here) draws life and comfort from a limited pool of resources. Recognition of this fact requires us to change the way we regard our relationship with nature, especially within our economic institutions.
2. **Practical policies for achieving a steady-state economy.** A set of well-conceived steady-state policies can replace and outperform the obsolete growth-oriented policies in use today. But people need a strong sense of these new policies before they'll be willing to embrace them.
3. **The will to act.** The economic changes that are required won't materialize on their own. We must dismantle the prevailing

institutions and policies that have produced a destructive and unfair economy. At the same time, we must initiate and nurture the required changes.

This book is organized around these three requirements. If you're already on board with the first one, you may recognize some familiar ideas in the next two chapters. Even so, it's worth spending some time considering the problem of "too much" before jumping to the solution of "enough." But the purpose of this book (in fact, the feature that sets it apart from others) is to describe how to establish a prosperous yet nongrowing economy. This is not a book that focuses on problems while relegating solutions to the last few pages.

That said, Part I, *Questions of Enough*, is more about *why* than *how*. It's where we summarize some of the scientific evidence that condemns the pursuit of continuous economic growth. Part I also considers what constitutes desirable levels of population and consumption, and then makes the turn toward *how* by describing the defining features of a steady-state economy.

Part II, *Strategies of Enough*, provides solutions—an escape route from the perpetual growth trap described in Part I. It's the part of the book that explains how, in a steady-state economy, we can:

- Limit the use of materials and energy to sustainable levels.
- Stabilize population through compassionate and noncoercive means.
- Achieve a fair distribution of income and wealth.
- Reform monetary and financial systems for stability.
- Change the way we measure progress.
- Secure meaningful jobs and full employment.
- Reconfigure the way businesses create value.

Taken together, the policies described in Part II form an agenda for transforming the economic goal from *more* to *enough*. But these policies will sit on the shelf unless we can gain extensive support for, and concerted action toward, achieving an economy of *enough*.

Part III, *Advancing the Economy of Enough*, provides the call for action. This part of the book contains ideas for moving past the culture of consumerism, starting a public dialogue about the downsides of growth and the upsides of a steady-state economy, and expanding cooperation among nations. All this discussion leads up to the presentation of an economic blueprint that summarizes the components and steps needed to build a steady-state economy.

This blueprint offers hope at a time when we need it most. It provides a viable way of responding to the profound environmental and social problems of our era. The ever-present drone of what we can't do has become both tiresome and unproductive. The time has come to figure out what we can do. We can build a better economy. We can meet our needs and care for the planet at the same time. We can live balanced lives, including time for the occasional game of checkers. This is *our* checkerboard, after all, and we don't have to play by the old rules anymore. Let's get to it. Enough is enough.

[CHAPTER 2]
WHY SHOULD ENOUGH BE THE GOAL?

*Anyone who believes exponential growth can go on forever
in a finite world is either a madman or an economist.*

KENNETH BOULDING[1]

To appreciate why an economy based on *enough* is worth striving for, it is useful to examine the failings of an economy that forever chases *more*. It's no secret that the dominant economic philosophy of modernity is *more*—more people and more production, more money and more consumption. Employees try to earn more income, business managers try to report more revenue on the balance sheet, and politicians try to ensure that the economy churns out more goods and services. On the surface, *more* seems like a good idea. For an employee, more money can mean financial security; for a business manager, more revenue can result in a promotion; and for a politician, more national income can generate votes in the next election. But if you dig beneath the surface, you begin to uncover the fatal flaws of *more*.

One person who has dug deeply is Jack Santa-Barbara. The story of his career serves as a personal case study for choosing *enough* instead of *more*. After earning a doctorate in psychology and working in academia for a while, he founded Corporate Health Consultants (CHC), a company with a mission to reduce stress on working people and help them improve their mental health. His company succeeded in both achieving its mission and turning a considerable profit. But money was never the motivation for Santa-Barbara. He says, "I've taken on work in my

15

career only because I thought it was useful and interesting," a sentiment that's supported by his determined pursuit of other interests.[2]

For example, he made volunteer trips to Nicaragua with International Physicians for the Prevention of Nuclear War, an organization that won the Nobel Peace Prize in 1985. Those trips intensified concerns he had about economic development as practiced in the West. Not one to ignore these concerns, he waded into the literature on sustainable development, including a book given to him by a friend: *For the Common Good*,[3] written by Herman Daly and John Cobb, Jr. Santa-Barbara says, "I had to read it a couple of times. The ideas needed to incubate for a while. That book laid out a radically different worldview." This worldview is based on themes from the emerging field of ecological economics, which accepts that there are limits to economic growth and questions the dominant philosophy of *more*.

Santa-Barbara was hooked—he saw promotion of ecological economics as the most useful way he could spend his time. "I wanted to get involved in ecological economics . . . but CHC was growing like stink, and I couldn't do both. I knew the business would survive without me, so I followed my passion and took a leap." He sold CHC, and since then has undertaken projects to help people understand the failings of *more* and the virtues of *enough*.

Jack Santa-Barbara made a profound transformation in his own life. He could have followed the path of *more* and kept growing his business. He could have pursued more money and more prestige, but something told him that path wouldn't lead to his desired destination. What exactly did he intuit? What's wrong with the philosophy of *more*, especially when applied to the economy as a whole?

In the remainder of this chapter, we explore the downsides of continuous economic growth, which fall into two broad categories:

1. **Environmental.** An economy that forever chases *more* is destined to fail environmentally as it exhausts natural resources and exceeds ecological limits.
2. **Social.** Diminishing returns to growth mean that, after a point, *more* fails to improve people's lives.

THE ENVIRONMENTAL FAILURES
OF ECONOMIC GROWTH

The main problem with pursuing never-ending growth stems from the fact that the economy is a subsystem of the biosphere. All of the inputs to the economy come from the environment, and all of the wastes produced by it return to the environment. As the economy expands, it consumes more materials and energy, and emits more wastes. But since we live on a finite planet, this process can't go on forever. Like an inner tube inside a tire, the subsystem can only grow so large compared to the system that contains it.

The size of the economy is typically measured using *gross domestic product* (GDP). GDP is the total amount of money spent on all final goods and services produced within a country over the course of a year. Since one person's spending is another person's income, GDP is also the total income of everyone in the country. GDP functions as an indicator of the overall level of economic activity—of money changing hands. Economic growth, as reported in the media at least, refers to GDP growth, which is essentially an increase in the amount of money changing hands.

A helpful place to turn for a long-term perspective on GDP growth is the work of economic historian Angus Maddison. During his distinguished career, Maddison compiled a remarkable data series on population and GDP starting in the year 1 c.e. and running to 2008. A graph of population and GDP per capita drawn from his data tells a compelling story (Figure 2.1).

For most of human history, the size of the economy was small compared to the size of the biosphere. But over the last hundred years or so, this balance has changed remarkably owing to the increase in the number of people in the world and the growth in each person's consumption of goods and services.

Between 1900 and 2008, world population increased from 1.5 billion to 6.8 billion people—more than a factor-of-four increase. At the same time, GDP per capita increased from $1,260 to $7,600—a factor-of-six increase. The result is that world GDP increased by an astounding factor of more than twenty-five over the last century, from about $2 trillion to $51 trillion (and this is after adjusting for inflation).[4]

On its own, an increase in GDP would not be a problem, except that economic activity is tied very closely to energy and resource use. As GDP increases, the economy requires more energy and resources, and produces more wastes. While Maddison's work provides a picture of the phenomenal growth of GDP, the work of ecological economists provides a picture of the growth in material and energy use that has accompanied it. As a result of GDP growth, humanity now uses eleven times as much energy, and eight times the weight of material resources every year as it did only a century ago (Figure 2.2). And most of this increase has occurred in the last fifty years.[5]

The connection between GDP and the use of materials and energy raises a subtle but important point. When we discuss "economic growth" in this book, what we're really concerned with is not GDP growth *per se*, but the increase in material and energy use that comes with GDP growth. Ultimately, the flow of materials and energy is what impacts ecosystems, not the exchange of dollars and cents (although the latter drives the process).

What is the environmental upshot of this growth? Plenty of evi-

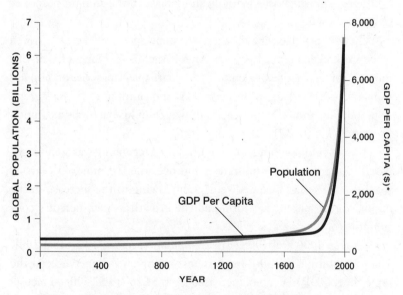

*GDP per capita is adjusted for inflation and expressed in 1990 dollars.

FIG. 2.1. Global population and GDP per capita have both grown exponentially, with the fastest growth occurring over the last two hundred years. SOURCE: see note 4.

dence suggests that the global economy is now so large that it is under-mining the natural systems on which it depends. This evidence presents itself as a wide range of global environmental problems: climate change, biodiversity loss, stratospheric ozone depletion, deforestation, soil degradation, collapsed fisheries—the list goes on.

In a landmark study published in 2009, Johan Rockström and his colleagues at the Stockholm Resilience Centre showed that the economy is placing an excessive burden on the biosphere.[6] In reaching their conclusion, the researchers analyzed nine planetary processes that profoundly influence life on earth:

1. Climate change
2. Biodiversity loss
3. Nitrogen and phosphorus cycles
4. Stratospheric ozone depletion
5. Ocean acidification
6. Global freshwater use
7. Changes in land use
8. Atmospheric aerosol loading
9. Chemical pollution

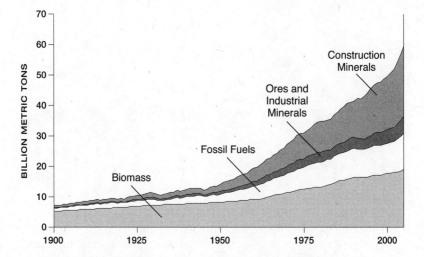

FIG. 2.2. Humanity's use of materials (including minerals, fossil fuels, and biomass) has increased steeply in the last fifty years.
SOURCE: see note 5.

Where sufficient data allowed, the authors of the study estimated how far humanity could go in altering these processes and still avoid dangerous levels of disruption. They were able to define "safe operating boundaries" for the first seven processes in the list above. A safe operating boundary is a sort of safety threshold—stay below it, and humanity incurs a low risk of abrupt and hazardous environmental change; go beyond it, and humanity faces a high risk. For three of the planetary processes (climate change, biodiversity loss, and the nitrogen cycle), humanity is now exceeding the planet's safe operating boundary, and by a large margin in some cases (Figure 2.3). The potential consequences are severe: the authors warn that transgressing one or more of the planetary boundaries could lead to catastrophic changes at the continental to planetary scale.[7]

Other analyses, such as those conducted by the Global Footprint

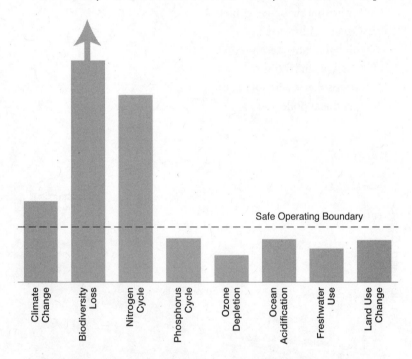

FIG. 2.3. Humanity is exceeding the safe operating boundary for three planetary processes: climate change, biodiversity loss, and the nitrogen cycle. Biodiversity loss is so far beyond the safe operating boundary that there's not enough space to draw it on this chart. Note that the safe operating boundary is measured differently for each planetary process. SOURCE: see note 6.

Network, corroborate the Rockström study. The ecological footprint is a measure of how much biologically productive land and water area a population requires to produce the resources it consumes and absorb the wastes it generates.[8] According to the latest data, humanity's ecological footprint is 50 percent larger than global ecosystems can accommodate.[9] This situation is called "ecological overshoot," and it's akin to living in debt (Figure 2.4). We can only continue to consume at our current rate by liquidating the planet's natural resources or overwhelming its waste absorption capacities. For example, we can cut forests faster than they can grow back and emit carbon dioxide faster than it can be absorbed by oceans and forests. Although we can behave in this way for a short time, ecological overshoot ultimately depletes the resources on which our economies and societies depend.

Indicators like the ecological footprint and scientific analyses like the planetary boundaries study suggest that the global economy has become too large for the encompassing biosphere. So long as this situation continues, we are risking environmental catastrophe. Even if we manage to avoid environmental collapse, the steady depletion of resources threatens to reduce the long-term carrying capacity of the planet, and with it the capability of future generations to flourish.

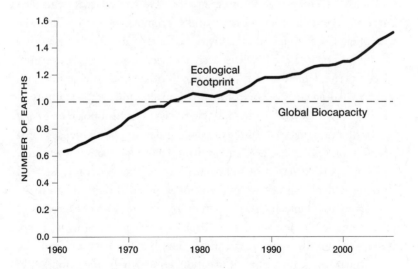

FIG. 2.4. Humanity's ecological footprint surpassed the capacity of global ecosystems to regenerate resources and absorb wastes in the mid-1970s. Since then, we have been living in "ecological overshoot." SOURCE: see note 9.

This unsettling state of affairs is causing some well-known advocates of economic growth to question their long-held views. Robert Solow, who won the Nobel Prize in economics in 1987 for his theories on economic growth, has said, "It is possible that the United States and Europe will find that, as the decades go by, either continued growth will be too destructive to the environment and they are too dependent on scarce natural resources, or that they would rather use increasing productivity in the form of leisure."[10] Economic journalist Thomas Friedman questions growth further. He asks, "What if the crisis of 2008 represents something much more fundamental than a deep recession? What if it's telling us that the whole growth model we created over the last 50 years is simply unsustainable economically and ecologically and that 2008 was when we hit the wall—when Mother Nature and the market both said: 'No more.'"[11]

The final year of Angus Maddison's dataset (2008) coincided with the implosion of the global financial system. Since that time GDP has stumbled on its upward march. And although it's too soon to discern whether the long-term trend has changed, more and more analysts are suggesting that substantial economic growth in the future may not be possible.

Richard Heinberg is one such analyst. He is a fellow of the Post Carbon Institute and one of the world's foremost experts on both the state of energy supplies and the history of energy use. He believes that the age of economic growth is over, the victim of three converging crises: (1) the depletion of fossil fuels and other critical resources, (2) the snowballing costs of environmental impacts, and (3) the inability of financial systems to adjust to the new reality.[12] In his book *The End of Growth*, he explains each of these crises in detail, but he focuses most intensely on oil depletion as the limiting factor for economic growth.

Why is oil depletion so important? A growing economy, with all of its individual sectors—from transportation to agriculture to manufacturing to financial services—requires supplies of cheap energy, and oil has fit the bill for decades. But the fact is, we're using it up. We're not on the verge of running out, but we have entered the era of peak oil production, a situation in which Exxon Mobil, BP, Shell, and other oil companies are unable to meet rising demand. The cheap and easy oil fields have been exploited. Now we're stuck with trying to wrest oil from places that require serious feats of engineering and carry significant risks. As a result, the price of a barrel of oil is susceptible to major price swings, and these swings produce cascading volatility in the rest of the economy.

One statistic that contains critical information for understanding the status of energy supplies and assessing the prospects for continued economic growth is EROEI. EROEI stands for "energy return on energy invested." It's a ratio that explains how much energy we have to put in (e.g., in exploration, extraction, and transportation) to get a certain amount of energy back when exploiting any given energy resource. The disconcerting news is that EROEI has been declining for a number of energy sources over the history of their extraction and use. In 1930, EROEI for oil extracted in the United States was greater than 100 to 1.[13] That means that for each unit of energy spent drilling and refining oil, we got back 100 units of energy. It was easy. All you had to do was sink a shallow well in the right place, and you could collect the gushing supply of energy-dense oil. By 1970, though, EROEI had decreased to 30 to 1. And by 2005, it was down to about 15 to 1.[14] Other sources of energy, both domestic and imported, also show declines in EROEI over time.

Meanwhile EROEI values for sources of renewable energy suggest that as we substitute solar panels and wind turbines for oil and coal, we can't expect the returns on investment we've become accustomed to. For example, EROEI on wind turbines is about 18 to 1. On photovoltaic solar panels it's 7 to 1. And on biodiesel fuel, it's only 1.3 to 1.[15] Declining EROEI has important implications for the economy because economic output is closely correlated with energy use (Figure 2.5).[16] As conventional supplies of energy dwindle and low-EROEI supplies are used as substitutes, it will be harder and harder to maintain (let alone increase) economic output.

However, in a report entitled *Growth Isn't Possible*, the New Economics Foundation suggests that declining supplies of oil and natural gas may be less of a threat to economic growth than the carbon dioxide (CO_2) emissions from burning them. The authors claim that peak oil production will not lead to economic collapse, but will likely result in greater use of liquid fuels derived from coal, resulting in even higher CO_2 emissions.[17] Thus, climate change may be the more pressing limit we face.

The concentration of CO_2 in the atmosphere has climbed 40 percent higher than its level at the beginning of the industrial revolution. In fact, CO_2 concentrations are higher now than they have been at any other time during the last 800,000 years, maybe even the last 20 million years.[18] In 2008, NASA climate scientist James Hansen and colleagues warned, "If humanity wishes to preserve a planet similar to that on which civilization developed and to which life on Earth is adapted, paleoclimate evidence and ongoing climate change suggest that CO_2 will need to be reduced from its current 385 ppm to at most 350 ppm, but likely less than that."[19]

Leaders of financial institutions have also begun to question the possibility of continued growth. Jeremy Grantham is the cofounder of GMO, one of the largest investment funds in the world. In his first newsletter of 2011, he wrote, "The purpose of this [letter] . . . is to persuade investors with an interest in the long term to change their whole frame of reference: to recognize that we now live in a different, more

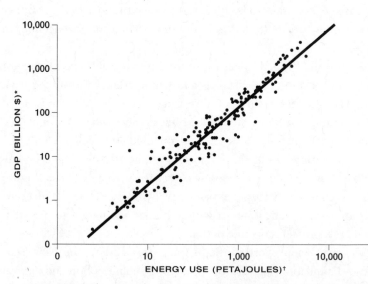

*GDP is expressed in purchasing power parity (PPP) dollars for the year 2005. Purchasing power parity is a technique used to calculate exchange rates between countries based on how much money would be needed to purchase the same goods and services in each country.

†One petajoule is the amount of energy contained in about 163,400 barrels of oil.

FIG. 2.5. Economic output (as expressed by GDP) and energy use are highly correlated. The data shown are for 175 countries in the year 2007. Exponential scales are used on both the x- and y-axes because GDP and energy use vary considerably across countries. SOURCE: see note 16.

constrained, world in which prices of raw materials will rise and short-ages will be common."[20]

In a similar vein, the 2011 annual report of Portfolio 21, a global mutual fund with investments in socially and environmentally responsible companies, states, "Although the news media continue to focus on the upheaval and volatility of the financial markets as the top story, ecological limits to economic growth is the real story of the century. Environmental disasters have been intensifying as economic growth struggles against natural and man-made limits."[21]

When leading scientists, economists, investment professionals, and journalists begin to concur about the impossibility of perpetual economic growth, then *enough* begins to look like more than just a responsible alternative. It starts to look like the only option. As the next section explains, it may be preferable for other reasons as well.

THE SOCIAL FAILURES OF ECONOMIC GROWTH

Although economic growth has come at a large environmental cost, it has also brought many benefits. People can acquire more stuff than ever before, and some of that stuff, such as new medicines, better diets, and communication technologies, can help increase well-being. But does *all* the extra stuff make us better off? Mainstream economists seem to think so. They accept a largely unchallenged assumption that GDP and well-being are directly linked, and this assumption drives the call for continuous economic growth. It seems crazy not to test an assumption that underpins such important economic policy decisions.

Let's suppose for a moment that we could find a way to increase GDP without using up resources or negatively impacting the environment. Would continued GDP growth in wealthy countries like the United States or the United Kingdom still be a worthwhile pursuit? Would a larger economy improve quality of life, alleviate poverty, and provide full employment—or does further economic growth stand in the way of achieving these goals?

Data from surveys of happiness and life satisfaction can help answer these questions. In such surveys, people are typically asked to rate their level of life satisfaction on a numerical scale (from zero to ten, for example). When these data are compared to GDP, a striking picture emerges. Although GDP per capita has more than tripled in countries like the United States and the United Kingdom since 1950, people have not become any happier (Figure 2.6).[22]

When data are compared across countries, the picture becomes even more interesting. Happiness and life satisfaction *do* tend to increase with income, but only up to a point. Beyond an average national income of about $20,000 a year, additional money does not appear to buy additional happiness (Figure 2.7).[23] That's precisely the point that Jack Santa-Barbara perceived when he changed his career and decided to pursue his passion instead of more profit. Once people can meet their basic needs and access enough goods and services, economic growth fails to improve their lives.

This finding seriously calls into question the continued pursuit of economic growth in wealthy nations. With global resource use already at an unsustainable level, further growth in these nations reduces the amount of ecological space available to poor countries, where economic growth could help lift people out of poverty.

Nevertheless, it is often argued that *global* economic growth is the best way to reduce poverty in poor countries. After all, reducing poverty without global growth would require the redistribution of income from rich countries to poor countries. Given that the rich are more

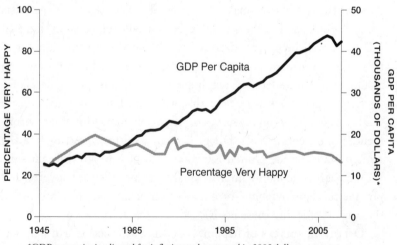

*GDP per capita is adjusted for inflation and expressed in 2005 dollars.

FIG. 2.6. Although GDP per capita has risen steadily in the United States since the end of World War II, the percentage of people who report being "very happy" has flatlined. SOURCE: see note 22.

powerful than the poor, redistribution is often portrayed as being a less feasible option than growth. In the view of Anne Krueger of the International Monetary Fund, "Poverty reduction is best achieved through making the cake bigger, not by trying to cut it up in a different way."[24]

The ever-expanding cake is a seductive idea (or would be in the absence of biophysical limits), but it has not solved the global poverty problem, and shows no signs of doing so. Despite the twenty-five-fold increase in the size of the global economy over the past century, more than 1 billion people still live on less than $1 per day, and a total of 2.7 billion people live on less than $2 per day.[25] Economic growth has been cited by the World Bank as the "essential ingredient for sustained poverty reduction."[26] But for every $100 of global economic growth that occurred between 1990 and 2001, only 60 cents went to people below the $1-per-day line. In other words, to get the poorest people of the world an extra $1 required a $166 increase in global production and consumption.[27] Someone is profiting from economic growth, but it's not the world's poor.

Nor is it the average citizen in wealthy countries. The benefits of

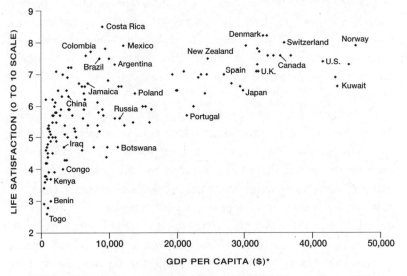

*GDP per capita is expressed in purchasing power parity (PPP) dollars for the year 2005.

FIG. 2.7. Life satisfaction data for 141 nations suggest that once average income reaches a certain level (let's call it *enough*), adding more income fails to buy more happiness. The data shown are average values for the years 2000 to 2009. SOURCE: see note 23.

economic growth have accrued mainly to the wealthiest members of society, and as a result income gaps have widened around the world. Over the past thirty years, the gap between the richest and poorest 10 percent of the U.K. population grew by almost 40 percent.[28] The richest tenth now have incomes 14 times higher than the poorest tenth. In the United States, the income gap is even larger at 16 times.[29] These gaps are deeply problematic. As Richard Wilkinson and Kate Pickett explain in their thoroughly researched book, *The Spirit Level*, high income inequality is associated with a multitude of health and social problems, including increased mental illness, more prevalent drug use, poorer physical health, lower life expectancy, inferior educational performance, heightened violence, and higher rates of imprisonment.[30]

Moreover, the social failures of the growth model are not just limited to quality of life, poverty, and income inequality. They also extend to the goal of achieving full employment. Despite persistently rising GDP, the unemployment rate has bounced up and down over time. For example, in the United States over the last several decades, the unemployment rate has ranged from a low of 3.5 percent in 1969 to a high of 9.7 percent in 1982, and it has recently climbed above 9 percent again.[31] The growth-based economy has not been able to guarantee full employment in the United States, largely because economic growth is an unstable "boom-and-bust" model. Periods of growth are inevitably followed by periods of recession, which are marked by significant job losses.

Perhaps it's not surprising that a policy of endless economic growth is destined to fail environmentally; common sense dictates that an economy cannot grow forever on a finite planet. What is surprising, however, is the way that growth is failing to achieve social goals. It is not providing lasting solutions to the problems of unemployment and poverty, and it is not making people any happier when they already enjoy enough goods and services. In the quest to lead fulfilling lives, consuming past the point of *enough* is an exercise in futility. The evidence suggests that most people living in wealthy countries already have enough material goods—the challenge is to figure out how to build an economy on something other than ever-increasing consumption.

John Maynard Keynes, probably the most influential economist of the twentieth century, recognized this point. He wrote, "The day is not far off when the economic problem will take the back seat where it belongs, and the arena of the heart and the head will be occupied or reoccupied, by our real problems—the problems of life and of human relations, of creation and behaviour and religion."[32]

Keynes understood that a society's ability to overcome scarcity—that is, to provision itself sufficiently with goods and services—could open a doorway to a better place. A society with *enough* as its goal could address higher needs and turn its attention to cultural and spiritual advancement. For wealthy nations, it appears that the day "not far off" has arrived.

[CHAPTER 3]
HOW MUCH IS ENOUGH?

This extraordinary ramping up of global economic activity has no historical precedent. It's totally at odds with our scientific knowledge of the finite resource base and the fragile ecology on which we depend for survival.

TIM JACKSON[1]

Determining how big the economy can grow with respect to the biosphere is a problem of scale, and scale is a concept that confounds many people. I met one such confounded person during a bike trip along the Chesapeake and Ohio Canal. The C&O Canal cuts a narrow path for 185 miles through the leafy, rock-strewn countryside of Maryland. After its completion in 1850, barges loaded with coal, timber, and food floated down the canal from the hills of Maryland into the heart of Washington, D.C. For seventy-four years, mules walked the towpath, pulling the barges, until competition from railroads and relentless poundings from floods put the canal out of business.[2]

But the C&O has lived a good life in its post-commerce years as a recreational respite from the hustle and bustle of Washington and other nearby towns. Along with its noteworthy scenery, the canal's route wanders through the tumultuous history of the American Civil War. It includes such destinations as Harpers Ferry, where the abolitionist John Brown seized the federal arsenal, and Antietam, one of the bloodiest battlefields of the war. This rich history helped the C&O attain its status as a National Historical Park and avoid being swallowed by the urban sprawl that radiated from the national capital after World War II.

The possibility of adventure along the canal and away from the city spurred my friend Dave and me to plan a bike trip from Washington to Antietam. Our itinerary called for a 60-mile ride to Harpers Ferry on the first day and a stay at a hotel there. Day two would entail an out-and-back 30-mile trip to Antietam. After another night's rest at the hotel, we'd make our triumphant return to Washington on day three.

It didn't work out that way. The forces of nature and the overconfidence of youth conspired against us. On the first day, a drenching thunderstorm turned the towpath into a shallow creek and then into a wheel-grabbing mud-fest. We were so grubby by the time we made it to the hotel in Harpers Ferry that the staff cordoned off a corner of the dining room to quarantine us from the respectable patrons. Exhausted and defeated, we scrapped our plan for day two and decided to spend it watching movies instead.

The next morning when we asked the smiling attendant at the hotel's front desk if there was a nearby theater, she responded affirmatively. She pulled out a map and showed us the location of the theater. From the previous day's ride, Dave and I had become experts at map reading; we had developed an almost supernatural ability to interpret a map route in terms of how we would feel riding it. The 10-mile distance to the theater was too far for our sore and weary legs. We handed the map back and told her as much. She pulled out a second map—a map showing a wider area—and in all seriousness said to us, "Hold on, it's not that far." She held her hand up at eye level, spread her thumb and index finger about an inch apart, and said, "Look, it's only *this* far."

Had there been a globe sitting on the desk, she might have magically condensed the distance to the theater to a hair's width. Dave and I traded a quick glance that said, "Is she for real?" and suppressed the urge to question the quality of public education in West Virginia. The cheerful concierge shared something in common with most economists. She had a poor grasp of scale.

SUSTAINABLE ECONOMIC SCALE

Scale is simply the size of one thing with respect to another. In cartography, it's the distance on the map with respect to the distance in the real world. A map can have a written scale, such as "1 inch on the map = 1 mile on the ground"; it can have a graphic scale bar with a line or rectangle that represents a specific distance on the ground; or it can have a simple fraction or ratio. Whichever way a cartographer represents it, scale is essential to the map's ability to convey useful information.

The scale of the economy is its size with respect to the capacity of the ecosystems that contain it, and *sustainable* economic scale means that the economy does not exceed that capacity. It's important to note that we're talking about the biophysical size of the economy, not the monetary size as measured by GDP (although the two are related, as discussed in Chapter 2). Unfortunately there's no simple scale bar or fraction to convey the scale of the economy, but let's run through a quick thought experiment and pretend there is.

Assume we have a scale of 1/8 for the world's economy. An interpretation of this hypothetical scale is that the global economy appropriates one-eighth of the capacity of the earth's ecosystems. In modern times, economists, financiers, and governments have sought to grow the economy at a rate of about 3 percent per year. If the economy achieves a 3 percent rate of growth, it doubles in size in about 23 years. (The rule of thumb for calculating the doubling time for exponential growth is to divide 70 by the percentage rate of growth; 70 divided by 3 comes out to about 23 years.)

So over the course of 23 years, the scale of the economy increases from 1/8 to 2/8. In another 23 years, it doubles again, and the scale changes to 4/8. After another 23 years, the scale increases to 8/8. At this point, 69 years later, the economy would be using all of the capacity of the earth's ecosystems. The numerator increases, but the denominator, which represents the capacity of our nonexpanding ecosystems, stays the same. If the Global Footprint Network's calculations are correct (see Chapter 2), then the current scale of the global economy is something like 12/8. Such a scale seems impossible, but it can happen if we are liquidating stocks of natural resources. When economic growth is the goal, and when that goal is achieved at an exponential rate, the size of the economy quickly catches up to the limits of its containing ecosystems.

This thought experiment simplifies reality a lot. It would be great to have such a straightforward scale calculation. If we knew the precise number of people that could occupy a given landscape and how much they could sustainably consume while living good lives, then we'd have a valuable reference point for deploying sound economic policies. The trouble is that the economy is a complex system, the biosphere is an even more complex system, and both are subject to a wide array of forces that can change how they function. Nonetheless, researchers have conducted some interesting studies to determine the sustainable scale of the human enterprise.

Before examining some of this research, however, it's worth stating a warning about predictions. Experts make awful predictions all the time. The best we can do in trying to sort out how things will go is to work with first principles, such as the laws of physics, and use the best data available. Even when experts employ such an approach, they are often laughably off target (weather forecasts offer a familiar example). That's the nature of the game when analyzing complex systems. Joel Cohen, a leading scholar of population dynamics, remarks, "The Law of Prediction asserts that the more confidence an expert attaches to a prediction about future human affairs, the less confidence you should attach to it."[3]

Cohen may be critical of predictions, but he has compiled plenty of them in his book, *How Many People Can the Earth Support?* Although somewhat dated, the book (published in 1995) provides comprehensive coverage of studies on the carrying capacity of the planet. Carrying capacity is defined as the maximum population of an organism that a particular environment can sustain. Having undertaken an exhaustive review of the literature, Cohen found that science-based estimates of the earth's human carrying capacity range from fewer than 1 billion people to more than 1,000 billion, with the most frequent estimates falling between 4 and 16 billion.[4] But he is quick to add that knowledge of population history, population projections, and ecological limits is insufficient to support a confident statement of how many people the planet can sustain.

The wide range in these estimates stems from the inexact science of calculating carrying capacity. It's a thorny challenge for an ecologist to gauge the potential population of perch in a pond, gazelles in a grassland, or jaguars in a jungle. Such calculations are tricky despite consistent life cycles and restricted habitats for the species involved. The calculations become even trickier when the species is *Homo sapiens*. People have spread all over the globe, so our habitats have fuzzier boundaries than those of other species. In addition, people do three things differently than other animals, and these differences make it difficult to pin down our numbers.

The first difference relates to the quantity of resources we consume. Whereas one sheep consumes about the same amount of stuff as any other sheep, some human individuals, communities, and societies consume a lot more than others (e.g., more food, more materials, and more energy). Our ability to alter how much we consume allows a trade-off between population size and standard of living. We can have a large population consuming relatively meager resources per person or a small population consuming more resources per person. The Worldwatch Institute estimates that the planet could accommodate roughly 13.6 billion people living low-income lifestyles, versus 2.1 billion people living high-income lifestyles (Table 3.1).[5] It's interesting to note that incomes in the high-income scenario are still about $10,000 less per year than the average income in the United States.

The second trait setting us apart from other animals and hampering determination of human carrying capacity is our ability to trade. Indeed, trade among early peoples may have catalyzed humans' rise to power. Researchers hypothesize that trade was a uniquely human advancement that allowed us to outcompete the Neanderthals. The thinking is that, through trade, we developed both specialization of labor and new technologies, while Neanderthals (who apparently were reluctant to trade) failed to develop either.[6] At the national scale, the flow of goods and services across boundaries—international trade—enables prolonged consumption beyond the capacity of local ecosystems. A nation, therefore, can expand its population and consumption to a greater extent than would be expected given the resources within its own territory.

TABLE 3.1. POPULATION AND INCOME SCENARIOS

Scenario	Sustainable Global Population (billions of people)	Annual Average Income per Capita (2008 dollars)
Low Income	13.6	$1,230
Middle Low Income	6.2	$5,100
High Income	2.1	$35,690
U.S. Income	1.4	$45,580

SOURCE: see note 5.

The third critical difference—the trait that muddles calculations of economic scale and carrying capacity the most—is technology. The unanticipated effects of technology have invalidated the claims of many scholars who have taken a pessimistic stance on the limits to population growth. In the late 1960s, the ecologist Paul Ehrlich expressed grave concern about the prospects for food production to keep pace with the demands of a growing population.[7] However, his forecasts of famine failed to materialize in the time frame predicted because he under-estimated the speed with which technological breakthroughs in agriculture would be adopted. On the flip side, the promise of technology has led some optimistic analysts to make outlandish assertions. Julian Simon was a rival of Ehrlich's and an oft-quoted professor of economics and business. In 1996, he claimed that human population could keep growing at the same rate for the next 7 million years—never mind that exponential growth over such a long period would produce a population greater than the number of atoms in the universe![8]

Putting aside predictions for the moment, it's clear that how much we consume, the effects of trade, and technological progress all influence how many people the planet can support. The story of Norman Borlaug demonstrates the point. Borlaug was a remarkable plant scientist. He directed an agricultural research program in Mexico and, over the course of twenty years, he developed a new strain of high-yield, disease-resistant wheat. He took what he learned and set out on a humanitarian mission to battle hunger by spreading his new strains, coupled with modern farming techniques, around the world. His effort came to be called the Green Revolution, and it prevented famine, suffering, and starvation for masses of people.[9] The technology of the Green Revolution and the subsequent trade in food created a caloric cushion that has provided sustenance for a larger global population. But Borlaug himself knew that the cushion was only temporary. In his acceptance speech for the Nobel Peace Prize in 1970, he stated that humanity would lose the fight against hunger unless it could figure out how to limit population size.[10]

Even with all the uncertainty attached to estimates of human carrying capacity, most economists, business leaders, government officials, and average Joes and Janes continue to buy into the model of *more*. They subscribe to technological optimism, a belief in the power of technology to overcome the limits to growth. The idea is that, if we employ technology to decrease the detrimental effects of economic processes, we can keep the numerator in the economic scale relationship from getting too big. But the question remains: how far can technology go in overcoming the failures of economic growth discussed in Chapter 2?

TECHNOLOGY'S POTENTIAL TO OVERCOME THE LIMITS TO GROWTH

Tim Jackson is an economist at the University of Surrey. He's a big-picture thinker who studies the connections between consumption, lifestyles, well-being, and the environment. One of the questions he poses in his research is whether technology can overcome the failures of economic growth. He asks, "Is it really possible for a strategy of 'growth with decoupling' to deliver ever-increasing incomes . . . and yet remain within ecological limits?"[11]

The term "decoupling" refers to the process of producing more economic output with fewer material and energy inputs. For decoupling to be a viable strategy, we would need to break the link between economic activity and resource use. The evidence to suggest we can do this, while by no means conclusive, is certainly discouraging. Between 1980 and 2007, the material intensity of the global economy (i.e., the amount of biomass, minerals, and fossil fuels required to produce a dollar of world GDP) decreased by 33 percent. It's worth celebrating this remarkable improvement in efficiency, as well as the technological innovations that made it possible. And yet, concurrent with these improvements, world GDP grew by 141 percent, such that total resource use still increased by 61 percent (Figure 3.1).[12] The gains made in efficiency were overwhelmed by the increase in the size of the economy. The picture is almost identical for global energy use: energy intensity decreased by 29 percent over the same period, but total energy use rose by 70 percent.[13] As economist Peter Victor remarks in his book *Managing without Growth*, "Americans have been more successful decoupling GDP from happiness than in decoupling it from material and energy."[14]

Although efficiency gains have so far failed to counteract the effects of growth, perhaps decoupling could still be a feasible solution for the future. To get a sense of its feasibility, Jackson has calculated the degree of decoupling that would be required in a world where economies continue to grow, and at the same time move toward global equity.

Jackson's scenario assumes wealthy economies will grow at about 2 percent per year between now and 2050, while the economies of poorer nations will grow more quickly, so that incomes in all countries will converge to those of the European Union by 2050. To keep the concentration of atmospheric CO_2 at 450 parts per million (a target higher than what many climate scientists believe is safe), the carbon intensity of each dollar would have to decrease by a factor of almost 130—a staggering improvement to achieve.[15]

Jackson has also run the numbers out to 2100, and finds that if global economic growth were to continue at 2 percent per year, we would need to achieve "a complete decarbonization of every single dollar."[16] If a stricter CO_2 target were imposed (say 350 parts per million instead of 450), Jackson says the carbon intensity would have to be less than zero. In other words, economic activity would have to remove CO_2 from the atmosphere, not add to it! These calculations have led him to call decoupling a myth, and to ask a series of thought-provoking questions such as "What kind of economy is that? What are its consumption activities? What are its investment activities? What does it run on?"[17]

Maybe there's still a chance that decoupling can work. Perhaps with

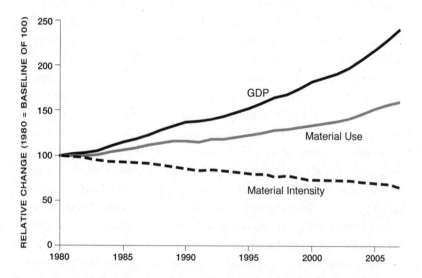

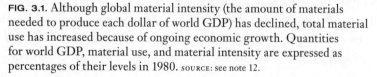

FIG. 3.1. Although global material intensity (the amount of materials needed to produce each dollar of world GDP) has declined, total material use has increased because of ongoing economic growth. Quantities for world GDP, material use, and material intensity are expressed as percentages of their levels in 1980. SOURCE: see note 12.

major investments in new technologies, we could improve resource efficiency fast enough to offset the negative effects of rising GDP. What if the desired technological breakthroughs are just around the corner? Chris Goodall, a researcher and writer on the topics of climate and technology, asserts that the United Kingdom may have already achieved decoupling of economic growth from overall material use. Based on his analysis of national material flow accounts, he suggests that the weight of material flowing through the U.K. economy peaked around 2001 to 2003, even though the economy continued to grow up until 2007. Goodall concludes that GDP growth may be spurring technological progress and more efficient use of resources, thereby reducing the environmental impacts of economic growth.[18]

If material use has indeed peaked in the United Kingdom, it's a striking achievement. However, Goodall offers no evidence of a causal link between GDP growth and improvements in resource efficiency. We think it is far more likely that material use stabilized in spite of GDP growth, not because of it. Moreover, Goodall's analysis overlooks important indicators, such as CO_2 emissions. Taking trade into account, U.K. emissions increased by almost 10 percent between 2001 and 2007.[19]

Continued tracking of material use, energy use, and pollution will be necessary to draw stronger conclusions about technology's role in mitigating the effects of GDP growth, but there are two major reasons to remain suspicious of a "techno-fix decoupling" strategy. The first is the "rebound effect," which was originally described by William Stanley Jevons in his 1865 book *The Coal Question*. Jevons observed that the invention of a more efficient steam engine made coal a viable fuel for many new uses. This efficiency gain amplified the demand for coal and led to a major increase in coal consumption, even as the amount of coal required for any particular use fell. As Jevons stated, "It is wholly a confusion of ideas to suppose that the economical use of fuel is equivalent to a diminished consumption. The very contrary is the truth."[20]

New technologies that reduce resource use also reduce costs; this frees up money that can then be spent on additional consumption, often undermining (or sometimes even overtaking) the original efficiency gains. Improvements in automobile fuel efficiency provide a good example. As cars have become more efficient, they have consumed less fuel per mile traveled, and the cost of driving has fallen. But drivers of more efficient cars may use the savings to drive more miles (an example of *direct* rebound). Alternatively, they might spend this money on a different activity altogether, such as a vacation abroad, increasing overall fuel use (an example of *indirect* rebound). Either way, because of the rebound effect, material and energy savings predicted on paper often fail to materialize in the real world.[21]

The second reason to be skeptical of the techno fix is that although some technologies (such as wastewater treatment) can help alleviate the environmental impacts of growth, others may cause unforeseen pollution and increases in energy and resource use. For example, some of the techniques used in the Green Revolution have caused soil erosion, water pollution, and other undesirable effects. The rapid evolution of computer technology provides another example. Technological progress in the field of miniaturization has vastly reduced the size of computers and expanded their processing power. The change is astounding, and it has provided many tangible benefits. For instance, a modern desktop computer can hold a library's worth of information. However, the miniaturization enabling this feat has also allowed us to build and operate machines that extract natural resources at rates previously unimagined. Without the power of modern computers (coupled with an abundance of cheap energy), it is unlikely that mining, fishing, farming, and energy production would be possible at the scale we see today.[22]

The key message regarding technological progress is that it can be helpful for managing some of the impacts associated with economic growth, but it may not be sufficient to overcome them. This doesn't mean that we should discourage innovation or abandon efforts to develop new technologies. On the contrary, we must invest heavily in the infrastructure for a low-carbon economy. But this alone will not be enough. To bring material and energy use within ecological limits, we must address the scale of economic activity as well.

The starting point may be to reform the education system so that people can gain a better understanding of economic scale. Most introductory economics textbooks devote plenty of ink to "economies of scale" (situations in which a firm can lower its average costs by increasing its output), but they fail to adequately consider sustainable economic scale. In his popular economics textbook, Harvard professor Gregory Mankiw takes less than one out of 896 pages to dismiss the notion that there may be a limit to how large an economy can grow.

The conclusion of the passage states, "Market prices give no reason to believe that natural resources are a limit to economic growth."[23] This statement may be true, but it reveals more about the failure of markets than the absence of limits!

Schools everywhere, from elementary to university, should include a curriculum on scale. To provide a particularly strong grasp of the concept, the curriculum could encourage students to complete a mapping exercise in which they exert their own energy to cross a great distance (a long bike ride down the C&O Canal would suffice for students in the Washington, D.C., area).

Suppose people did develop a better understanding of economic scale and realized that the economy had grown beyond what's sustainable. Or suppose that, even if such understanding failed to blossom, people generally concluded that *enough* was preferable to *more*. Then a pressing question would arise. What sort of economy provides *enough*—that is, how would the economy be different from what we've experienced in the age of growth?

CHAPTER 4

WHAT SORT OF ECONOMY PROVIDES ENOUGH?

It is not enough simply to attack the progrowth orthodoxy;
we must have an alternative vision.

HERMAN DALY[1]

Students in college economics courses occasionally express their frus-
trations, and when they do, it can be both loud and public. Each fall at
the University of Pennsylvania, home of the Wharton School of Business, students enrolled in Economics 101 participate in a curious ritual
that can fairly be described as loud and public. The night before the
first midterm exam, students abandon the library early, even though
you'd expect them to linger among the dusty rows of books for one last
look at their production-possibility frontiers and supply-and-demand
curves. It doesn't take a reconnaissance team to track down the missing
students—they can be found hanging out on the Junior Balcony and
grassy field of the lower Quad.

More and more students make their way to the Quad as the hour
approaches midnight. A nervous energy begins to pulse through the
crowd, and windows open in the dorm rooms above, so that residents
can get a good look at the gathering horde. A minute before midnight,
an unsettling quiet descends on the students as they take a collective
inward breath. Then the quiet is broken by a countdown, much like the
one in Times Square on New Year's Eve. Ten, nine, eight, seven, . . .

At the stroke of midnight, the Econ Scream erupts. Normally mild-
mannered students hang out of windows screaming, "I HATE ECON!"

Members of the crowd, some of them shirtless, scurry in all directions, spewing unintelligible grunts from the depths of their souls. The Econ Scream is an outpouring of emotion and a massive release of stress. A few moments later, the students shuffle back to their dorm rooms, and the Quad rests peacefully for the remainder of the night.

What causes students to build up and then blow off steam over a simple test of economic knowledge? Mostly it has to do with the pressure accompanying the first exam of their college careers. But there's more to it than that. After all, it's not the Math Scream or the English Scream. Students often take exception to economics because they sense a disconnect between what they're learning and what they experience in the real world.

The Econ Scream offers a lighthearted example of this attitude among students. A more serious example took place on November 2, 2011, at Harvard University. On that day, seventy students walked out of their economics class, which was being taught by Gregory Mankiw, author of one of the most popular introductory economics textbooks. An open letter from the students to Mankiw stated, "Today, we are walking out of your class, Economics 10, in order to express our discontent with the bias inherent in this introductory economics course. We are deeply concerned about the way that this bias affects students, the University, and our greater society."[2]

The Post-Autistic Economics Movement provides another example of student discontent. In the year 2000, a letter from French economics students to their professors ignited an international uprising. The students wrote the letter to express their dissatisfaction with the teaching of economics and to demand more attention to history, functioning institutions, and concrete realities. They declared, "We no longer want to have this autistic science imposed on us." As the letter generated media coverage, the movement leapt across the ocean. Students from Cambridge, England, to Cambridge, Massachusetts, identified with the themes of the letter and made similar requests at their colleges.[3] The themes are still gaining traction in a journal that emerged from the movement, the *Real-World Economics Review*.

What's going on with these students of economics? Perhaps they want an education that will help them build a better society. They are coming of age in an era when the economy isn't working (see the daunting environmental and social problems described in Chapter 2), and they seem to crave a hopeful and credible vision for the economy. The orthodoxy they're learning appears unfit for the challenge. The growth-centric economy explained in their classes and instituted around the world fails to address the environmental and social issues of the day. A different sort of economy is required, but what exactly?

Scholars and activists have attached a variety of names to this different sort of economy, names like green economy, ecological economy, sustainable economy, stationary state, dynamic equilibrium, eco-economy, biophysical economy, and even the "new economy." Given the title of this book, we could conceivably call it the economy of *enough* (or, at the risk of diverging into absurdity, enough-o-nomics). But for the sake of clarity, we'll stick with Herman Daly's original name—the steady-state economy—at least until something catchier comes along.

WHAT IS A STEADY-STATE ECONOMY?

At its simplest, a steady-state economy is an economy that aims to maintain a stable level of resource consumption and a stable population. It's an economy in which material and energy use are kept within ecological limits, and in which the goal of increasing GDP is replaced by the goal of improving quality of life.

A steady-state economy would require striking a balance between the stock of natural capital and the stock of built capital, with both remaining relatively constant over time. A constant stock of natural capital implies the preservation of wilderness areas and the maintenance of important ecosystem services, such as climate regulation. A constant stock of built capital means maintaining and improving the quality of infrastructure, such as buildings and roads, but not constructing more and more of these over time.[4]

It's important to distinguish between what's on and what's off the list of things to hold steady in a steady-state economy. Only a few items need to be held steady—the number of people, the stock of artifacts (built capital), and the quantity of material and energy flowing through the economy (this flow, also called throughput, will be discussed in detail in Chapter 5). In contrast, the list of items that can change is long. It includes knowledge, technology, information, wisdom, the mix of products, income distribution, and social institutions, among other things.[5] The objective is to have the items on this second list improving over time, so that the economy can develop qualitatively without growing quantitatively.[6]

In short, a steady-state economy is an economy with *enough* as a goal. It prioritizes well-being above consumption, and long-term health above short-term gains. It focuses on innovation and development instead of growth. The pursuit of endless economic growth, with all of its downsides, is clearly unsustainable in the twenty-first century. A steady-state economy is the sustainable alternative to perpetual economic growth.

Four main features characterize a steady-state economy. The first, and arguably most critical, is *sustainable scale*. As explained in Chapter 3, sustainable scale requires that the economic subsystem is able to function within the capacity provided by the earth's ecosystems. The economy should grow only if the benefits of growth (e.g., more income, more consumer products) exceed the costs (e.g., climate change, species extinctions). However, as soon as the costs catch up to the benefits, growth becomes uneconomic.[7] At this point, each additional dollar of growth actually makes us poorer, not richer. Uneconomic growth continues, in part, because the benefits accrue to a few rich and powerful people, while the larger costs fall increasingly on the poor and disempowered. This circumstance provides the rationale for adopting the second feature of a steady-state economy: *fair distribution* of income and wealth.

Recall from Chapter 2 that Anne Krueger of the International Monetary Fund said, "Poverty reduction is best achieved through making the cake bigger, not by trying to cut it up in a different way."[8] But if the size of the oven prevents us from baking a bigger cake, then we'd better start considering how to slice the pieces and how big a slice each person is entitled to eat. The good news is that fair distribution of income and wealth may be the key to alleviating a wide range of social problems, such as violence, crime, and drug abuse.[9] In addition, there's a strong environmental argument for shrinking the gap between the rich and poor: high levels of inequality lead to status competition and associated increases in material consumption across society as everyone tries to "keep up with the Joneses."

The third important feature of a steady-state economy is *efficient allocation*. The allocation of scarce resources among competing interests lies at the heart of conventional economics. The dominant thinking holds that free and competitive markets, where prices are determined by supply and demand, lead to the efficient allocation of goods and services (at least when consumers have access to good information about products). A steady-state economy includes a strong role for markets, but it is critically important to recognize where markets work and where they don't, and to deploy the power of markets appropriately. A steady-state economy aims to strike the right balance between markets, the state, and civil society. In recent years, this balance has become skewed. We've put too much faith in the ability of markets to solve problems that they are not equipped to solve, including some problems they created in the first place (e.g., burning too much fossil fuel).

A steady-state economy works toward these first three features (sustainable scale, fair distribution, and efficient allocation) in order to achieve the fourth feature, a *high quality of life* for all citizens. Currently, GDP serves as the main measure of economic progress, but increases in GDP are not translating into increases in well-being for people in high-consuming countries. A steady-state economy would use different indicators of progress to assess whether quality of life is improving. It would shift the focus of measurement away from the production and consumption of goods and services, and toward things that really matter to people, such as health, well-being, secure employment, leisure time, strong communities, and economic stability. All in all, it would transform the goal of the economy from producing more stuff to enabling people to live better lives.

CAN WE REALLY DO THIS?

The vision of a steady-state economy described above is a profoundly positive one. It promises that the transformation of the economic system from growth to stability, from *more* to *enough*, would allow us to solve critical environmental problems, while maintaining (or even improving) quality of life. It almost seems too good to be true. Can such an economy really work in practice? Is it possible to have full employment, no poverty, fiscal responsibility, and reduced environmental impacts without relying on economic growth?

To help answer this question, economist Peter Victor created a model of the Canadian economy to test what would happen in various growth scenarios over a thirty-year period (from 2005 to 2035).[10]

Although a computer model doesn't serve as a substitute for experience in the real world, it can help us understand what policy changes are required to achieve various economic outcomes.

If the model is run under a business-as-usual scenario in which past trends continue, then the economy will continue to grow (Figure 4.1).[11] Between 2005 and 2035, GDP per capita roughly doubles, the unemployment rate goes up slightly and then comes back down, government debt falls (as a percentage of GDP), and greenhouse gas emissions increase. Despite the large expansion of the economy, however, poverty (as measured by the United Nations Human Poverty Index) continues to rise, with more Canadians living in poverty at the end of the period than at the beginning.[12]

While the business-as-usual scenario is appealing in many ways, it is unrealistic because of environmental constraints that are not part of the model. Leading climate scientists have warned that the current concentration of carbon dioxide in the atmosphere (let alone a higher concentration) poses a danger to maintaining a stable climate.[13] Victor, who teaches environmental management courses, is keenly aware of the downsides of the business-as-usual scenario. In fact, his motivation

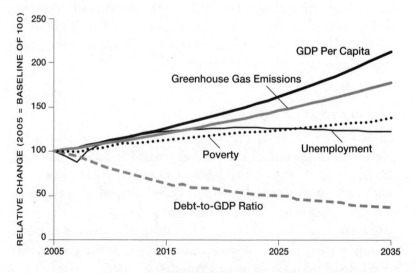

FIG. 4.1. Computer model 1: Peter Victor's business-as-usual scenario for the Canadian economy assumes that past growth trends continue. GDP per capita doubles, but greenhouse gas emissions reach dangerous levels, while poverty still increases. SOURCE: see note 11.

for developing the model was to see if he could find a safer path for the economy. He has taken up the challenge put forth by Larry Elliott, the economics editor of *The Guardian*, who wrote, "The real issue is whether it is possible to challenge the 'growth-at-any-cost model' and come up with an alternative that is environmentally benign, economically robust and politically feasible."[14]

If increases in all of the sources of economic growth (i.e., consumption expenditure, investment, government expenditure, trade, population, and productivity) are eliminated over a ten-year period beginning in 2010, a very different scenario emerges from the model: a no-growth disaster (Figure 4.2). Poverty skyrockets, unemployment actually climbs off the chart, and the level of government debt becomes completely untenable. As GDP per capita levels off, so do greenhouse gas emissions, but at the cost of economic collapse.[15]

Fear of this nightmare scenario keeps nations chasing economic growth. It has prompted them to respond to the global recession by propping up the existing system and trying to return to something resembling the business-as-usual scenario.

Fortunately, the model also demonstrates that it is possible to

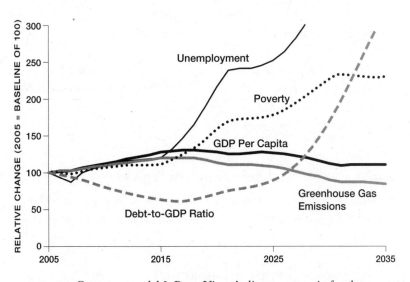

FIG. 4.2. Computer model 2: Peter Victor's disaster scenario for the Canadian economy is based on eliminating traditional sources of economic growth, but without adopting steady-state policies. Skyrocketing unemployment, poverty, and debt are the result. SOURCE: see note 15.

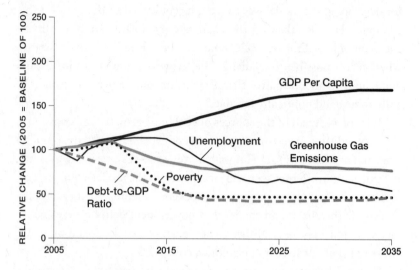

FIG. 4.3. Computer model 3: Peter Victor's scenario for a successful transition to a steady-state economy in Canada. With the right policies in place, a low-growth or no-growth economy can achieve important social and environmental goals. SOURCE: see note 16.

achieve a no-growth success (Figure 4.3). If growth slows over time and the size of the economy stabilizes under the right set of policies, unemployment drops to historically low levels, leisure time increases, poverty is virtually eliminated, greenhouse gas emissions decrease, and government debt falls to a healthy level—all without the need for continuing economic growth.[16] This scenario offers hope that it is possible, at least in a technical sense, for a national economy to make the transition to a successful nongrowing economy.

WHAT NEEDS TO HAPPEN IN THE TRANSITION?

Significant changes are required to achieve the economic results shown in Figure 4.3. According to Victor and other economists, these changes include:

- New meanings and measures of progress
- Limits on material and energy consumption, waste production, and conversion of natural lands
- A stable population and labor force

- A more efficient capital stock
- More durable, repairable products
- Better pricing, including a carbon price
- A shorter work year and more leisure time
- Reduced inequality
- Fewer status goods
- More informative and less deceptive advertising
- Better screening of technology
- More local (and less global) trade of goods and services
- Education for life, not just for work

But the transition to a steady-state economy will require more than just the important policy changes listed above, as economist Tim Jackson points out.[17] It will also require rethinking some of the core ideas underpinning the economy, such as investment, productivity, ownership, and environmental values. Let's examine each of these ideas.

Investment. Investment has come to mean using money to make money. Capital flows to enterprises that generate financial returns, often by means that are not necessarily in society's best interests. But investment is not about—or should not be about—throwing over the old in favor of the new, simply because it sells. Investment represents a simple relationship between the present and the future. It entails forgoing present-day consumption and using the resources saved to build a better future. A steady-state economy would require us to embrace this deeper view of investment.[18] Instead of viewing investment only as a way to generate financial returns, we must also see it as a way to generate social and environmental returns.

Productivity. The current economic system seeks to maximize labor productivity—to produce more output from each hour of work. But the assumption that increasing productivity furthers the best interests of society is not always valid. In a service-based economy, for example, pursuing labor productivity makes little sense; it simply leads to job losses. Instead of seeking to maximize productivity, the economic system should work toward optimizing it. It's worth pursuing productivity gains to minimize unpleasant work, but we need to take care not to displace work that brings joy and meaning to people's lives.[19] As

E. F. Schumacher wrote: "If a man has no chance of obtaining work he is in a desperate position, not simply because he lacks an income but because he lacks this nourishing and enlivening factor of disciplined work which nothing can replace."[20]

Ownership. Ownership of the means of production has been the subject of fierce debate for generations. The debates have largely regressed to shouting matches about the merits and drawbacks of capitalism. But ownership is not limited to the black-and-white choice between the public and private realm—there are many shades of gray in between, along with opportunities to design new ownership structures that achieve better results for society.[21]

Environmental values. Perhaps the most important thing we need to rethink is our relationship to nature. Across all sectors of the economy, it's easy to find environmentally unsustainable practices. In the agricultural sector, for example, many farms around the world are consuming groundwater supplies faster than they can be replenished. Groundwater depletion in California's Central Valley has become severe enough that researchers are concerned it may impact U.S. economic and food security.[22] In the energy sector, drilling for oil in offshore areas provides another example of an unsustainable practice. BP demonstrated the volatility of this practice in 2010 when the explosion of its *Deepwater Horizon* rig cost the lives of eleven workers and spilled a massive amount of crude oil into the Gulf of Mexico.[23] Such practices have become commonplace because of a worldview that sees the economy and its institutions as somehow independent of the natural world. Technology has given us a false sense of separation from our environment. In reality, we are part of nature, and we must respect and abide by its laws. The sooner we begin to reconnect with the natural world around us, the sooner we can begin building an economy that fits on the planet.

Reconfiguring our ideas about investment, productivity, ownership, and the environment would unravel and reweave the current economic tapestry. But the transition to a steady state requires another change—one that would reverse the current economic dogma by 180 degrees. As explained in the preceding chapters, for an economy to last over the long run, its footprint must fit within the capacity of the ecosystems that contain it. Recognizing that our collective footprint now exceeds available biological capacity, many scholars maintain that the scale of the global economy needs to contract. Instead of managing economic institutions to achieve growth, we need to manage them to achieve *degrowth*.[24]

Although the exact meaning of the term "degrowth" is subject to debate, it is increasingly interpreted as a socially sustainable and equitable reduction of society's material and energy throughput.[25] However, as with perpetual growth, perpetual contraction of an economy is neither possible nor desirable. Degrowth is a process of transition, and the ultimate goal of this process is a steady-state economy. The declaration from the first international conference on degrowth, held in Paris in 2008, makes this point while providing a more detailed definition:

> We define degrowth as a voluntary transition towards a just, participatory, and ecologically sustainable society. . . . The objectives of degrowth are to meet basic human needs and ensure a high quality of life, while reducing the ecological impact of the global economy to a sustainable level, equitably distributed between nations. . . . Once right-sizing has been achieved through the process of degrowth, the aim should be to maintain a "steady state economy" with a relatively stable, mildly fluctuating level of consumption.[26]

Degrowth may very well be necessary to make the transition to a sustainable economy, but the remainder of this book focuses on the ultimate goal of a steady-state economy. There are three reasons for this focus: (1) it is critically important to establish a working model for the steady state, because this is where the economy must end up; (2) if we can determine how to make a steady-state economy work, then the steps required in the degrowth transition will become clearer (it's easier to get someplace if you know where you're going); and (3) the economic policies needed to achieve a steady-state economy, and to manage the degrowth transition to one, appear to have much in common.

One final factor must be considered for an economic shift from *more* to *enough*—politics. Although Peter Victor's model offers hope that a steady-state economy is technically achievable, it says little about whether it is politically feasible. Political feasibility is certainly increased by demonstrating (with the model) that such an economy can work. However, a wide gap still exists between a successful computer model and real-world implementation, especially considering the needed changes. Victor himself says, "The dilemma for policy makers is that the scope of change required for managing without growth is so great that no democratically elected government could implement the requisite policies without the broad-based consent of the electorate. Even talking about them could make a politician unelectable."[27]

Given the stakes (e.g., environmental catastrophe and social upheaval), opening some space in which pundits and politicians can sensibly discuss the limits to growth makes sense. The Center for the Advancement of the Steady State Economy (CASSE) is one of a handful of organizations that have been trying to create this space. Toward this end, CASSE has created a position statement on economic growth that can be endorsed by individuals and organizations.[28] This statement recognizes the conflict between economic growth and environmental protection, and calls for the transition to a steady-state economy. At the time of writing, the position statement had been signed by more than 9,000 individuals, including a large number of well-known economists and scientists. It had also been endorsed by 185 organizations, including professional societies, nonprofit organizations, businesses, and political parties. CASSE's position statement may provide political cover for engaging in discussions about the limits to growth, but for people to embrace the concept of a steady-state economy, they need to understand how it would work and why it would be preferable to what they've become accustomed to.

The concept of a dynamic economy that does not require growth to improve quality of life and that finds equilibrium with nature is highly appealing, but many questions remain about how to achieve it. Now that we've summarized the case for shifting from *more* to *enough* and reviewed the basic features of an economy that embraces *enough*, we're ready to tackle these questions. Part II of this book, *Strategies of Enough*, offers workable proposals to:

- Limit the use of materials and energy to sustainable levels.
- Stabilize population through compassionate and noncoercive means.
- Achieve a fair distribution of income and wealth.

- Reform monetary and financial systems for stability.
- Change the way we measure progress.
- Secure meaningful jobs and full employment.
- Reconfigure the way businesses create value.

To organize the information consistently, we have structured each of the next seven chapters around three questions: What are we doing? What could we do instead? And where do we go from here? Although the proposals provide the starting point for a remarkable economic transformation, they should not be viewed as the definitive answer for how to achieve a steady-state economy. However, they do provide a basis for further discussion and action.

An enlightened transformation to a steady-state economy is a profoundly hopeful prospect. Alignment of economic scale with the realities of ecosystem limits would address many of the world's most serious environmental problems. Explicit attention to fair distribution of income and wealth would alleviate some of the most grievous social injustices. Recalibration of the reach of markets would eliminate some of the worst abuses of the corporate age. Taken together, these economic changes would help secure a high quality of life for this and future generations. As a bonus, students might even change their attitudes about economics. It's unlikely that they'd take to shouting, "I LOVE ECON!" in the Quad, but maybe economics would give them something they could believe in.

[PART II]
STRATEGIES OF ENOUGH

CHAPTER 5

ENOUGH THROUGHPUT

Limiting Resource Use and Waste Production

The Earth has no way of registering good intentions or future inventions or high hopes. It doesn't even pay attention to dollars, which are, from a planet's point of view, just a charming human invention. Planets measure only physical things—energy and materials and their flows into and out of the changing populations of living creatures.

DONELLA MEADOWS[1]

WHAT ARE WE DOING?

Whether a mansion in Monaco, an apartment in Argentina, or a cottage in Cambodia, every household has a measurable metabolism. Materials, from trash cans to ceiling fans, from apple pies to French fries, flow into the household from external sources. Each household also obtains supplies of energy, such as electricity, sunshine, and natural gas, from the outside world. Members of the household consume the materials and use the energy to support their lifestyles. And finally, the household completes the metabolic process by expelling wastes to the environment through carbon dioxide emissions, wastewater discharge, and trash disposal. This metabolism, the flow of materials and energy and the emission of wastes, can be called the throughput of the household.

Some households have a larger throughput than others. For proof, there's no better source than *Material World*, an eye-catching book by photographer Peter Menzel. Like a doctor examining a patient to get to the bottom of a metabolic mystery, Menzel takes the pulse of typical households in thirty countries by photographing families and their possessions in front of their homes. The collection of material goods surrounding the Getu family (from Ethiopia) in the foreground of their 320-square-foot hut is small, especially when compared to the possessions of the Skeen family (from the United States) in front of their 1,600-square-foot suburban house.[2] The difference in accumulation of material goods between the two households is obvious. A closer inspection of the photographs and captions also reveals the difference in energy throughput. The Getus rely on dung collected from their oxen corral for cooking fuel; the Skeens import electricity to power their appliances and control their home's temperature, and they use gasoline to power their three motor vehicles. Interestingly, the Skeens' throughput looks modest compared to that of other Americans today. Since the book was published in the mid-1990s, the typical American family has stepped up its consumption. New single-family homes in the United States in 2010 averaged 2,392 square feet, about 50 percent larger than the Skeens' home.[3]

Many conclusions may be drawn from *Material World*, and one of the clearest is that American households boast a high metabolism—Americans are the unofficial throughput champs. A recent news story reported that if everyone in the world consumed like the average American, we'd need about six earths to sustain ourselves.[4] Such statistics are telling, but perhaps a deeper understanding of America's burgeoning household throughput emerges from the portrait of a curious industry: self storage.

Self storage has been the fastest growing segment of the U.S. commercial real estate sector over the last thirty-five years.[5] Self-storage units, which usually occupy row upon row of garages in metal- and concrete-trimmed warehouses, provide a place for households to keep excess stuff. In the not-too-distant past, a small number of self-storage businesses catered to homes in transition (for example, when people were moving from one place to another), but the industry has grown significantly in recent years. The United States now has over 2.2 billion square feet (78 square miles) of rentable self-storage space, more than three times the size of Manhattan Island. Nearly one out of every ten American households leased a unit in 2007, up from one in seventeen in 1995.[6] On top of that, one of the most common reasons that customers rent self-storage units is to store items they no longer need or want.[7]

The flow of materials into American homes has grown so much that it has surpassed the capacity of many of these homes (which have themselves been growing impressively) to contain it. The result is the rise of a self-storage nation.

At the household scale, getting a handle on throughput is relatively easy, even without dragging everything into the front yard like the families in *Material World*. An audit of household throughput requires tracking how much stuff is coming in and how much waste is flowing out (including exports to the self-storage unit). It also requires documenting energy consumption. For the most part, an auditor would need to collect receipts from shopping, extract data from utility bills, and do some arithmetic—a straightforward, although somewhat tedious, task. But what about a really big household like the economy?

The word "economy" actually derives from two Greek words, *oikos* (household) and *nomos* (management). Economics is literally the management of the human household. The larger the household, the more difficult it is to analyze, but researchers have devised useful tools for tracking throughput at broad scales. Material flow analysis is one such tool—a systematic way to assess the flow of materials through an economy. Rooted in the law of conservation of matter, material flow analysis uses mass balance equations to track the flow of materials from environmental sources, through consumptive processes in the economy, and back to the environment in waste streams.[8]

Like a household in which the family rents three self-storage units to manage its overflow of stuff, an economy can also have an overactive metabolism. Material flow analysis suggests that the metabolism of the global economy is much higher than it used to be. Humanity now uses eight times more material resources (by weight) than it did a century ago.[9] Researchers have concluded that "if the present metabolic rate is maintained, there will ultimately be constraints for development. These may occur as resource scarcities at the supply side, or as environmental degradation at the disposal side."[10]

This conclusion resembles what's being communicated by the ecological footprint, another useful tool for understanding the flow of materials and energy through an economy. As described in Chapter 2, estimates of the global economy's footprint suggest that humanity is consuming resources and emitting wastes at a rate that is 50 percent faster than what's sustainable.

These findings suggest we are mismanaging our global household, pulling too many resources in the front door and pushing too much waste out the back door. Current approaches to resource management have become outdated. They are founded upon economic models developed when the world was relatively full of nature and relatively empty of people and manufactured goods.[11] During that era, the evolution of agriculture, the spread of colonialism, and the industrial revolution provided seemingly endless frontiers of untapped resources. Coupled with new technologies, expanding economic activity enabled novel, more efficient, and faster use of resources. The worldview that became dominant at that time is captured in the words of the political economist Henry George, who in 1884 wrote:

> It is a well-provisioned ship, this on which we sail through space. If the bread and beef above decks seem to grow scarce, we but open a hatch and there is a new supply, of which before we never dreamed. And very great command over the services of others comes to those who as the hatches are opened are permitted to say, "This is mine!"[12]

The relentless increase in throughput over the last two hundred years has provided humanity with a dizzying array of goods and services and an accompanying rise in material well-being. This growth dynamic has also allowed for a rapid increase in population, which, in turn, has driven even greater levels of resource use. Scholars estimate that humans entirely dominate 36 percent of the earth's biologically productive surface area.[13] The appropriation of materials, energy, and land for economic activity has significantly reduced the space available for nonhuman species, leading to ecosystem breakdowns, extinctions, and decreased biological diversity.[14] Excessive levels of throughput are destabilizing the natural systems (e.g., a stable climate, nutrient cycling, fresh water provision, and so on) on which humanity ultimately depends. Overconsumption of nonrenewable resources, such as fossil fuels, and overexploitation of renewable resources, such as forests and fish, may mean that future generations will have to get by on less. Despite the pressure that the economy is placing on the biosphere, the dominant economic model still calls for *more*. But the boundless economic frontiers envisioned by Henry George appear, at last, to be bounded.

WHAT COULD WE DO INSTEAD?

It's time to consider a new household management plan. At the planetary scale, there is no off-site self-storage unit where we can extract resources or send wastes. To succeed over the long term, the new plan must incorporate three important operating rules, which were first proposed by Herman Daly:

1. Exploit renewable resources no faster than they can be regenerated.
2. Deplete nonrenewable resources no faster than the rate at which renewable substitutes can be developed.
3. Emit wastes no faster than they can be safely assimilated by ecosystems.[15]

The economy, as currently configured, does not play by these three rules. Prices often fail to capture the effect of resource depletion, waste generation, and loss of ecosystem services. As a result, the market sends improper signals—if it sends any signal at all—regarding the sustainability of throughput levels. We need to eliminate this market failure and make sure the economy abides by Daly's three rules. Doing so will require throughput-limiting policies that strike a balance between maintenance of healthy ecosystems and provision of sufficient goods and services.

Some throughput-limiting policies are relatively simple and could be implemented within current institutional arrangements, while others would require the establishment of new institutions.[16] Choosing the right policies is a high-stakes game. The urgent environmental problems facing humanity demand prompt action to reduce the flow of materials and energy to sustainable levels. At the same time, policies intended to accomplish this reduction would likely impose constraints on what people could do. On the one hand, the need for safety and security (to avoid resource scarcity and environmental catastrophes) calls for direct methods to lessen throughput immediately. On the other hand, the need for autonomy (from rules and regulations) may make it tough for people to stomach throughput-limiting policies, especially if the policies are viewed as too restrictive. The challenge is to enact policies that reduce throughput with minimal impingement on personal freedom. This challenge calls for careful consideration of when to use direct methods and when to try less direct methods.

Direct Methods to Limit Throughput

The simplest and most direct policy to limit throughput is an outright ban. A ban prohibits the use of a specific material or a particular process in the economy. For example, banning lead as an additive to paint and gasoline has provided significant benefits to society. Lead's toxic properties can cause debilitating mental health effects. Bans have dramatically decreased exposure and reduced lead-related health problems worldwide.

Rationing is another type of direct policy to limit throughput. Rationing schemes provide each person or company with the right to use a specified amount of a resource. For instance, each person could be allocated a certain number of kilowatt-hours of electricity per month. Such a scheme could decrease both the quantity of resources drawn from mines (e.g., coal and uranium) and the amount of wastes flowing into the environment (e.g., carbon dioxide and nuclear waste).

Bans and rationing have been used effectively to achieve desired reductions in harmful substances, and they could be applied more widely, but they are on the coercive end of the spectrum. With an eye toward less coercive means, Herman Daly and other economists have proposed a tradable permit system as an efficient method of limiting throughput.[17] Like bans and rationing, tradable permit systems set direct limits on the use or emission of a substance, but they offer more flexibility in how the limits are achieved. Such systems can come in several flavors, but most contain these basic elements:

- Based on the best available scientific information (and following the three operating rules proposed above), a public authority determines an overall quota for the use of a resource or emission of a pollutant.
- The public authority then distributes or auctions off a number of permits within this quota.
- Each permit mandates the amount of a resource the permit holder

can use or the amount of a pollutant the permit holder can emit over a specified period.

• Permit holders can trade their permits (or shares of them) in a competitive market.

The idea is to give permit holders as much autonomy as possible without allowing them to overuse resources or overtax waste absorption capacity.

An intriguing spinoff of tradable permit systems is "cap and share" (Figure 5.1). A cap-and-share scheme sets an overall cap on the use of a

1 THE CAP

A scientifically sound cap is set
each year for carbon emissions.

↓

2 THE SHARE

Government distributes annual
emission permits to all citizens.

↓

3 THE SELL

Citizens sell their permits in
an easy-to-access market.

↓

4 THE BUY

Fossil fuel companies buy permits
to cover the emissions that will be
produced by burning coal, oil, and gas.

↓

5 THE ENFORCEMENT

Inspectors match permits to fossil fuel
emissions, and then cancel the permits.

FIG. 5.1. A cap-and-share scheme for CO_2 management, in which citizens are allocated emission permits to sell to energy companies, could achieve desired reductions in carbon emissions while providing a fair method for citizens to earn income. SOURCE: see note 18.

resource and divides the cap into equal permits that are distributed to all citizens. Citizens may then sell these permits to industries, which must purchase them in order to use the resource. Each individual in the scheme effectively owns a share of the resource and sells a permit to producers seeking to profit from the resource. This setup assigns property rights for resources to citizens rather than to corporations. Income from the sale of permits compensates individuals for the increased prices that result from limiting the supply of the resource. As a bonus, individuals who consume less than their fair share of the goods and services produced from the resource are financially rewarded for their virtuous behavior.[18]

Direct methods of limiting throughput, such as bans, rationing, tradable permits, and cap-and-share schemes, have the benefit of offering security. Assuming throughput limits are determined with sound science, they have a high likelihood of accomplishing their purpose—maintaining throughput within ecological limits. But given the relative coerciveness of throughput limits, less direct methods may also prove worthwhile.

Indirect Methods to Limit Throughput

When economists consider ways to alter consumption habits, most of them sooner or later hit on taxation schemes. Taxes are able to influence behavior to some degree. For example, a "sin tax" on tobacco products attempts to reduce the unhealthy behavior of smoking by making it more costly. In addition to the deterrent effect, the revenue generated from sin taxes can be used to help mitigate the impacts of the undesirable behavior (e.g., paying the costs of medical care for smoking-related health problems). *Ecological tax reform* is a proposed system of sin taxes for curbing consumptive and waste-generating behavior. Ideally the tax burden is shifted onto items and activities that need to be limited in order to prevent environmental problems (e.g., pollution or vehicle miles traveled). The revenue generated from ecological taxes can replace revenue from other taxes, which can then be lowered or abolished (e.g., income taxes). As Herman Daly puts it, we should tax "bads" instead of goods.[19]

Sifting through an economics toolbox, you'd expect to find the tools for tax reform. But economists would do well to consider another tool for restricting throughput to a sustainable level—one found more often in an ecologist's toolbox: the conservation of natural areas.

Jurisdictions all over the world, from communities to nations, have gained extensive experience establishing and managing protected areas. These protected areas, such as national parks, wildlife refuges, and marine sanctuaries, are excluded from economic production—laws prohibit exploitation of these lands and waters and the resources they contain. Yet despite their importance, existing protected areas aren't getting the job done. In the United States, the majority of ecosystem types have relatively little of their area conserved.[20] Biologists have found that land protection efforts in North America are more likely to focus on scenic, economically unproductive lands at high elevation—essentially, rocks and ice.[21] Globally, the protected areas network has grown impressively in the last few decades and now covers more than 11 percent of the planet's land surface, but it falls short of providing security for the long-term survival of many vertebrate species.[22]

One prescription for enhancing the effectiveness of protected areas is to emulate the new vision for investment introduced in Chapter 4: we need to invest in more protected areas and locate them strategically to conserve a wider range of ecosystem services and biological diversity. Doing so would reduce throughput by taking more lands and natural resources off the market and by helping restore the ability of ecosystems to assimilate wastes (e.g., uptake of carbon dioxide by forests). Filling this prescription, however, is a thorny political and financial problem, because the majority of high-priority conservation regions around the world exist in low-income nations where paying the costs of establishment and enforcement is difficult.[23] Wealthy nations could help by employing "payment for ecosystem services" schemes, which offer financial incentives to farmers or landowners in exchange for managing their lands to provide some sort of ecological service.

Aldo Leopold, an early American ecologist whose work had a profound effect on the science of wildlife management, offered another prescription. He believed it was necessary to apply conservation approaches more broadly across the landscape—to adopt what he called a "land ethic." In Leopold's words, a land ethic "reflects the existence of an ecological conscience, and this in turn reflects a conviction of individual responsibility for the health of the land. Health is the capacity of the land for self-renewal. Conservation is our effort to understand and preserve this capacity."[24] Following Leopold's ideas, societies need to embrace a philosophy of stewardship and work toward conserving the health of all lands, instead of just fencing in a collection of protected areas.

WHERE DO WE GO FROM HERE?

Humanity sits in a precarious position. The global household is consuming too much stuff, and it's time to cut back. Success will likely require a combination of both direct and indirect policies, which may impinge on personal freedom to some degree. But regardless of the mix of policies, there are four prerequisites for moving forward.

First and foremost, we need to achieve a more equitable distribution of income and wealth (Chapter 7 discusses this topic in depth). As throughput-limiting policies take effect, available resources will decline. When this occurs, each person must be assured access to a fair share. What would happen if we maintained the current distribution of natural resources (and the goods and services that flow from them) in a scenario of limited resource use? The wealthy would capture an ever-greater proportion of the supply, and the poor would suffer. Therefore, any policy limiting the use of a resource must explicitly address how the value embodied in that resource can be fairly distributed among all citizens.

Second, we need a comprehensive monitoring system. Tracking economic throughput (and assessing whether that throughput is sustainable) requires good data collection and analysis systems. To see why, consider a limit on the use of fossil fuels. Such a limit would likely stimulate a significant increase in the production of biofuels, which could have unintended consequences on land use and food prices. Without monitoring, we'd have no way of tracking these indirect impacts, let alone the direct impacts of burning less fossil fuel. The information provided by monitoring programs could also help refine policies (e.g., changing the cap in a cap-and-share scheme in the event of unforeseen consequences), which would be very useful, as we undoubtedly will have to tinker with new policies to get them right. A good starting point for a nation to monitor throughput is to adopt green accounting procedures, such as the United Nations System of Environmental-Economic Accounts (SEEA 2003).[25] SEEA 2003 provides a framework for consistent analysis of the contribution of environmental resources to the economy, and the impact of the economy on the environment.

Third, we need to adopt an incremental approach. Imposition of resource-limiting policies would require considerable cultural and institutional changes across society. Applying such policies incrementally would allow space for people to alter their behavior and restructure economic institutions.

Fourth, we need to improve cooperation and coordination across all levels of government. The power to regulate the extraction and consumption of resources primarily resides at the national level, but the impacts from the use of such resources are often experienced globally. For example, oil supplies and forests fall under the jurisdiction of nations, but the management of these resources affects global common goods, such as climate and biodiversity. In addition, if one nation enacts limits on throughput, there's a real risk that capital and industry could flee to other countries that have not imposed such limits. A nation trying to establish sensible resource-use policies may face difficulties if other nations continue to pursue growth-based policies.

Resource limits, therefore, should ideally be set from the top down, starting at the global level and filtering through international regions, nations, and local communities. But the power to manage resources within these limits should reside with individuals and organizations at the local level. Such a process will require close cooperation among nations and coordination among smaller jurisdictions. Even though humanity has struggled to achieve such cooperation and coordination, encouraging precedents exist. The Montreal Protocol successfully restricted the use of chemicals that deplete stratospheric ozone (ozone protects life on earth from harmful UV radiation). Adoption and enforcement of the Montreal Protocol's rules required intense negotiations and buy-in from the international community.

Limiting throughput to sustainable levels requires fundamental alterations to the economic landscape. These alterations will no doubt come with costs, but the greater costs to fear are the costs of doing nothing. Is it worth the risk of wrecking our global household by cramming it full of more stuff than is necessary for people to live good lives? It will be a challenge to convince entrenched, pro-growth elites to accept needed changes, but maybe the 88 Percent can tackle the challenge.

Most people have heard of the 99 Percent—the self-proclaimed group of people fed up with the exorbitance of the top 1 percent of income earners—but who are the 88 Percent? In a survey of residents (eighteen and older) of the state of Oregon, 88 percent of respondents agreed that the United States "would be better off if we all consumed less."[26] It's hard to find any topic in politics on which 88 percent of people can agree—that's a strong majority calling for *enough*, and a solid base of support for maintaining a healthy household metabolism.

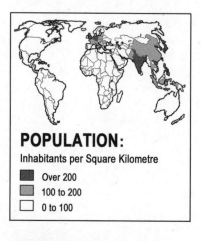

POPULATION:
Inhabitants per Square Kilometre

- ■ Over 200
- ▨ 100 to 200
- ☐ 0 to 100

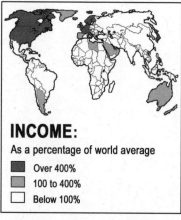

INCOME:
As a percentage of world average

- ■ Over 400%
- ▨ 100 to 400%
- ☐ Below 100%

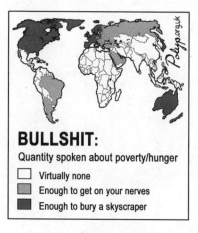

BULLSHIT:
Quantity spoken about poverty/hunger

- ☐ Virtually none
- ▨ Enough to get on your nerves
- ■ Enough to bury a skyscraper

[CHAPTER 6]
ENOUGH PEOPLE
Stabilizing Population

I've never seen a problem that wouldn't be easier to solve with fewer people. The same problem becomes harder, or ultimately impossible, when more people are involved.

SIR DAVID ATTENBOROUGH[1]

WHAT ARE WE DOING?

An unusual house sits in a typical middle-class neighborhood in the suburbs of Atlanta. Fifty homes that look like an early 1970s vision of the American dream line the neighborhood's shady cul-de-sacs. The mass-produced houses sit on parcels carved out of the forested red-clay slopes typical of Georgia's Piedmont region. These houses mostly look alike, since they share the same cultural and architectural roots, but the very last house at the end of the street stands out. It's a custom job with unusual coffee-colored brickwork, small built-in courtyards for rock gardens, and a design that still strikes most observers as being modern. It is the home of a Chinese-American family, and the youngest of the family's four children was my best friend when I was a kid.

It was obvious, even to a second-grader, that David's house was different on the outside, but I also noticed something different the first time I saw the inside. On the wall of the study, the room where we spent time discussing crucial matters such as Halloween costumes and the best design for a bicycle seat (banana or standard?), was a row of framed photos of U.S. presidents, from Lyndon Johnson to Jimmy Carter. Now that's an odd choice for a wall decoration, especially in a home adorned with scrolls, sculptures, and pottery from the Far East. Even odder was that each photo had a hand-written message and signature on it.

David's big brother, Bobby, who was born in 1967, came into this world as the 200-millionth American. His baby photos appeared in a spread on the pages of *Life* magazine. Bobby gained a sort of fame, because people were interested to watch his life unfold, to see how this random representative of America's population measured up. As a result, on each birthday, he received a signed photo from the president.

I hadn't thought about Bobby's status as the 200-millionth American for a long time, until a news story on October 17, 2006, brought it to mind. On that day, the 300-millionth American was born, and something about that fact unsettled me. It was the speed of the population growth. In less than forty years, we added 100 million people to the country. That's like adding ten more states the size of Georgia (with today's population) to the Union, or 185 more cities the size of Atlanta.

On the other side of the Atlantic, the population of the United Kingdom is also on the rise, projected to increase from its 2010 level of 62 million to 67 million in 2020, and 73 million in 2035.[2] The fact that the United States and United Kingdom populations are growing is troubling, since both countries have ecological footprints that are already higher than their biological capacity. The U.S. footprint is twice the size of its capacity, and the U.K. footprint surpasses its capacity by nearly four times.[3] Without further judgment of the sustainability of such population growth, it's safe to say that it makes for big changes to the economics and social fabric of a nation.

Panning out to the global scale, at the time of Bobby's birth, the earth held about 3.5 billion people.[4] In the years since, we've doubled the population to 7 billion. Seven billion is a number that's mostly outside of human experience, but the National Geographic Society has tried to make sense of it with a couple of compelling statistics:

- It would take two hundred years to count to 7 billion out loud.
- In 7 billion steps, you could circumnavigate the globe 133 times (assuming you could walk on water).[5]

Seven billion is still difficult to conceptualize, but understanding the very large effect that can arise from a very small rate of growth is even more difficult. The physicist Albert Bartlett has highlighted our mathematical shortcomings in his presentations, stating, "The greatest failing of the human race is our inability to understand the exponential function." Recall that the rule of thumb for calculating doubling time is to divide 70 by the percentage rate of growth, so a growth rate of only 1 percent per year applied to a population of 7 billion means that in about seventy years, the population will double to 14 billion. In short, a small, but constant, rate of growth causes a rapid rise in population. Currently, both the world and U.S. populations are growing at a little over 1 percent per year.[6]

Population growth over the past few centuries provides a striking example of the exponential function at work. Now demographers are trying to figure out what will happen to population numbers in the future. In its "medium" population projection, the United Nations estimates that global population will reach 9.3 billion by the year 2050, and over 10 billion by 2100 (Figure 6.1).[7]

Although sometimes construed as a North-versus-South issue, population growth and overpopulation affect a diverse range of nations. As Figure 6.2 shows, some of the most densely populated countries, such as the Netherlands, Japan, and the United Kingdom, are in

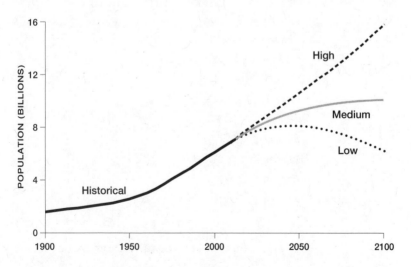

FIG. 6.1. Demographers expect world population to grow by another 1.2 to 3.7 billion people by 2050. The line from 1900 to 2010 shows historical data, while the three lines from 2010 to 2100 show the United Nations' three population growth projections (low, medium, and high). SOURCE: see note 7.

the global North.[8] Even so, there is a demographic difference between the more- and less-industrialized nations. Most nations in the North have lower population growth rates than those in the South.

Much has been said about the decline in population growth rates in industrialized nations. In European countries, Japan, and Russia (among other nations), fertility rates have dropped below the level associated with a stable population (generally around 2.1 children per woman in industrialized nations).[9] Population size is already shrinking in some of these countries, and it will likely fall soon in more (the United States is an exception—even though the rate of population

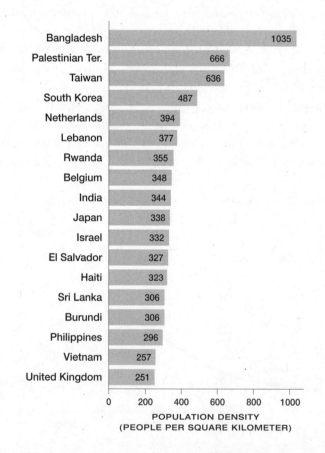

FIG. 6.2. The world's most densely populated nations form a diverse group, both geographically and culturally. Data are for the year 2007 and exclude small city and island states. SOURCE: see note 8.

growth is not as high as it used to be, record numbers of babies are being born, and population growth remains robust).[10] In light of the environmental consequences of overpopulation, stabilization and decreases might be viewed as a positive development. But nations with falling populations seem to fear this trend. They worry about what an aging population and a declining workforce will mean for pensions and social programs. Perhaps they're also worried about waning influence on the world stage, as the most populous nations tend to play bigger roles. In some cases, nations have acted on these worries by offering incentives to increase births. The Russian government initiated a program in 2006 to pay 250,000 rubles ($9,200) to women choosing to have a second baby—a huge payment that was higher than the average salary that year.[11]

It's a different story in many of the less-industrialized nations, where fertility rates remain high. For example, Niger has the highest total fertility rate of any nation at 7.6 children per woman. Fertility rates in nineteen other countries are above 5 children per woman.[12]

A cursory exploration of the numbers allows us to draw a simple conclusion: we live on a crowded planet, and it's growing more crowded, despite declining fertility rates. What are the implications of an increasing population? The total resource use of a country will increase when either the number of people living in the country increases, or the amount that each of these people consumes increases. The "I-PAT equation" summarizes how population interacts with other variables to produce environmental impacts.[13] It states that

$$I = P \times A \times T$$

where I quantifies total impact on the environment, P stands for population size, A represents affluence (calculated as income per person), and T explains the effect of technology (calculated as the environmental impact per unit of income).

To prevent I from growing too large and undermining planetary life-support systems (e.g., by destabilizing the climate), societies must manage the values of P, A, and T. Frugality and sufficiency can constrain A, and environmentally benign behavior and technological progress can constrain T, but there are limits to these capabilities.[14] Stabilization of P is necessary as well to construct an economy in balance with nature.[15] Such a balance will not be achievable if current population growth trends continue.

As described in Chapter 2, the ecological footprint of the global population is too large, and we are pushing beyond the safe operating space of planetary boundaries. But overpopulation is more than just an environmental issue; it's also an issue of social justice. The greater the world's population, the smaller the share of natural resources available to each person.

If the planet's resources were divided equally among all people, it's questionable whether there would be sufficient resources to provide a good life for all in a world headed toward 9.3 billion. Even if the situation could be sustained, it would be far from optimal. To alleviate poverty, citizens in wealthy nations must consume less, and population levels in all countries must be stabilized or reduced. We need smaller footprints, but we also need fewer feet.

Unfortunately the issue of population growth invites controversy, and people struggle to discuss it in a constructive way. Population growth is tied to divisive topics such as poverty, reproductive health, women's rights, immigration, and cultural and religious beliefs. People on both the left and right tend to shun the issue. Some fear that focusing attention on population detracts from what they view as more pertinent social justice issues, such as redistributing wealth from the rich to the poor.[16] Others fear that discouraging population growth will encourage abortion, or that halting population growth will cause economic hardships.[17] Still others see addressing population growth as an attack on human rights (e.g., the free movement of people or the right to reproductive choices).[18] The issue of population growth lives, politically speaking, in a limbo.

To be fair, population growth is a tricky topic, and population stabilization efforts have a sordid history, including compulsory abortions and forced sterilizations. With that backdrop, it's important to recognize that hidden in population numbers are real people—mothers and fathers, sons and daughters. Focusing solely on the numbers obscures the faces and personalities. Bobby ceases to be Bobby; instead, he becomes just the 200-millionth American.

Viewing population stabilization through a humanistic lens raises issues that need to be considered in any discussions of future policy. Marq de Villiers, an award-winning Canadian writer, embraces this humanistic perspective and raises questions about how we can arrive at the "right" number of people without being coercive.[19] Failure to contemplate such questions—failure to put a human face on our numbers—could lead to the development of immoral policies. To sidestep such an unwelcome possibility, we need to keep the social consequences of population policies firmly in mind as we attempt to stabilize the number of people on the planet.

WHAT COULD WE DO INSTEAD?

Many people, pundits, and politicians are content to take a wait-and-see approach to population growth. Most agree that stabilizing population is a worthy goal, but at the same time, they are relying on some sort of "natural" path to stability. It's easy to dodge the issue or hope the problem will take care of itself, but doing nothing, in light of evidence that we are already transgressing important environmental limits, may be the riskiest course.

Taking action is a more prudent approach, and there's a simple strategy that all nations can put into practice together—providing education about family planning and ensuring access to condoms and other contraceptives. Globally, roughly 80 million unintentional pregnancies occur each year. By coincidence, 80 million is also about the size of annual global population growth.[20] Widespread knowledge of contraceptives and more ease in obtaining them could significantly decrease the number of unplanned pregnancies and go a long way toward stabilizing global population. The high potential of this strategy explains why the Center for Biological Diversity, which recognizes the link between overpopulation and biodiversity loss, runs a project to distribute condoms.

Distribution of condoms can help avoid unwanted pregnancies, but there's a lot more work to do to reach population stability. Appropriate policies for any given nation depend on where its population increase is coming from: domestic births or immigration. Some nations with growing populations have high fertility rates and low—or negative— immigration rates. These tend to be low-income nations like Uganda and Mali. Other countries have low fertility rates and high immigration rates. These tend to be high-income nations like the United States and the United Kingdom (Table 6.1).[21] There are exceptions to this

TABLE 6.1. ESTIMATES OF INCOME, TOTAL FERTILITY RATES, AND IMMIGRATION RATES FOR SELECTED NATIONS IN 2011

Country	Income (GDP per capita, adjusted to account for purchasing power)	Total Fertility Rate (children born per woman)	Immigration Rate (immigrants per 1,000 residents)
Uganda	$1,300	6.69	–0.02*
Mali	$1,300	6.44	–5.23
United States	$48,100	2.06	4.18
United Kingdom	$35,900	1.91	2.60

SOURCE: see note 21.

*Negative values indicate that emigration is larger than immigration.

categorization, but generally we can declare two policy tracks, one for low-income, high-fertility countries and another for high-income, low-fertility countries.

Stabilizing Population in Low-Income, High-Fertility Nations

China introduced its one-child-per-family policy in 1980. Although the policy succeeded in slowing population growth, it is viewed mostly in a negative light for three main reasons. First, it has placed substantial constraints on personal freedom. Second, although taxes and propaganda have been the preferred ways of enforcing the policy, there have been cases of forced sterilizations and abortions. Third, the policy has produced an unforeseen demographic imbalance—the cultural preference for boys has skewed China's gender ratio, since many couples went out of their way to make sure that their one child was a boy. China now has perhaps 30 million single men called *guang gun* (bare branches).[22]

With the bad taste of China's one-child policy still lingering, demographers and activists have almost unanimously settled on a less coercive way to decrease fertility rates: the empowerment of women. Such empowerment requires that women have the same rights and opportunities as men. It also requires that girls have access to education. Girls who go to school and obtain an education tend to grow up to be mothers of fewer children.[23] The economist Jeffrey Sachs lists four reasons:

- Girls in school are likely to postpone marriage and child rearing.
- When girls learn about sex, contraception, reproductive health, and the trade-offs associated with having lots of children, they are more likely to aim for having smaller families.
- Having an education can empower a young woman to be a stronger negotiator with her spouse about family size and child rearing.
- Having an education can help a young woman develop a career, something that often leads her to desire a smaller family.[24]

The strategy of educating girls has benefits beyond reducing fertility rates; it also has the potential to help alleviate poverty—a true win-win for societies with high birth rates and low incomes. The challenge is to make sure families are able to send their daughters to school. This challenge requires a society to prioritize education and come up with the financial resources to pay for it. Education, often hailed as a key to growing the economy, is actually a key to stabilizing population and setting the stage for a transition to a steady-state economy. The high-income nations, whose fate is connected to the low-income ones, have a role to play in supporting education around the globe, but they also need to attend to population issues within their own borders.

Stabilizing Population in High-Income, Low-Fertility Nations

Roger Martin is a former U.K. diplomat. In that role, he participated in many negotiations to protect the environment. The more he examined environmental problems, the more he came to understand that most of them could trace their roots to there simply being too many people. Realizing that continuing population growth in the United Kingdom was undermining efforts to achieve a sustainable society, he decided to accept a position as chairman of the Optimum Population Trust (now Population Matters). In this capacity, Martin has made a number of recommendations for stabilizing population in the United Kingdom—recommendations that apply equally well to other wealthy nations.

One of his main recommendations is to raise the profile of sustainable population as a topic on the government's agenda. To accomplish that, he suggests appointing a high-ranking, inter-departmental official whose job description includes two main duties: (1) helping government agencies assess how their policies affect population growth, and (2) recommending a range of population stabilization measures.

Among such measures, Martin especially supports incentives to keep family size to two children or fewer. But another of his policy recommendations—the most important one for a nation with the United Kingdom's demographics—is to change immigration policy to achieve equal levels of immigration and emigration. Striking such a balance would require decreasing the number of people admitted through immigration.

On the other side of the Atlantic, famous lines from a sonnet inside the Statue of Liberty read:

> Give me your tired, your poor,
> Your huddled masses yearning to breathe free,
> The wretched refuse of your teeming shore.
> Send these, the homeless, tempest-tost to me,
> I lift my lamp beside the golden door![25]

Lady Liberty has been conveying this unofficial U.S. immigration policy since 1886 when she settled on her island near the tip of Manhattan. But in 1921, when waves of immigrants were making their way past her gaze to the entrance station at Ellis Island, Congress added some rules limiting the size of the huddled masses. Nowadays, the United States places strict limits on immigration, but its policies retain much of the humanitarian spirit of Lady Liberty's pronouncement. According to the Congressional Budget Office, U.S. immigration policy has four goals:

1. Admit workers with desired skills to fill job openings.
2. Reunite families by admitting immigrants who have relatives in the United States.
3. Provide refuge for people at risk of political, racial, or religious persecution.
4. Ensure diversity by admitting people from countries with historically low rates of immigration to the United States.[26]

These goals divide immigrants into three categories: (1) workers, (2) relatives, and (3) refugees (immigrants admitted under the fourth goal fall into one of these three categories). Other wealthy nations, like Canada, also apply similar categories.[27] Any plan to reduce the number of immigrants forces a decision about which categories of immigrants to reduce. We can't maintain the humanitarian spirit of immigration policy if we prevent families from reuniting or turn away refugees. That leaves workers as the primary category for cuts, but such cuts, it turns out, can actually strengthen the humanitarian nature of immigration policy.

The United States and other wealthy countries are recruiting immigrant workers, especially highly educated and skilled workers, for the purpose of spurring economic growth. This practice creates a "brain drain," in which the top talent in developing nations is lured away.[28] The practice is inappropriate for wealthy nations needing to make the transition to a steady-state economy—not only are they increasing their populations in the name of economic growth, but they're doing so at the expense of poorer countries. The home nations of these talented immigrants are often the very places that need their skills the most. Instead of recruiting educated and entrepreneurial people from abroad, wealthy nations should cultivate talent at home and encourage nations abroad to retain their most capable workers. This change would serve the humanitarian purpose of alleviating the conditions that induce emigration in the first place.

Immigration reform is necessary to stabilize populations in wealthy nations and around the globe, but it's a sensitive subject. So is the development of policies aimed at reducing birth rates. Think of the controversies and ideological battles swirling around family planning, contraception, immigration, and reproductive rights. That's why any policies in this area must be founded upon the principles of compassion and noncoercion—not just from an ethical standpoint, but also from a practical one. Without these two principles, proposed population policies will likely be rejected, and rightfully so. Compassion is necessary to avoid past mistakes and to establish policies beneficial to people of all nations. Noncoercion is necessary to put aside fears about trampling people's rights. After all, what impinges on our freedom more—noncoercive policies designed to limit family size, or the inevitable exhaustion of resources that will come from continued population growth? The answer is clear, but even compassionate, noncoercive population-stabilization policies will be a nonstarter unless we can open space for civil discussion.

WHERE DO WE GO FROM HERE?

If starting an intelligent conversation is the first step toward gaining traction on population policies, then we're fortunate to have a role model who can show us how to get the conversation going. Despite the gray in his hair, Bill Ryerson projects youthful energy. He's quick on his feet and can recall population statistics from an impressive reservoir of knowledge. His job title is founder and president of the Population Media Center (PMC), a nonprofit organization concerned about overpopulation. But really Ryerson's job title should be "soap opera producer."

PMC's soap operas are different from the standard fare—yes, there are plenty of melodramatic conflicts and betrayals, but their purpose is to help people consider and talk about reproductive options, which, in turn, helps them make healthy decisions about family size. The soap operas, broadcast in both TV and radio formats, might seem like an unscientific way to influence behaviors related to sex and family planning. But in reality, the storytelling framework stems from peer-reviewed research, and PMC statistically analyzes the results of each soap opera to assess how well the message is being received.

The process starts with customized plotlines and characters to reflect a targeted audience. The serial dramas are entertaining (some of PMC's programs have topped the ratings), but the real intent is to provide role models. Albert Bandura, a widely cited psychologist, has demonstrated that mass-media role models can be powerful teachers of attitudes and behavior.[29] As the characters in PMC's soap operas deal with the consequences of their decisions regarding sex—exposure to sexually transmitted disease, treatment of wives and daughters, and pregnancy—the audience gets to live vicariously and absorb some take-home lessons. Audiences cringe as "bad-guy" characters make dubious decisions and their lives spiral out of control. But the truly influential characters are those who overcome obstacles and uncertainties to make positive changes in their lives.[30]

Some of the plots are heartwarming, but not nearly as heartwarming as the results. For example, PMC broadcast 257 episodes of the radio drama *Yeken Kignit* (Looking over One's Daily Life) in Ethiopia between 2002 and 2004. An independent study, which surveyed both listeners and non-listeners before and after the program aired, found:

- Nearly half of Ethiopia's population tuned into *Yeken Kignit* regularly.
- The fertility rate fell from 5.4 to 4.3 children per woman.
- Demand for contraceptives increased by 157 percent.
- Listeners were five times more likely than non-listeners to know three or more methods of family planning.
- There was a 50 percent increase in communication between mothers and their children about sexuality issues.[31]

PMC's TV and radio projects provide an artistic way to get the conversation started. Another encouraging way has been demonstrated by the Global Population Speak Out. Organizers of the Speak Out recruit participants who are asked simply to fulfill a promise to deliver a public presentation on population issues. Up and running for only a few years, the Speak Out program has been active in fifty nations on six continents. The theme of reaching a global population of 7 billion dominated the Speak Out in 2011.[32]

There's that unfathomably large number again—7 billion. With 7 billion of us on the planet, the passing of the torch from the 200- to the 300-millionth American seems like a nonevent. In fact, news articles about it took a human-interest angle, with whimsical titles like "Time to Move Over, Mr. 200 Millionth."[33] Few questioned the environmental or social sustainability of adding 100 million more people to the U.S. population. But the reality is that it was a major event, and world population growth to 7 billion is a mind-blowing event. Unprecedented numbers of people are using unprecedented quantities of resources. If we want to achieve a sustainable economy, conserve some natural ecosystems on this finite planet, and give people—including those not yet born—a fair piece of the pie, we need to stabilize our numbers.

[CHAPTER 7]

ENOUGH INEQUALITY

Distributing Income and Wealth

> *Among the new objects that attracted my attention during my stay*
> *in the United States, none struck me with greater force than the*
> *equality of conditions. I easily perceived the enormous influence*
> *that this primary fact exercises on the workings of the society.*
>
> ALEXIS DE TOCQUEVILLE (1835)[1]

WHAT ARE WE DOING?

In 1897 two tremendously influential artists were born in the American South. One lived a life of poverty, died in his forties among the ashes of his burned-down house, and remained anonymous until years after his death. The other lived into his mid-sixties, garnered international fame, and accumulated plenty of money and prestigious awards.

If you have a name like Blind Willie Johnson, then you just might be a blues musician. In the life stories of blues artists, it's hard to separate myth from fact, but according to a mishmash of sources, Johnson was raised by his father and stepmother, both of whom had a mean streak. When Johnson was seven years old, his father beat his stepmother when he caught her with another man. In a ghastly moment of revenge, she picked up a handful of lye and threw it into the face of her attacker's son.[2] Blind as a result of this violent act, Johnson turned to religion and gospel music. He went on to preach and perform on street corners. He played a soulful slide guitar while singing with a gravelly bass voice "that could grind glass."[3] He caught the attention of Columbia Records and recorded a set of songs between 1927 and 1930. Despite his musical talents, he lived his whole life in poverty. When his home burned down in 1945, he had nowhere else to go, so he remained among the ruins. In the open air, he fell ill and died.[4]

The details of Johnson's life stand in stark contrast to what happened after it. Is there another musician whose obscurity blossomed into such far-reaching influence? Musical acts such as Bob Dylan, Led Zeppelin, Eric Clapton, the Grateful Dead, Beck, and the White Stripes have commended his work and covered his songs. But the pinnacle of his posthumous career is the inclusion of his song "Dark Was the Night, Cold Was the Ground" on the *Voyager* satellites' Golden Records. The emotive force of Blind Willie Johnson's music is hurtling through space on its way to distant star systems.

Johnson's contemporary and fellow Southerner, William Faulkner, lived a different sort of life. He was born into a well-to-do family in Mississippi, and he received a good education. While Johnson was recording his songs, Faulkner was writing his novels, including *The Sound and the Fury* (1929) and *As I Lay Dying* (1930). In 1949, he won the Nobel Prize for Literature for "his powerful and artistically unique contribution to the modern American novel,"[5] and he also collected a Pulitzer Prize in 1954 and a second one in 1962, the year of his death. His passing was widely reported in the media, including coverage of his funeral by the novelist William Styron in *Life* magazine.[6]

Faulkner deplored the inequalities that mired Johnson in a life of poverty. He wrote, "To live anywhere in the world today and be against equality because of race or color is like living in Alaska and being against snow."[7] All his life he witnessed the social ills of inequality at home in Mississippi, and he wrote frequently and forcefully about it—a brave thing to do in the Deep South.

The racist and segregationist policies that created the disparities between Willie Johnson and William Faulkner have largely disappeared, and attitudes about justice and equality have changed with the times. In the years after Johnson and Faulkner died, it appeared that income inequality was also fading. But over the last few decades it has staged a comeback. In the 1950s and 1960s, top corporate executives in the United States took home 25 to 30 times the income of typical workers. In 1980, CEOs earned 40 times more than workers. By 1990 the gap had widened to 100 times. And in 2007, the difference was an astonishing 350 times.[8] More and more, wealth is concentrating at the top of the pyramid.

Economic growth is frequently used as an excuse to avoid dealing with such inequality. The conventional wisdom is that "a rising tide lifts all boats," but this trickle-down approach has not worked. The richest fifth of Americans make eight and a half times more than the poorest fifth, while the richest fifth in the United Kingdom make over seven times more than the poorest. Such income gaps are much larger than in most other high-income countries (Figure 7.1).[9] It appears that the rising tide is lifting the yachts and swamping the rowboats.

FIG. 7.1. The gap in income between the richest 20 percent and poorest 20 percent of earners varies across countries. The ratios shown are averages for the years 2003 to 2006. SOURCE: see note 9.

As the fruits of economic growth have continued to concentrate in the storerooms of the rich, negative consequences have piled up for people across the income spectrum. As Richard Wilkinson and Kate Pickett show in their groundbreaking book *The Spirit Level*, less equal societies have a powerful tendency to become dysfunctional. Inequality, both among high-consuming countries and among the fifty U.S. states, is correlated with the signs of "broken societies" (Figure 7.2).[10]

The hierarchical structure that forms in unequal societies results in widespread mistrust, crime, violence, and a host of related problems.[11] Inequality produces the conditions for social ills, but it also contributes to environmental problems. Large income gaps lead to unhealthy status competition and consumption of materials and energy beyond what's necessary to meet people's needs. These higher levels of throughput, as described in Chapter 5, can degrade ecological systems.

The growing gap between the rich and the poor could be a product of human nature (if we believe that people are inherently greedy), or it

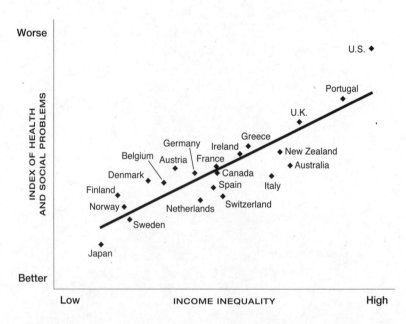

FIG. 7.2. Nations with greater income inequality have more health problems (e.g., mental illness, shorter life expectancy, obesity) and more social breakdowns (e.g., high rates of imprisonment, homicide, and teenage motherhood). The close-fitting trend line demonstrates a strong correlation. SOURCE: see note 10.

could simply be the result of an economic system that encourages this type of behavior. Conventional economic theory paints people as "rational utility maximizers." This theory assumes that individuals make decisions to maximize personal gains, and under this assumption, people are justified in attempting to earn as much as possible. But scholars who study behavior are finding that people often behave with fairness in mind, and not according to purely selfish motivations. Sociologists Gerald Marwell and Ruth Ames designed an experiment decades ago that demonstrates this finding.[12]

In the experiment, participants are given a number of tokens and presented with a choice: invest their tokens in a "private bank" that guarantees a small payout per token invested, or invest tokens in a "community bank." The community bank pays a return to all participants, whether they invest in it or not. But the more participants invest in the community bank, the higher its payout. And with only modest investment, this payout quickly surpasses the payout of the private bank. A rational utility maximizer would invest all his tokens in the private bank to gain the biggest payout, acting like a "free rider" on the virtuous investments of other participants who put tokens in the community bank. But that's not what happens in practice. Instead, people put a substantial share of their tokens (about 42 percent) in the community bank. Interestingly, students of economics had the lowest rate of investment (20 percent) in the community bank.[13]

Evidence of the preference for fairness-seeking over self-serving behavior can also be seen in the public's increasing frustration with income inequality. Outrage is in the air—you can breathe it on the streets. Protestors around the world, from Wall Street to Syntagma Square, have expressed their indignation over the inequality between the top 1 percent of income earners and the remaining 99 percent. Having experienced a series of economic crises, starting with the subprime meltdown of 2008, growing numbers of citizens are finding that the idea of a more equitable distribution of income and wealth resonates with their sense of fairness.

WHAT COULD WE DO INSTEAD?

Henry Wallich (1914–1988), a distinguished American economist and central banker, once said, "Growth is a substitute for equality of income. So long as there is growth there is hope, and that makes large income differentials tolerable."[14] Wallich's sentiment may be true, but if so, then the reverse is also true. Greater equality of income is a substitute for growth, and it's a desirable one in a world where the economy is bumping up against biophysical limits.

More than just a *desirable* substitute for growth, equality of income may also be a *necessary* substitute. In a steady-state economy with a stable level of resource use, total income would remain relatively stable—in correspondence to the finite quantity of resources flowing through the economy. To adapt to this situation (and prevent the political turmoil that would result from an unfair distribution), society needs to develop customs, laws, and institutions to distribute the nongrowing stream of income in an equitable way.

The good news is that the benefits of a more equitable distribution are well documented. As Wilkinson and Pickett show, more equal societies perform better on a variety of health and social measures. The list of positive outcomes that accrue to more egalitarian societies is remarkable:

- People enjoy better health and a higher life expectancy.
- Fewer citizens develop drug addictions.
- People are less victimized by violence.
- Birth rates among teenage girls are lower.
- Children experience higher levels of well-being.
- The rate of obesity declines.
- Mental illness is less common.
- Fewer people end up in prison.
- Opportunities for social mobility are more widespread.

In addition, the benefits of equality are not confined to the poor—they flow to all members of society. For instance, the wealthiest people in societies with narrow income gaps tend to live longer than the wealthiest people in societies with large income gaps.[15]

But wait, doesn't the possibility of receiving higher pay serve as an incentive for hard work and innovation? That's a common argument made against policies that encourage greater equality. The thinking is that monetary incentives, in the form of large salaries and big bonuses, provide motivation for entrepreneurs and inventors. But do societies really need high levels of inequality to foster innovation? If this were the case, you'd expect more patents to be issued in societies with larger income gaps, but that doesn't happen.[16] In fact, research suggests that larger financial incentives lead to poorer performance on almost anything but the most rudimentary tasks. People perform best when they are given the freedom to direct their own work, the opportunity to improve their skills, and when they feel that their work has meaning and purpose.[17]

Such insights lead to the conclusion that wealthy nations can improve their living conditions by focusing on equality rather than economic growth.[18] Improvements in quality of life within these countries depend more on social relations than on higher levels of consumption,[19] and the reduction of income gaps provides a golden opportunity to enhance such relations. Greater equality can improve social relationships by lessening status competition, suppressing unnecessary and conspicuous consumption, and improving psychological well-being. In short, an economy that features greater equality is likely to have both healthier citizens and a healthier environment.

The question, then, isn't about whether we would benefit from greater equality; the question is how to achieve it. There are two basic strategies. The first is straightforward redistribution of wealth and income through the use of taxes, social programs, and minimum income requirements. Sweden and the state of Vermont are good examples of societies that achieve high equality using taxes and generous social programs. The second strategy is to encourage a smaller difference between the wages of high and low earners to begin with, so that redistribution is less necessary. Japan and the state of New Hampshire achieve high equality without large taxes and redistribution by maintaining a smaller wage gap.[20] Regardless of how a society goes about achieving greater equality, changes can happen quickly. At the end of World War II, Japan had an inequitable distribution of wealth, and the United States had an equitable one. The two nations have since swapped positions.[21]

Progressive taxation and social programs have been used effectively in many places to attain a more even distribution of wealth. Programs like Social Security and Medicaid in the United States provide a boost and essential services to people with low incomes. Many nations have become comfortable with applying taxes and using such programs, but another untried intervention could more directly address income in-equality and the social ills that accompany it.

A *citizen's income* (also known as a minimum income or basic in-come) provides an unconditional, automatic payment to each individual in a society as a right of citizenship.[22] A high-profile U.K. study found that insufficient income is associated with diminished prospects for long-term health and life expectancy. A citizen's income could provide better prospects by placing everyone on the same starting line—a line that allows each person to meet basic needs related to nutrition, physi-cal activity, housing, social interaction, transportation, medical care, and hygiene.[23]

As a universal benefit, a citizen's income could replace other direct benefits provided by the state. Elimination of such benefits would free up money to fund a citizen's income. It could also be funded by estab-lishing a ceiling on income or the accumulation of wealth. Consider the wealth held by the heirs of Sam and Bud Walton. When the two brothers who founded Walmart died, their heirs received a huge in-heritance. Today these six people, born into their positions of privilege (actually, one of them married into it), have as much wealth as roughly the bottom 30 percent of Americans.[24] That's more than 90 million people! Enough money sits in the accounts of the super-rich (with more flowing in by the day) to cover the costs of a citizen's income. In ad-dition, an income ceiling would further reduce the gap between rich and poor.

The strategy of redistribution through taxes or a citizen's income may be effective, but it comes with a risk. A government can easily abolish taxes or overturn income policies. And governments have been known to be influenced by special interests and the wealthiest members of society. That's a large part of the story behind the widening income gap from the 1950s to the present day.

The second strategy, which is on display in Japan and New Hamp-shire, overcomes this risk by narrowing income differentials from the outset. This strategy can be categorized as workplace democratization; its thrust is to weave democracy into the fabric of economic institutions. Policies that address inequalities where they originate (most notably in the workplace) are likely to be the most effective way to achieve long-lasting equality. The key is to put control of companies, government agencies, and nonprofit organizations into the hands of the people who work in them, use their services, or live in the communities affected by them.[25] Some approaches to do this include the following:

Set maximum pay differentials. Some organizations have successfully instituted pay-scale ratios, such that the highest-paid employee can earn only a certain percentage more than the lowest-paid employee. For example, the Mondragon Cooperatives in Spain have a range of pay differentials from 3:1 to 9:1 (with an average of 5:1).[26] Other cooperatives in the United Kingdom have established similar ratios, and a 20:1 ratio has been proposed for U.K. public sector employees.[27]

Establish more employee-owned companies. In such companies, employees are the shareholders, and profits are reinvested into activities that the employees consider to be valuable. There is less of a tendency to undertake speculative or needlessly risky actions in pursuit of profit, and employees have more say in company policies, including those that determine wages.

Transform enterprises into cooperatives. A cooperative is a member-owned and member-governed organization that exists to serve its members and share its profits. Democratic control is a cornerstone of cooperative enterprises, and examples of flourishing cooperatives can be found in a variety of economic sectors (see Chapter 11 for a broader discussion).[28]

Improve gender balance. Having more women in positions of power within economic institutions could help drive income equality. As institutions reexamine their cultural climates, they may be able to dismantle social hierarchies that inhibit income equality (along with gender equality).

The strategy of workplace democratization may also produce cascading effects that help ensure fair distribution of wealth and income over the long run. Democratization could help build a culture that values income equality, which would make it easier to establish and maintain tax policies and social programs that contribute to even greater equality.

WHERE DO WE GO FROM HERE?

If you listen to "Cold Was the Night, Dark Was the Ground," you can practically feel the hardship in Willie Johnson's voice. In all likelihood, he would have been healthier and happier had he lived in a more equitable society. Reduction of inequality can certainly help individuals struggling with poverty, but it can make everyone else better off as well. The inspiring benefits of greater equality are waiting to be taken advantage of. The key is to attack inequality on a variety of fronts, starting with a strong movement to democratize economic institutions. Oftentimes an external threat compels such a fundamental social or economic shift. For example, Japan's modern-day equality sprang from its horrendous experience in World War II. Whether such a threat or crisis appears or not, we can build a stronger and more resilient economy by actively seeking the transformation of economic institutions to provide greater equality.

But even with good intentions and well-designed policies, it may still prove difficult to reduce inequality because of certain aspects of human nature. Base human emotions such as fear, greed, and desire for status may drive inequality and push society toward wide income gaps. Although human beings also have other, more altruistic motivations, our negative emotions are reinforced and exploited by advertising, news stories, television, movies, Internet sources, and other forms of consumer culture that send misguided messages about the benefits of having *more*. But what's the point of material success amid social failure—can we be truly wealthy in a broken society? A cultural shift away from the endless and exhausting pursuit of *more* to the satisfying and secure recognition of *enough* is a prerequisite to implementing the required changes to economic institutions (see Chapter 12 for more about this cultural shift).

Cultural shifts and big policy changes require a home that provides an enduring base of support. The Occupy movement, which began as a protest on Wall Street in September 2011 and morphed into a worldwide phenomenon, may turn out to be such a base for establishing greater income equality. The movement's call for greater income equality can be seen as a continuation of past efforts to win other types of equality. As such, it and other future movements could benefit by looking to and learning from those efforts, especially the Civil Rights movement, which would have put Willie Johnson and William Faulkner on an equal footing if they were alive today. Thanks to these past efforts, racism, sexism, and homophobia have become socially unacceptable. The goal now is to make greedy behavior just as unacceptable.

Two big lessons from past movements can guide action toward achieving greater income equality. Lesson number one is that people will only accept a big social change if they believe that they and their families will be secure after the change. New economic institutions must demonstrate that they can provide this security. We need to build and nurture working examples of democratized workplaces. The Evergreen Cooperative Laundry in Cleveland, Ohio, provides one inspiring model. It's an employee-owned, environmentally conscientious enterprise that's meeting community needs and offering jobs and hope within a poverty-stricken urban area.[29]

Lesson number two is that public education is a critical component of the cultural shift; people have to understand the benefits of equality and democratized workplaces before they'll support them. Corporate board members who understood equality would refrain from authorizing oversized salaries and bonuses. Legislators who understood it would maintain fair tax laws and eliminate loopholes. Most of all, neighbors who understood it would see one another in a different light. They would realize that there is no prosperity unless it is a shared prosperity.

[CHAPTER 8]

ENOUGH DEBT

Reforming Monetary and Financial Systems

> *Even the apparently simple question of where money comes from is hard to answer. It's not the government printing press; money really originates when banks make loans. And since they charge interest for those loans, part of the endless-economic-growth model is in place right from the beginning—without the growth, you can't pay off the interest.*
>
> BILL MCKIBBEN[1]

WHAT ARE WE DOING?

In the early 1990s when financial derivatives were taking off in the world of securities trading, one of Wall Street's rising stars, John Fullerton, was taking off on a flight bound for Tokyo. It was his inaugural trip as the manager of J. P. Morgan's commodities investment business in Asia, and it was a heady time. He was young—in fact, he was the second-youngest person ever to have become a manager at the renowned bank—and, as he remembers it, he was "running with the big dogs."[2]

When the flight got under way, he smiled to himself as he unfolded a copy of the *New York Times*. In addition to the demands of his rising career, he faced the demands of having a two-year-old and an infant at home. The first-class seat seemed like a luxury, but it was nothing compared to the luxury of being able to relax in peace with a newspaper. He should have felt like a million dollars, but instead he had an uneasy sense that he was in the wrong place. The fact that it was Father's Day weekend undoubtedly played a role. As they might say in the financial industry, leaving his family behind on that particular weekend had a "deflationary effect" on his excitement about his new job. But something else also troubled him.

As he browsed the business section of the *Times*, two articles caught his attention. The first was about a struggling federal housing program. He wasn't particularly interested in housing issues, but the article reminded him that there were plenty of problems in the world in need of attention besides a portfolio of bank investments. The second article was about media business icon Walter Annenberg, who had donated huge sums of money to several schools near the end of his life. The article quoted the head of one of the schools as not knowing what to do with the massive cash infusion. Fullerton thought, "What was the point of accumulating so much money—enough to become a philanthropist—if you couldn't make intelligent decisions about how to invest it?" It seemed that even the financial success of someone like Walter Annenberg came with a downside. Contemplating these news stories reinforced Fullerton's emerging doubt about spending his whole career in the high-flying world of investment banking. These thoughts contributed significantly to what he calls his "rolling epiphany"—a growing awareness of fundamental flaws in the way the financial system works.

A number of people around the world are rolling along with Fullerton toward the same epiphany. Protests in the United States have showcased public outrage about the way Wall Street operates, and in Greece and other European countries, people have expressed anger over the austerity programs proposed to deal with high levels of debt. The problem is that both the financial system and its lifeblood—money—are becoming increasingly unhinged from real assets.

Fullerton has some ideas about how to reform the financial system based on his years as a banking industry insider, but when considering the basics of money, he's refreshingly open about what he doesn't know. He says, "I frankly don't understand money. It's way more complicated than any of us realize." And he's not alone. In their textbook *Ecological Economics*, Herman Daly and Joshua Farley write, "Anyone who is not confused by money probably hasn't thought about it very much."[3]

Money serves three key functions in modern society. First, it's a *medium of exchange*, an intermediary used in trade to avoid the inconveniences of a barter system. Second, it's a *unit of account*, as things are sometimes assigned money values even if they are not being bought or sold (e.g., unsold inventories in warehouses). And third, it's a *store of value*, in that it can be saved and used in the future to purchase goods and services.[4] These three functions of money make it a very useful tool for helping people get what they need. But even with these well-defined functions, three key misconceptions about money and finance cause us to use them in unsustainable ways.

Misconception Number 1: Money Is Wealth

Wealthy characters in comic books, such as Scrooge McDuck and Richie Rich, often make a sport of diving into vast piles of gold. In calmer moments, they might take a stroll through a personal vault that contains bags of money stacked from floor to ceiling. The gold and cash are proof of their "wealth," but money is not real wealth—it's a *claim on wealth*.[5] Real wealth takes the form of housing, land, fertile soil, medical care, dinner, and computers—actual resources, goods, and services that have value. Money itself has no intrinsic value. Its value is derived from the fact that we accept it in exchange for real wealth. The only reason anyone wants money is to be able to trade it for a bundle of goods and services (or, more cynically, to have the status and power that accrue to someone who can make many such trades).

The fact that money serves as a claim on wealth poses a problem when its supply surpasses the supply of real wealth. When there are too many claims on real wealth, prices go up (i.e., inflation occurs) as more and more money chases the same volume of goods and services.[6] Unfortunately the system is rigged for this to happen because of the mathematics of compound interest. Take, for example, a simple investment in which a millionaire deposits a million dollars in a savings account at 5 percent interest per year. His interest earnings in that first year total $50,000. With compound interest, that $50,000 payment is added to the principal, and the next interest payment is calculated based on the new total. So the following year's earnings come to $52,500. And then it's off to the races. No physical law prevents the claim on wealth in this savings account from expanding indefinitely—it could increase as high as we can count. However, the supply of goods and services that this money can buy can grow only according to the laws of physics and ecology that govern the real world.

Around the globe, claims on wealth (in the form of debt) have been ballooning. An example from the United Kingdom demonstrates the trend (Figure 8.1).[7] Between 1965 and 1985, the money supply and GDP grew at a similar rate, but following deregulation of the finance industry in 1986, the money supply began to grow much faster than GDP. In recent years, the money supply has become almost completely detached from the real economy, as new financial instruments have allowed banks to pump more and more money into the economy. The disconnect has caused much of the economic and financial instability in the world today..

As long as our claims on wealth are growing, there's a strong incentive to produce enough real wealth to keep pace. Imagine the potential for social chaos if people suddenly found that their money couldn't buy what they thought it could—that there was too much money and not enough real wealth. (Actually, you don't have to imagine it; you can study historical instances of hyperinflation or the effects of the subprime mortgage crisis.) Growing the economy has been the strategy for preventing the financial system from collapsing, but this is a case of the tail wagging the dog. Money should *serve* the economy, not *govern* it.

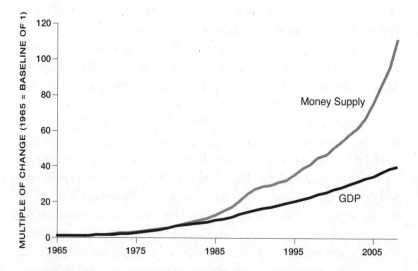

FIG. 8.1. The money supply (claims on wealth) is becoming increasingly detached from economic output (as measured by GDP) in the United Kingdom. Quantities for the money supply and GDP are expressed as multiples of their values in 1965. SOURCE: see note 7.

Misconception Number 2:
Governments Are the Primary Money Creators

Another common belief holds that money originates from the print-ing presses and coin mints of governments. Some of it does, but only a small fraction. In the United Kingdom, for example, the Bank of England and the Royal Mint create about 3 percent of the money in circulation as banknotes and coins. Private banks create most of the money in the form of interest-bearing loans.[8] Banks do this by a simple trick of bookkeeping. An example helps explain the process.

Suppose you want to buy something expensive like a car, but you don't have the money to pay for it up front, so you go to the bank for a loan. Assuming we're not in the subprime mortgage era, the bank might do a little research on your financial health. After judging you to be creditworthy, it grants you a loan. In one column of its books, the bank enters a *liability*, the money loaned to you. In the other column, it enters an *asset*, the money owed by you. Everything balances out be-cause the two numbers are equal.[9] With a few keystrokes on the com-puter, the bank simply transfers money into your account. The money didn't come from the bank's vault. It didn't come from a central bank like the Federal Reserve. It came from nowhere.

How can banks operate in this way? Banks are able to create money out of thin air because they can legally issue loans far in excess of the money they hold on deposit. In the United States, the Board of Gov-ernors of the Federal Reserve Bank sets reserve requirements, which specify how much money a bank must have on deposit in comparison to its liabilities.[10] Over time reserve requirements have become more and more lenient.[11] In fact, the reserve requirement for some types of accounts is zero.[12] The result is that banks have very few restrictions on how much money they can create.

But the story doesn't end there. Money that is created by a bank in the form of a loan must be paid back by the borrower. The borrower has to go out and earn this money by engaging in economic activity (e.g., doing a job). In addition to the principal, the borrower has to pay inter-est, which generates even more economic activity. Debt-based money creation, therefore, drives economic growth, the primary reason why a steady-state economy requires a different sort of monetary system.

Another reason is that the current money system also fuels an upward spiral of debt. Since loan recipients must pay back more money than they borrow, the total money supply must expand over time to avoid defaults. This additional money can only come from one place: more loans. As a consequence, the total amount of debt must increase over time for the financial system to continue functioning under its current conventions. It's a bit like using your Visa to pay off your Mastercard—except applied to the whole economy.

This method of money creation is inherently risky. If banks stop lending, the whole system collapses. That risk became clear in the meltdown of 2008. The flow of credit from banks slowed and threatened to topple a number of financial institutions. National governments intervened with taxpayer-funded bailouts to keep the system running, at least in the short term. In the aftermath, many taxpayers felt they had been fleeced, and rightfully so. Money that could have been spent on salaries for school teachers, vaccinations for children, repairs to crumbling infrastructure, or other worthy public projects went, instead, to big banks.

The meltdown and bailouts eroded some of the trust people have in the system of finance. For money to work, people must trust it. After all, who would be willing to accept money as payment if no one believed in its value? Trust in money largely exists because the government guarantees the currency and is willing to back it up in times of crisis. Yet control of this necessary public resource, and the profit made from producing it, is given to a small number of private banks. The ability to create money and lend it at interest provides banks with huge profits, while taxpayers receive only a small amount of revenue from the issue of banknotes and coins.[13] Moreover, this right to create money gives the banking sector incredible power to decide where to direct investments in society.[14]

Misconception Number 3: The Current Financial System Needs to Be Maintained for Economic Health

Financial institutions have a legitimate role to play in the economy—to facilitate investment of scarce resources in enterprises that will make the best use of them. For providing this service, financial institutions should earn a modest return. However, instead of allocating capital efficiently, financial institutions are using a variety of convoluted financial instruments to create and redistribute money to themselves, at great cost to the rest of society. The financial sector is capturing vast sums of money through speculation, as banks buy and sell securities and profit from fluctuations in their prices. In these transactions, the *underlying* value of the assets is not important—it may not even change. What matters is the *perceived* value and whether the assets can be sold for more than their original purchase price. Money is being created and shuffled about in a shell game where nothing tangible is produced, and where, at the end of the game, the banks have all of the money. In fact, a third of the money created by banks in recent years was simply loaned to other banks.[15] In a phenomenon called "financialization," the U.S. financial sector has accounted for more and more of the nation's total economic activity (Figure 8.2),[16] but it is questionable whether this activity has produced anything useful.

A contributing cause of financialization is that financiers fail to understand how the financial system relates to three broader systems. The financial system is a subsystem of the economy, the economy is a subsystem of human society, and human society is a subsystem of the biosphere. Without recognizing these relationships, financiers and their institutions are driving global processes that negatively impact the biosphere.

Unlike most of his colleagues, John Fullerton understands the

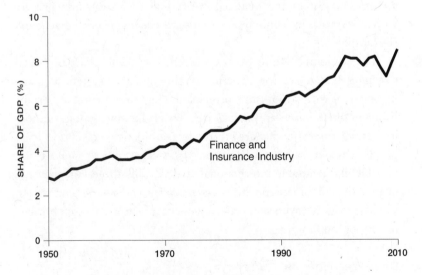

FIG. 8.2. The finance and insurance industry has accounted for an increasing percentage of total economic output in the United States over the last few decades. SOURCE: see note 16.

financial system's modest position within these other systems, but he's not a typical financier. After studying the bigger picture and realizing that the financial system was having a negative influence on the three broader systems, his "rolling epiphany" was complete, and he knew he had to reinvent his career. In a striking transformation from Wall Street insider to Wall Street reformer, he founded the Capital Institute in 2009.

The Institute approaches finance with a worldview grounded in the science of the biosphere rather than unrealistic economic theories. This worldview demands an overhaul of monetary and financial systems. As Fullerton says, "If there are limits to economic growth, then there are also limits to debt and limits to investment." The challenge is to design a monetary and financial system that respects these limits—a system that promotes stability instead of growth.

WHAT COULD WE DO INSTEAD?

To achieve a steady-state economy, we need to eliminate the growth imperative that is built into the current monetary and financial system. Such a change means overhauling the process of money creation and accepting a more modest role for financial institutions. We need a monetary system and financial institutions that are commensurate with a nongrowing economy, and that serve the interests of society and the biosphere.

The economists Molly Scott Cato and Mary Mellor have proposed sweeping changes to the structure of the monetary system to make it consistent with steady-state principles. They recommend the establishment of (1) a *debt-free national currency* created by a public authority, (2) *local currencies* that are created by communities to support local production and trade, and (3) an *international currency* to support sustainable and equitable international trade.[17] This three-currency approach, in combination with a *restructuring of financial institutions*, would provide a way to support economic transactions without breaching ecological limits.

Debt-Free National Currency

The most important change needed in the monetary system is to prohibit private banks from issuing money as debt. To accomplish this, the reserve requirement should gradually be raised to 100 percent, so that banks are no longer able to create money out of thin air.[18] The practice of creating money as debt should be made illegal, just as counterfeiting is. At the same time, the power to create money should be transferred to a public authority such as a central bank. The central bank would decide how much money is necessary to facilitate exchange in the economy, create this money debt-free, and transfer it to the government to spend into existence.[19]

Under this system, savings and investment would be separated. A customer could choose to save money by depositing it in a bank, where it would remain without being loaned or invested. No interest would be paid on such a deposit, and the bank might charge the customer a fee for this safe-keeping service. Alternatively, the customer could invest the money through a bank or other financial intermediary, and potentially earn interest. In this case, the customer would have no access to the money until the loan was repaid.

As the public reclaims the power of money creation, the priorities for investing newly created money should be determined democratically. The money could, for example, be used to build the infrastructure for a low-carbon economy (public transport, insulation for homes, improved electricity transmission grids, and so on) or to finance social programs, such as public education.

To prevent inflation, taxation and government spending would need to be linked to the system of money creation. If prices started to rise, money could be removed from circulation using taxes. Conversely, if prices started to fall, additional money could be created and spent into existence. This system would allow the size of the money supply, and hence inflation, to be controlled more directly than is possible with the current debt-based banking system.

Local Currency

A local currency is money that is issued by a community and valid for transactions only within that community. It can serve as a substitute for the national currency in local transactions, as long as businesses agree to accept it, citizens are willing to use it, and a bank or local exchange provides a service to swap the local currency for units of the national currency. This rather modest idea can produce far-reaching social and environmental benefits.

Since a local currency is accepted only within a small area, its use encourages the purchase and production of local goods and services.

As the currency circulates to people and businesses within the community, more benefits accrue to the community, and less money drains out to other parts of the country or world—a recipe for enhancing the local economy. In addition to the economic benefit, the use of a local currency can improve community trust by encouraging neighbors to rely on one another to meet their economic needs. As residents become accustomed to spending and receiving a local currency, they also build community security. In an age of financial uncertainty, it's reassuring for a community to know that it can rely on a local currency in the event of a breakdown in the broader monetary system. And as the currency encourages more consumption of locally produced goods, the community can reduce its dependence on products that are transported long distances.

Many communities around the world have launched local currencies and are using them successfully (although typically on a small scale). In the Berkshire region of Massachusetts, BerkShares are accepted by nearly four hundred businesses, and five area banks will gladly exchange 95 dollars for 100 BerkShares.[20] On the south side of London, the Brixton Pound made its debut in 2009. In addition to paper money, Brixton Pounds are conveniently available as an electronic currency. After setting up a "B£e" account, a customer can complete a transaction by sending a text message to the B£e Bank to authorize payment to a participating business.[21]

Despite these encouraging developments, many local currencies remain consigned to the fringes of the economy. An important step needed to promote the circulation of local currencies is for governments to accept them for tax payments. In Bristol, U.K., the local government has recently decided to take this step, a decision that should help the Bristol Pound achieve mainstream acceptance among residents and businesses.[22]

International Currency

The international economic playing field is quite uneven, and since fairness is one of the key characteristics of a steady-state economy, nations should consider adopting a new international currency to help level the playing field. The unevenness stems from the use of the U.S. dollar and the euro as the main "reserve currencies" in the world. Central banks in other countries hold reserves of dollars and euros to support their national economies and help balance trade deficits. Widespread reliance on these currencies gives a tremendous advantage to the United States and Eurozone countries, because other countries are willing to export goods and services to the United States and Europe, but they use little of the money they receive as payment to buy American and European products. Instead, they leave this money sitting in their central banks. The result is that the United States and Europe have received billions of dollars worth of imports, while giving little in return except for paper notes and electronic credits.[23]

An international currency, which could be issued by an independent organization to settle trade balances between nations, could put a stop to this unfair arrangement. John Maynard Keynes proposed an idea along these lines in the 1940s at the United Nations Monetary and Financial Conference in Bretton Woods, New Hampshire. Keynes suggested establishing a currency (which he called the "Bancor") and an international clearing union to regulate currency exchanges. Unfortunately the dollar won out over the Bancor at the conference and became the main reserve currency—not because of flaws in Keynes's proposal, but because the United States was the dominant economic power and largest international creditor.[24]

Now, more than ever, the world needs a neutral international currency that is not controlled by any single country or group of countries. The new international currency could either be created as *fiat money*, meaning that its value would be derived only from its declaration as legal tender (this is the case for all reserve currencies today), or it could be given value by linking it to a physical resource, such as the right to emit carbon dioxide.[25]

Restructuring Financial Institutions

The proposed three-currency system, with a debt-free national currency, an abundance of local currencies, and a neutral international currency, represents a seismic shift in the monetary landscape that would shake the foundations of financial institutions. The changes that we propose seek to balance claims on wealth with the supply of real wealth, promote local production and consumption, provide greater equality among the economies of different nations, and encourage commerce commensurate with ecosystem capacities. Financial institutions need to follow suit and square their operations with these aims, so they can support a sustainable and equitable monetary system.

A number of organizations have proposed promising ideas for restructuring banks and other financial institutions. In addition to John Fullerton's Capital Institute, other nonprofit organizations, such as the New Economy Working Group, the New Economics Foundation, Positive Money, Slow Money, and RSF Social Finance, are calling for major reforms. A common theme emanating from all these sources is the need to decrease the size and power of financial institutions. "Too big to fail" means too big, period.

The 100-percent-reserve requirement proposed for the switch to a debt-free national currency would go a long way toward tempering the power of banks. But other policy changes are probably needed as well. A tax on international financial transactions, sometimes called a Tobin tax (named after an influential economist) or a Robin Hood tax (named after an influential social worker), would further discourage the "wheeling-and-dealing" culture of banks. The merits of this idea have been discussed for decades, and it now appears that someone is willing to give it a try. The French government has announced plans to collect a tax of 0.1 percent on financial transactions, with the hope that other countries will follow suit.[26]

Measures like the 100-percent-reserve requirement and Tobin tax can rein in financial institutions that have run wild in the era of economic expansion. Shortly after banks such as Goldman Sachs and Citigroup were reduced to groveling for federal bailout funds, they were siphoning off record profits from a distressed economy.[27] The era of ecologically sound economics will be fundamentally different, with changes in who creates money, how it circulates, how it is invested, and how benefits from its use accrue to people across society.

WHERE DO WE GO FROM HERE?

In a sense, the financial sector can be viewed as a cost. It's the cost of helping money flow to where it's needed in the economy. The fewer resources needed to accomplish this service, the better off society is. So we should aim to minimize the cost represented by the financial sector—it should account for as small a percentage of total economic activity as possible. That's the opposite of financialization and counter to the way banks have been accumulating money and consolidating power. Instead of focusing on using money to make more money, financiers should be focusing on serving a stable economy, an equitable society, and a healthy biosphere.

Banks will not concede their power easily, and they have formidable resources at their disposal to oppose change. Needed financial reforms will not originate from bank boardrooms, and the speedy delivery and size of the bailouts of 2008 suggest that they will not originate from the halls of government either. That means the impetus to overhaul the system of finance must come from citizen action outside the establishment.[28] Worldwide movements and protests have demonstrated that people are willing to oppose the status quo, but greater momentum is needed to overcome what has turned into a financial plutocracy. Two main ingredients for generating this momentum are widespread understanding of the financial system and utilization of financial crises.

If more people understood how inequitable and unsustainable the current debt-based money system is, it would be much easier to change it. But the financial system is complex, and many of the concepts involved are challenging to communicate. In order to raise awareness, ideas for monetary and financial reform need to be translated into a simple message that can capture the public imagination. Hopefully more financiers will find their way to a Fullerton-esque epiphany and help draft and communicate such a message.

However, even with a well-crafted message, requisite policy changes may not materialize without the forcing hand of a crisis. The monetary system negotiated at Bretton Woods emerged from the smoldering battlefields of World War II. In the transition to a steady-state economy, the goal is to avoid such a devastating crisis (in fact, it would be preferable to avoid any crisis). The meltdown of 2008 exposed serious flaws in the financial system and cost taxpayers vast sums of money. It kindled outrage and helped generate the desire for change, but banks have retained much of their power, and the monetary system remains essentially unchanged.

Another crisis or series of crises may be necessary to clear the way for more fundamental changes. But we'd better be prepared. As the economist Milton Friedman wrote, "Only a crisis—actual or perceived—produces real change. When that crisis occurs, the actions that are taken depend on the ideas that are lying around. That, I believe, is our basic function: to develop alternatives to existing policies, to keep them alive and available until the politically impossible becomes the politically inevitable."[29]

[CHAPTER 9]

ENOUGH MISCALCULATION

Changing the Way We Measure Progress

[T]he gross national product does not allow for the health of our children, the quality of their education, or the joy of their play. It does not include the beauty of our poetry or the strength of our marriages, the intelligence of our public debate or the integrity of our public officials. It measures neither our wit nor our courage, neither our wisdom nor our learning, neither our compassion nor our devotion to our country; it measures everything, in short, except that which makes life worthwhile.

ROBERT F. KENNEDY (1968)[1]

WHAT ARE WE DOING?

"Almost heaven, West Virginia, Blue Ridge Mountains, Shenandoah River . . ." I was in a backwoods bar late one evening with three friends, when one of them dropped a quarter in the jukebox and selected John Denver's "Country Roads." The four of us, already on our third round of beer, began singing along. Soon enough, the other five or six patrons in the bar had joined our chorus. It would have been a typical scene in this particular bar, located in rural Virginia alongside the very Blue Ridge Mountains referenced in the song, except for one oddity. My three friends, Sonam, Tchewang, and Jigme, hailed from the Himalayan kingdom of Bhutan. It was quite a sight to see the solemn, bearded faces of the locals across the bar singing their hearts out with the three Himalayan visitors. When the song was over, all of us, Bhutanese and Americans, raised our beer bottles in a salute to happy times and the universal appeal of music.

That was the fondest of many fond memories from a six-week-long professional course on ecology and biodiversity sponsored by the Smithsonian Institution in the summer of 2001. It was the first time I had met anyone from Bhutan. Truth be told, it was the first time I had ever heard of Bhutan, a fascinating place that rocketed to the top of the list of places I'd like to see before I die. (In fact, so many Westerners yearn to experience a place sequestered from the burdens of their over-grown, techno-worshipping lifestyles that Bhutan has imposed a limit on the number of tourists it admits.)

The Smithsonian course offered an intensive curriculum to students from around the world. We spent twelve hours a day in lectures and hands-on activities to learn methods for conserving species and habitats. Sonam was my roommate at the course, and once I learned a little bit about his homeland, I spent more than a few of my free hours interrogating him.

Bhutan's geography ranges from lowland tropical rainforests to the high Himalaya. A network of national parks and wildlife sanctuaries provides habitat for tigers, snow leopards, and plenty of other rare and endangered species. The people are proud and protective of their eco-systems and their culture, which is rooted in Buddhist pacifism. Sonam told me that the nation was modernizing, but, unlike the rest of the world, the people were making a concerted effort to prevent the invasion of Western-style consumer culture. I found all these facts fascinating, but one Bhutanese concept stood above all the rest in my mind: *gross national happiness.*

When I heard the term "gross national happiness," it immediately clicked. I knew it was a play on "gross national product," and I was intrigued by the contrast in those two terms. From my study of economics, I had a firm understanding of gross national product (and its more widely cited sibling, gross domestic product, or GDP), but I found something distasteful about using "product" or economic output as an indicator of the health of a nation. Why shouldn't a nation strive instead to maximize its happiness over the long haul?

In 1972 Jigme Singye Wangchuck, the king of Bhutan, answered this question by declaring that gross national happiness was more im-portant than gross domestic product.[2] The Bhutanese government and others who subscribe to gross national happiness believe that measure-ments of national wealth should include more than economic output—

environmental preservation and quality of life, for example. They have identified four pillars of gross national happiness: (1) promotion of equitable and sustainable socioeconomic development, (2) preservation and promotion of cultural values, (3) conservation of the natural environment, and (4) establishment of good governance.[3]

It's one thing to coin a clever term; it's another thing altogether to expand that term into operational policy. How can you measure gross national happiness? Dasho Karma Ura of the Centre for Bhutan Studies established a partnership with Michael Pennock, a Canadian public health expert, to work on it. Together they developed a survey to collect information from citizens on personal health, psychological well-being, time use, environmental quality, cultural preservation, and other topics. Bhutan uses the survey results to help craft its national policies with an eye toward ensuring that such policies will increase happiness and well-being. Applying this approach, the government concluded that membership in the World Trade Organization would not improve well-being, so it declined the invitation to join.[4]

The ideals embedded in gross national happiness are catching on in other countries as well. For example, the U.K. government is pursuing an index of happiness to steer government policy.[5] The Australian Bureau of Statistics runs a program called Measures of Australia's Progress (MAP) that's designed to address the question, "Is life in Australia getting better?"[6] The United Nations issued a resolution in July 2011 calling on member nations to pursue measures of happiness and well-being to guide public policies.[7] And the Japanese government recently drafted a set of happiness indicators to supplement economic data.[8]

Gross national happiness is gaining popularity based on its own merits, but it's also gaining popularity in response to disillusionment with gross domestic product as a measure of societal success. Such disillusionment has been building for decades, as evidenced by Robert F. Kennedy's quote from 1968 at the beginning of this chapter.

Gross domestic product is the main economic indicator in use today, and probably the most politically influential of all indicators. Its importance in policy-making is hard to overstate. New policies and technologies are assessed in terms of their impact on GDP. Government budgets are evaluated in terms of their predicted effect on GDP. National progress has become synonymous with increasing GDP.[9] But what is GDP, and is it a good indicator of progress?

In simple terms, GDP is a measure of economic activity—of money changing hands. Consumer spending on food, clothing, or entertainment contributes to GDP. Government investment in education also counts toward GDP. These are expenditures that most people would consider to be desirable. However, if there is an oil spill, such as the BP disaster in the Gulf of Mexico, the money spent by government on cleanup also contributes to GDP. If more people get cancer and require treatment, their medical costs count toward GDP. The costs of war, crime, and family breakdown all cause GDP to rise. In the language of economics, GDP does not distinguish between benefits and costs, but lumps everything together under the banner of economic activity.

Although GDP per capita has been on the rise (it has more than tripled in the United States since 1950),[10] surveys of life satisfaction indicate that people have not become any happier. Beyond the level of income required to meet people's basic needs and provide for some comforts, additional income does not appear to improve our lives.[11] Studies suggest that a variety of other factors, such as living with a partner, enjoying good health, holding a secure job, having trust in institutions, volunteering, and limiting the amount of time spent watching television, do improve well-being, however.[12]

Our main economic measuring stick, GDP, appears to be a very poor indicator of progress, even in an economy where the goal is growth. It would be an even less useful indicator of progress in a steady-state economy, where the goal is to achieve sustainable scale, fair distribution, efficient allocation, and a high quality of life. GDP provides little information on whether we are achieving these goals. Although GDP growth and increases in resource use tend to go hand in hand, zero growth in GDP would not necessarily be indicative of a steady-state economy. Zero growth in GDP could still be accompanied by declining stocks of natural capital or increasing inequality, both of which are counter to the goals of a steady-state economy. For these reasons, new indicators are required to replace GDP.

In addition to the work on gross national happiness, several initiatives around the world are investigating alternatives to GDP. These include the European Commission's Beyond GDP initiative, the OECD's Better Life Initiative, and the Commission on the Measurement of Economic Performance and Social Progress launched by former French President Nicolas Sarkozy.[13]

Governments in many countries, such as France, the United Kingdom, Costa Rica, Ecuador, and (naturally) Bhutan, are seriously considering alternative ways of measuring progress. They are doing this partly because of the criticisms of GDP, but also because of growing recognition that societal goals and priorities are changing.[14] A U.K. poll found that 81 percent of people support the idea that the government's main objective for its citizens should be the "greatest happiness" rather than the "greatest wealth."[15] Similarly, an international survey found that three-quarters of respondents believe health, social, and environmental indicators are just as important as economic indicators and should be used to measure progress.[16]

Even with such popular support for change, society still employs measures that are failing to get the job done. Members of the mainstream media religiously report the Dow Jones Industrial Average, with cheers of delight when it rises and howls of protest when it falls. The Dow Jones is an index that tracks the stock prices of thirty supersized U.S. corporations. If Boeing's stock price increases because it is expected to sell more weaponry, or if Exxon Mobil's stock goes up because it can exploit tar sands (with accompanying impacts on the landscape and climate), then the Dow Jones tends to go up. Are the activities that increase these stock prices necessarily good for society? Newscasters, investors, and the public overlook the repercussions of a rising Dow Jones because they have become accustomed to shooting for a higher score. CEOs manage corporations specifically to maximize their stock prices.

Just as an obsession with stock prices can promote corporate growth that may harm society, obsession with GDP can promote economic growth that may also be detrimental to society. The current state of global ecological overshoot was at least partially caused by our focus on, and attempt to maximize, a narrow set of economic indicators. Economic growth could not have become such a high priority if indicators such as GDP had never been invented. GDP has undermined the goal of economic welfare that it was supposed to support because people have ended up serving the abstract (but quantitative) indicator instead of the concrete (but qualitative) goal.[17]

"We manage what we measure" is a cliché often uttered in business boardrooms, but it rings true. You could also say that we "mismanage what we mismeasure." In this case, we mismanage the scale of the economy because we're treating an indicator of its size—GDP—as if it were a measure of social performance. If we want to achieve a sustainable and fair economy that provides a high quality of life, it's crucial to get the measures right.

WHAT COULD WE DO INSTEAD?

When a lightbulb burns out, the obvious remedy is to replace it (preferably with an energy-efficient alternative). That's what we need to do with GDP. As a measure of progress, GDP burned out decades ago, and many people and organizations have noticed that we are fumbling in the dark. For example, the declaration from the first international degrowth conference, held in Paris in April 2008, calls for such a replacement. It says that we need to develop "new, non-monetary indicators (including subjective indicators) . . . to assess whether changes in economic activity contribute to or undermine the fulfillment of social and environmental objectives."[18] In August 2008, just prior to his election as president, Barack Obama acknowledged that it's time to try something else. He told *New York Times Magazine* writer David Leonhardt how much he admired Robert Kennedy's speech about gross national product, and he stated that environmental concerns require something of a paradigm shift for economics.[19]

How, then, should we measure economic progress? Researchers have come up with some good ideas. For example, Herman Daly and John Cobb, Jr., devised the Index of Sustainable Economic Welfare (ISEW), which has been developed by other scholars into the Genuine Progress Indicator (GPI).[20] These two indicators draw on some of the same consumption data used to calculate GDP, but they take the calculations further. They add in the value of positive actions that take place outside of the market, such as volunteer labor and work in the home. At the same time, they subtract undesirable expenditures on crime, pollution, and family breakdown, as well as the costs of environmental damage and the depletion of natural resources. When GDP and GPI are compared, an interesting picture emerges. While GDP per capita has increased rapidly in the United States since 1950, GPI per capita peaked around 1980, and has flatlined since then (Figure 9.1).[21] These data suggest that the benefits of additional economic activity are roughly being canceled out by the costs. For every step forward, we take another step back—all the while increasing the pressure we place on the environment.

One of the most intriguing and most positively named new economic measures is the Happy Planet Index (HPI), an efficiency indicator developed and published by the New Economics Foundation.[22] HPI measures the ecological efficiency with which we are achieving good lives. As an equation, it may be expressed as follows:

$$\text{Happy Planet Index} = \frac{\text{Happy Life Years}}{\text{Ecological Footprint}}$$

The numerator in the equation, "Happy Life Years," is a composite of life expectancy (an objective indicator) and life satisfaction (a subjective indicator, the value of which is obtained from surveys). While life expectancy measures physical health, life satisfaction measures how people actually experience their lives.

HPI measures something very different than GDP. Whereas GDP sums up the money exchanged in market transactions, HPI gauges how well we transform the limited resources available to us into long and happy lives.

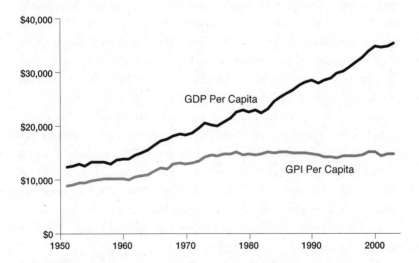

FIG. 9.1. Although GDP per capita increased rapidly in the United States between 1950 and 2004, the Genuine Progress Indicator (GPI) per capita has remained relatively flat since 1980. All data are adjusted for inflation and expressed in year 2000 dollars. SOURCE: see note 21.

Rankings based on GDP are unsurprising—the leading "performers" are populous and industrialized (or rapidly industrializing) countries. The top ten nations (adjusted for purchasing power parity) are the United States, China, Japan, India, Germany, Russia, the United Kingdom, Brazil, France, and Italy.[23] Many Americans pride themselves on topping this list—on having the biggest economy—and they fret about the way China is gaining ground. Meanwhile, countries like Vietnam (41st), Costa Rica (88th), and Jamaica (113th) don't measure up. HPI rankings, however, tell a very different story. The New Economics Foundation calculated HPI for 143 countries in the year 2005.[24] As Table 9.1 shows, many nations at the top of the GDP list have plenty of room to improve their performance when it comes to translating resource use into well-being.

GPI and HPI are both summary indicators of economic progress—they attempt to accomplish a difficult task, to paint a picture of economic achievement with a single number. The benefits of a single number are easy reporting and easy scorekeeping. But the danger of using such indicators is that they greatly simplify reality, and, as with GDP, we might end up focusing too much attention on the number and not enough on what's happening around us. Some researchers, therefore, propose using multiple measures, something of a dashboard approach. The U.K. Department for Environment, Food and Rural Affairs, for example, measures progress in sustainable development through a suite of 68 sustainable development indicators.[25] That's quite a dashboard!

One of the developers of the Happy Planet Index is a psychologist named Saamah Abdallah. Abdallah understands that a steady-state economy requires very different measures of progress than those used to assess our current growth-centric economies, and he recognizes the value inherent in having both summary indicators and a suite of measures. He has therefore proposed creating a set of indicators that takes a hybrid approach.[26] This set of indicators would contain three groups: the Environment, the Economic System, and Human Well-Being. Each group would include one headline indicator and a number of more detailed sub-indicators (Figure 9.2).

This grouping helps to separate ends from means—a critical distinction. In the proposed indicator system, *sustainable and equitable human well-being* is the ultimate end, or key outcome to strive toward. Other economic goals are means in support of this end.

TABLE 9.1. SELECTION OF NATIONS
RANKED BY HAPPY PLANET INDEX

Ranking	Nation	HPI Score (out of a possible 100)
1.	Costa Rica	76.1
2.	Dominican Republic	71.8
3.	Jamaica	70.1
4.	Guatemala	68.4
5.	Vietnam	66.5
9.	Brazil	61.0
17.	Bhutan	58.5
20.	China	57.1
35.	India	53.0
51.	Germany	48.1
74.	United Kingdom	43.3
75.	Japan	43.3
89.	Canada	39.4
106.	Russia	34.5
114.	United States	30.7
115.	Nigeria	30.3
143.	Zimbabwe	16.6

SOURCE: see note 22.

To achieve a high level of well-being in society, the economy must provide jobs, stable prices, and equal opportunities to earn income. The economic system, in turn, is dependent on the environment, because all resources used by the economy come from nature, and all wastes produced by it return to nature. The environment also affects human well-being directly, by providing goods and services that are essential to life on earth, such as fresh water and a stable climate. Without these ultimate means (nature's goods and services) there would be no humans, let alone sustainable and equitable human well-being.

The ecological footprint would make a good headline indicator for the Environment Group of indicators. As described in Chapter 2, the footprint calculates the biologically productive area of land and water needed to generate the resources consumed in a country, and absorb the wastes produced.[27] The footprint accounts for the environmental impacts of trade, meaning that goods produced in China, but consumed in the United States, are captured in the U.S. ecological footprint rather than the Chinese footprint. Other environmental indicators, such as measures of material and energy use, would be important sub-indicators to complement the footprint.

A potential headline indicator for the Economic System Group is income equality. A high degree of equality in society is critical to achieving the goal of sustainable and equitable human well-being. As discussed in Chapter 7, studies have shown that societies with lower levels of inequality tend to have fewer health and social problems, among the rich and poor alike. The ratio of the incomes of the

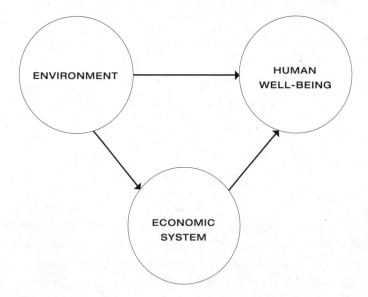

FIG. 9.2. The proposed system of indicators considers human well-being to be the ultimate end. This end requires environmental sustainability and economic equality. Arrows point from means to ends. SOURCE: see note 9.

richest 20 percent to the poorest 20 percent of society is a simple measure to calculate and understand, and could be used as a headline indicator for this group. Other measures of how well the economy is functioning, such as unemployment and inflation rates, remain important and should be included as sub-indicators.

The Human Well-Being Group could use happy life years (the numerator in HPI calculations) as the headline indicator. Of course, well-being is about more than just life expectancy and life satisfaction, and sub-indicators that measure people's ability to flourish should be included in this group. These sub-indicators should assess how well people are able to meet their psychological needs (for example, needs for autonomy, competence, and connection with others). Multiple indicators of well-being are needed to measure whether people are both "feeling good" and "doing well."

This three-group system of indicators to replace GDP is embryonic in its development. There are still many stones to turn over in the quest to develop worthy indicators of progress. In fact, one of us (Dan) is currently measuring how close countries are to achieving a steady-state economy, and what this means for their social performance. In a recent paper, he has proposed a set of environmental and social indicators that fits neatly into an ends-and-means framework.[28] Further research will continue to identify improved ways to measure progress, but we already have enough knowledge to adopt better national accounting systems and gain a much clearer understanding of how well our economies are performing.

WHERE DO WE GO FROM HERE?

The main obstacle to creating and using a new system of indicators, such as the one proposed in this chapter, is the dominant position society has given to GDP. The problem is not so much that social and environmental data are unavailable, but that GDP always trumps other indicators. As long as the public and private sectors remain united in the hunt for what they view as the ultimate trophy—a bigger economy—we are unlikely to give alternative indicators the attention they deserve. But we would be wise to support efforts to adopt new indicators. As Donella Meadows, one of the authors of the influential book *The Limits to Growth*, writes:

> Indicators arise from values (we measure what we care about), and they create values (we care about what we measure) . . . [C]hanging indicators can be one of the most powerful and at the same time one of the easiest ways of making system changes— it does not require firing people, ripping up physical structures, inventing new technologies, or enforcing new regulations. It only requires delivering new information to new places.[29]

In order to knock GDP off its pedestal and replace it with something more sensible, people need to care about indicators. If your financial fortunes are tied to the ups and downs of the stock market, then you tend to watch the market. If you're a public official and you believe that job creation and progress are possible only with a rising GDP, then you tend to watch GDP statistics. At the moment, most people have little idea about what GDP measures, but if they did, they would probably be a lot less enthusiastic about policies designed simply to increase GDP. Education has a key role to play in helping people, especially government and business leaders, understand that there are other indicators that more closely measure what we truly care about. If the goal of society were to change from increasing GDP to improving human well-being and preventing long-term environmental damage, then many proposals that are currently seen as "impossible" would suddenly become possible.

In the end, most people care much more about spending time with their families, performing well in a meaningful job, or pursuing their hobbies than they do about collecting consumer products and expanding the economy. If we believe that human progress is synonymous with a bigger economy, then GDP is the right measure. If, however, like Robert Kennedy, we believe progress flows from the health of our children, the beauty of our poetry, the strength of our marriages, or the intelligence of our public debate, then we must demand more appropriate measures of progress.

[CHAPTER 10]

ENOUGH UNEMPLOYMENT

Securing Meaningful Jobs

> *Ultimately society, not the economy, determines*
> *how many people are out of work.*
>
> BLAKE ALCOTT[1]

WHAT ARE WE DOING?

Deb Wren is the ideal employee, and her work ethic is one reason why. She grew up on a dairy farm where hard work was the norm, and she routinely helped with chores during her school years. Although she left home to attend college, farm life left a strong impression on her, so after earning her degree, she returned to the family farm to work alongside her father. Wren's warmth and positive attitude shine through, even as she describes her struggles tending a herd of cows in the frozen winter of upstate New York.

"It was so cold, and we had fifty or sixty new calves—a huge number for our small operation. We were doing our best to keep them warm and well fed. It was aggravating, because calves generally don't know what they're doing. But the heifers were even more of a problem. We'd spend the first two hours each morning milking them, and some of them had frostbitten teats—they were hard, scarred, and sore, and the cows would kick like crazy."[2] Considering days like that, a nice, warm office might sound appealing, but Wren looks back on those times with fondness; she thinks that farm work strengthened her bond with her family and helped her develop a healthy appreciation of animals and the outdoors.

Working hard is important, but there's more to being an ideal employee than just that. You have to care about the work you do. From an early age, Wren found deep meaning in her work. "Growing food became so important to me. I never had to question the validity or purpose behind what I was doing." Her sense of purpose blossomed into a quest to do meaningful work. And she seems, for the moment, to have found the right place to focus on her passion for both food and nature.

ECO City Farms is a nonprofit organization inside Washington, D.C.'s Beltway that serves as a prototype for sustainable, local urban agriculture. Its purpose is to reenvision farming to improve soil fertility, restore environmental health, provide sufficient income for farmers, and make nutritious food available to all. Even though she's a part-timer at ECO City, Wren has a wide range of responsibilities. On Mondays she's an administrator, working with the CEO to write grant proposals, arrange meetings, and develop partnerships with other organizations. On Tuesdays she's a farmer, feeding the chickens, transporting worms from the compost bin to the aquaculture tanks, watering plants in the hoop houses, amending soil, and transplanting seedlings. On Thursdays she's a harvester, spending her time picking fruits and vegetables to be distributed through ECO City's community food subscription program. And on Fridays and weekends, she's back to being an administrator.

With a penchant for hard work, a strong commitment to her values, and a positive attitude, Deb Wren can do it all. She really is the ideal employee, except for one thing. She's not actually an employee—she's a volunteer at ECO City with hopes that a paying job will materialize.

Playing down her situation, she quips, "Yeah, it's a bummer not to be paid." But she's clearly willing to make sacrifices. To pursue her dream job, she has strung together a series of unpaid or low-paying internships. Since earning a graduate degree in sustainable development, she has found employment as a babysitter and food-and-drink server to bring in enough income to keep doing some of the other work she believes in.

Wren remains hopeful that she'll be able to find a paying job that suits her calling, but she's not free from worry. Jobs to grow food sustainably and restore urban and suburban lands are hard to find. "It's frustrating," she says. "[Work like we do at ECO City] is not generally profitable, at least not in a conventional sense, and the nonprofit organizations can't afford to hire." She asserts that many young people would like to work in sustainable food systems and related fields, but "the jobs just aren't there."

Plenty of people face tough competition for scarce jobs in their chosen fields. However, it's troubling that a smart, hard-working, educated, and personable job seeker faces such long odds, especially when her desired job makes so much sense in the transition to a sustainable economy. A functional economy should be able to provide an important job to such a valuable employee. What is it about the current economic setup that makes stories like Deb Wren's all too common?

To answer this question, it's helpful to examine our motivations for seeking paid employment in the first place. To a certain extent, people work because they enjoy doing so, but they also work for the paycheck. We need income from our jobs to pay the rent and buy food, clothing, and other goods and services. But people also work because of social pressure to do so. Having a good job is an avenue for gaining esteem. One of the most common questions people ask each other when they first meet is, "What do you do for a living?" Moreover, people with gaps in their resumes, say a year or two when they are out of work, may be seen as uncompetitive in the labor force. As a result, many people stick with jobs they don't really like, especially if they are providing for children or other family members. In some cases, people may like their jobs, but they work more hours than they would choose if they felt they had more freedom.

The problems of unemployment, under-employment, and unsatisfactory employment stem from three main flaws in the economic system. The first flaw is the misuse of gains in labor productivity. Technological progress has allowed businesses to become more efficient at producing goods and services, such that it now takes less labor to produce the same amount of stuff than in the past. However, instead of using new technologies to reduce working hours, we have largely used them to produce more goods and services, while keeping working hours relatively constant. This choice has made economic growth a requirement for creating and maintaining jobs. As economist Peter Victor explains, "The shortage of employment has become more important than the shortage of products. Whereas in the past we needed to have more people at work because we needed the goods and services they produce, now we have to keep increasing production simply to keep people employed."[3]

But the strategy of increasing production and consumption to secure employment has become untenable, especially for those economies that already use too many resources and emit too much waste. Indeed, the transition to a steady-state economy, in which resource use and waste emissions remain within ecological limits, requires *reduced* production and consumption. Less production in the current economic configuration, however, leads to less work and rising unemployment—in short, not enough jobs to go around.

The second flaw is that employers frequently lack flexibility. In trying to cut costs by standardizing their operations, firms often institute one-size-fits-all rules for work schedules and hours. For example, some companies offer only full-time positions with no opportunities for alternative work schedules. As a result, many employees end up in arrangements that are far from their ideal.

The third flaw is a mismatch between the kinds of jobs supplied by the economy and the kinds of jobs that society really needs. Available jobs reflect societal values, but we are undervaluing the maintenance of healthy communities and ecosystems while overvaluing the consumption of stuff. The mock newspaper *The Onion* hit the nail on the head with a disconcertingly realistic article about consumer-product diversity exceeding biodiversity. The article joked, "Last year's introduction of Dentyne Ice Cinnamint gum, right on the heels of the extinction of the Carolina tufted hen, put product diversity on top for the first time."[4] Many jobs that need doing don't get done because it's unprofitable to do them (e.g., repairing damaged ecosystems). At the same time, people perform many jobs that don't really need doing, but that are supported by the market (e.g., brokering purely speculative financial deals).

These three flaws are hindering effective employment—they are preventing willing workers from landing jobs that would provide benefits for society. These flaws need to be fixed as we make the transition to a steady-state economy, and two key policies can help.

WHAT COULD WE DO INSTEAD?

The goal for employment in a steady-state economy is straightforward: secure enough jobs for people who want them, and make sure labor is directed toward constructive and meaningful tasks. The economy should value the services of talented people like Deb Wren and dedicated organizations such as ECO City Farms as they strive to do important work. The ecological economists Martin Pullinger and Blake Alcott propose two key policies to help people secure meaningful jobs in a steady-state economy: work-time reduction and guaranteed jobs.

Work-Time Reduction

Work-time reduction provides a way to reallocate the fruits of increasing labor productivity. Instead of using productivity gains to boost production, we could gradually shorten the working day, week, year, and career.[5] In Western economies, the quantity of goods and services that a worker produces per hour of labor has typically increased by about 2 percent per year. Assuming that labor productivity continues to increase at this rate, we could have a four-day workweek in twelve years, a three-day week in twenty-five years, and so on, with no decrease in incomes.[6] Of course, there are limits to increasing productivity, and some industries may have slim prospects for gaining more productivity. For example, it's difficult to increase productivity in human-service industries, such as physical therapy or counseling, in which effective results depend upon people spending time in direct (and often one-on-one) contact.[7] Even so, trends in technological progress and productivity suggest that working hours can decline significantly from present levels.

Using the benefits of technological progress to reduce working time, rather than increase production, would likely appeal to many people. Survey data indicate that, given the choice, the majority of people would rather work less than earn more money. In a U.S. Department of Labor study, 84 percent of respondents said that they would like to trade some or all of their future income for additional free time.[8] Moreover, even if reduced working time resulted in a decrease in pay, a large number of people would still be on board. A study conducted in fifteen countries found that 41 percent of people would prefer to spend less time at work (and earn less), compared to 10 percent who would prefer to spend more time (and earn more).[9]

There are many potential ways to achieve work-time reduction. Perhaps the most obvious is to shorten the standard workweek. In the United States, the forty-hour workweek traces its roots back to the 1930s when Franklin D. Roosevelt, the unions, Congress, and the courts butted heads over the length of the workweek. At the time, the

$0.25-per-hour minimum wage was regarded as a more controversial measure, even though the forty-hour workweek had plenty of powerful detractors.[10] The minimum wage has changed with the times, but the standard workweek has not. The number of hours has stood firm for decades, and it seems arbitrary. Why not thirty or thirty-five hours? Even with a supposed forty-hour workweek, actual working hours have risen. Many college graduates are working more than fifty hours per week, and married couples with children are working many more hours than they were a generation ago, despite evidence that working such long hours is unhealthy.[11]

Another simple way (at least conceptually, if not politically) to achieve work-time reduction is to lower the retirement age or offer workers options for early retirement. Unfortunately the quest for economic growth and fiscal balance is leading governments to *raise* the retirement age. For example, in 2010 the Italian government enacted a plan to raise the retirement age from sixty-five to sixty-eight in an attempt to reduce pension payouts, retain a larger workforce, and decrease spending deficits.[12] An even simpler reform would be to increase vacation time. The contrast between minimum paid vacation time in the United States (none legally required, but typically two weeks) and Europe (around five weeks) is striking.

Other progressive policies, such as increased opportunities for part-time work, job sharing (in which two or more people combine part-time work to make up a full-time job), options to take career breaks, and parental leave, can also reduce working time. These are often called "work–life balance" policies, and several European countries have been practicing variations on them for years.[13]

The European experience provides valuable examples of how work-time reduction could succeed in a steady-state economy. In the United Kingdom, parents with children under the age of eight (or eighteen if the child is disabled) can choose to work shorter hours, with a proportionate reduction in pay. In the Netherlands, work–life balance has been integrated into the overall employment strategy. Under the Wassenaar Agreement, signed in the 1980s, unions and employers agreed to reduce unemployment by sharing the available work.[14] Individuals also have the right to request reduced working hours in their jobs, and the right to take career breaks of up to three years in length under the Life-Course Savings Scheme, introduced in 2006. The Life-Course Savings Scheme offers people greater sovereignty over their time, allowing them to enter and leave the labor market more easily, with protection from adverse impacts on their career or future employability.[15] It also provides them with greater financial security by allowing workers to spread income more evenly over their lifetimes.

These policies have helped the Netherlands to achieve the lowest working hours among high-income countries—about 1,377 hours per year. For comparison, the average American works 1,778 hours per year, and the average Brit works 1,647 hours per year.[16] That means the Dutch work about ten fewer weeks per year than Americans and six fewer weeks than the British! The Dutch have also achieved low rates of unemployment (below 4 percent in 2009) and a high labor force participation rate (almost 80 percent of the working-age population).[17]

Work–life balance policies, such as those that exist in the Netherlands, explicitly address the flaw of employer rigidity by institutionalizing flexibility in the workplace. In addition, work-time reduction addresses the flaw of misused gains in labor productivity by spreading the decreased number of working hours more evenly throughout the population. As increasing productivity decreases the need for labor, everyone does a bit less paid work, and fewer people are forced out of their jobs. Applying work-time reduction policies more generally would not only prevent job losses, but also reduce financial burdens on governments that pay unemployment benefits.

In addition to providing relief for unemployment, work-time reduction is likely to produce a well-being dividend. Spending fewer hours on the job opens opportunities to seek purpose and fulfillment outside of work. Once we've acquired the basics, most of us don't need more consumer goods; we need more time. Less time at work means individuals can pursue well-being in less materialistic ways, such as spending time with friends and family, participating in community events, engaging in creative activities, and embarking on personal or spiritual development. We are faced with the "inconvenient truth" that current lifestyles cannot continue due to environmental limits, but the "convenient truth" is that working and consuming less can lead to increases in well-being.[18]

Work-time reduction also has the potential to generate environmental dividends, by reducing resource use and waste emissions. If working hours went down at the same rate that labor productivity is going up, people could work less and still earn the same income. They could spend the same amount of money and consume the same volume of goods and services as before. With stable levels of consumption, the environmental impact of the economy would likely decrease over time as methods of production became cleaner and goods and services became less resource-intensive. Alternatively, if paid working hours decreased faster than labor productivity is increasing, people would earn less, spend less, and consume less. In this case, total consumption would fall and the environmental impact of economic activity would be reduced more quickly.

Let's suppose that a society embraced work-time reduction and established appropriate policies. We'd begin to accrue the social and environmental benefits, but people might still struggle to find jobs, especially ones that are truly needed by society. A policy beyond work-time reduction—one that addresses the mismatch between the kinds of jobs supplied by the economy and the kinds of jobs we need—might still be necessary to achieve all the employment goals of a steady-state economy.

Guaranteed Jobs

A guaranteed-jobs policy appoints the state as the employer of last resort and creates jobs for those wishing to work but unable to find employment. Guaranteed jobs may seem like a radical idea, but the right to work is included in Article 23.1 of the 1948 Universal Declaration of Human Rights and has been partially enacted in India, Argentina, and some European cities (e.g., Zurich).[19] In the same way that the public sector guarantees primary schooling, garbage collection, and medical care (in most industrialized countries), it could also guarantee jobs, and, in the process, decouple the goal of full employment from the size or growth rate of the economy.

Traditionally, indirect means have been used to fight unemployment. Economic growth, deficit spending, and even work-time reduction policies are examples of indirect economic approaches to achieve full employment. Although they create conditions that may generate jobs, there is no guarantee that jobs will be created. The alternative is to battle unemployment head-on. A guaranteed-jobs policy directly ensures success in achieving full employment, and at the same time furthers three important goals:

1. It provides income for people who need it.
2. It uses relatively cheap labor to accomplish useful public works (e.g., caring, cleaning, gardening, building, and so on).
3. It relieves the psychological and social problems that arise when people want to work but can't find a job.[20]

Of these three goals, the third is arguably the defining one, because the first two can largely be achieved by other means. For example, the first goal could be achieved through a minimum income (see Chapter 7), while the second could be achieved by financing public works through conventional means.

The Civilian Conservation Corps (CCC) is one of the most famous and successful guaranteed-jobs programs in U.S. history. The CCC existed only from 1933 to 1942, its life cut short by the onset of World War II, but it accomplished remarkable works over that brief time span.[21] With the Great Depression draping a shroud of unemployment over the economy, many young men were desperate for jobs, including Isaac Louderback. "I wasn't doing anything. I needed the job—that's the reason I got into the CCC."[22] Louderback enlisted as a nineteen-year-old after having completed high school and one year of college, joining 275,000 other young men nationwide who had enrolled within the first ninety days of the program's inception.[23] He was stationed on the high ridges of Shenandoah National Park among the mountain meadows and undulating forests of Virginia's countryside. The park had been established only seven years before, and Louderback worked on forest health projects—surveying sites to remove nuisance shrub species—in addition to rock-breaking assignments on Skyline Drive, the scenic roadway that rolls over the spine of Shenandoah.

When asked about camp life in the CCC, Louderback says, "It was a wonderful experience, it was wonderful training. It made you more self-reliant." But more important, the experience helped shape the rest of his life. "I think maybe the successes that I've had . . . came from my early training with the CCC. [It] gave you a lot of trades and things that you could do that would help you later on."[24] Many of the men who started with the CCC went on to careers in forestry, carpentry, mechanics, engineering, masonry, and wildlife management.[25]

The experience also provided immediate relief for families in urgent need of income. Enlistees came from families who were on, or eligible for, welfare. Each man received $30 per month in pay (the equivalent of about $500 today), but by law, he had to send $25 of it home to his family.[26] Enterprising recruits like Louderback often found ways to earn supplemental income. He made a deal with his fellow recruits to stay behind and clean the barracks over weekends when everyone was on leave. His barracks-mates paid him 10 cents each for this chore. With his earnings, he was able to help put his younger brother through business school.[27] In the end, 3 million men found employment through the CCC.[28] They restored natural areas that had suffered from generations of abuse and built some of the most enduring and beautiful structures on the American landscape. From his time in the hills and hollows of Shenandoah, Isaac Louderback could look back proudly and say that the CCC "was a wonderful thing—it actually accomplished something."[29]

Economic growth presents us with a dilemma: on the one hand, we rely on growth to generate employment; on the other hand, continuous economic growth is undermining the life-support systems of the planet. More than anything else, it's the specter of unemployment that haunts economists and public officials when they contemplate the end of economic growth and prevents them from considering the alternative to growth. Policies like work-time reduction and guaranteed jobs offer a way out of the dilemma. They provide reassurance to economists, public officials, and everyone else across society that we can maintain full employment in the transition to a steady-state economy. And the changes might just help us get some useful things done, too.

WHERE DO WE GO FROM HERE?

The economic system has serious flaws if it constantly puts people out of work. It has flaws if many of its jobs really don't need to be done. And it has flaws when people find themselves stuck in unfulfilling occupations. Policies such as work-time reduction and guaranteed jobs have the potential to eliminate, or at least mitigate, these flaws. But like many of the changes required for the transition to a steady-state economy, the changes in employment policies will require a shift in values, especially a shift toward stronger environmental and community values. The shift is necessary to confront the challenges of today's environmental and social conditions, which stem from too many people consuming too much stuff. The social and environmental landscape now contains degraded ecosystems, broken communities, shrinking supplies of energy, and declining government services. This may seem like a scary landscape, but it's also full of opportunities, especially opportunities for securing employment.

Ecosystems are in need of restoration, and communities are in need of healing. The end of the era of cheap oil will likely mean a greater demand for human labor. Helping children learn to read, tending community gardens, caring for the elderly, restoring native plants along stream corridors—these are examples of labor-intensive tasks that could employ many more people if we were to make them higher priorities. In a nutshell, there's plenty of work waiting to be done, many hands ready and able to do it, and practical policies to match people to the work. But first we have to change our values so that we can properly value the work that needs to be done.

Along with values, business structures also need to change. In today's business environment, higher labor productivity is almost always converted into higher production. This happens because business owners, who are beholden to the profit motive, have every incentive to increase sales, and little incentive to reduce working hours. Businesses with different, more democratized ownership structures, different criteria for making operating decisions, and different indicators of success (beyond financial returns) would be more likely to convert productivity gains into reduced working time. As we'll see in the next chapter, new forms of business have the potential to meet societal needs while at the same time dampening the imperative for growth.

The impetus for all of these changes—shifting values, reforming businesses, and adopting new employment policies—has to come from outside the economic establishment. After all, the establishment is what got us into this mess in the first place. In discussing how to secure well-paying, meaningful jobs for her generation of young workers, Deb Wren says, "We have to do it ourselves—it's not going to be done for us." But secure and meaningful jobs will only come as values change and economic policies change in response. Where Wren's sentiment really applies is in the push to introduce such changes. When enough people across society demand meaningful work that is valued appropriately, the system of employment will adapt to get the job done.

CHAPTER 11

ENOUGH BUSINESS AS USUAL

Rethinking Commerce

Business is the economic engine of our Western culture,
and if it could be transformed to truly serve nature as
well as ourselves, it could become essential to our rescue.

KARL-HENRIK ROBÈRT[1]

WHAT ARE WE DOING?

What's the most influential book that takes a critical view of the environmental excesses of business? There's an argument to be made for Henry David Thoreau's *Walden*, Rachel Carson's *Silent Spring*, and E. F. Schumacher's *Small Is Beautiful*, but our award goes to *The Lorax* by Dr. Seuss. Seuss created a fanciful landscape and populated it with a technicolor forest of Truffula Trees, a menagerie of curious critters, and two main characters—a clever entrepreneur named the Once-ler and a tenacious environmentalist called the Lorax.[2] In part, the book's influence is due to Dr. Seuss's legendary rapport with children (and adults who stubbornly cling to a childlike sense of wonder). His eccentric illustrations, lyrical rhymes, and inventive language give the book staying power, but its influence also stems from its universal storyline—a storyline that resonates with readers who have observed the downsides of modern business practices.

The enterprising Once-ler, roaming the countryside to seek his fortune, arrives in the land of the Truffula Trees and senses a business opportunity. From the tuft of a tree, he knits a "Thneed," and finds it hard to suppress his excitement:

> A Thneed's a Fine-Something-That-All-People-Need!
> It's a shirt. It's a sock. It's a glove. It's a hat.
> But it has *other* uses. Yes, far beyond that.
> You can use it for carpets. For pillows! For sheets!
> Or curtains! Or covers for bicycle seats![3]

With a knack for selling Thneeds, the Once-ler grows his operation into a sprawling factory with dozens of employees. His meteoric rise is the stuff of corporate legend, but as his business grows, so do its impacts on the surrounding environment. These impacts, which include pollution and deforestation, provoke the Lorax to visit the factory and scold the Once-ler for causing a decline in the health of the forest and its endemic species:

> "Once-ler!" he cried with a cruffulous croak.
> "Once-ler! You're making such smogulous smoke!
> My poor Swomee-Swans . . . why, they can't sing a note!
> No one can sing who has smog in his throat."[4]

But the Once-ler, who built a business empire using only his wits and the resources of the forest, has no intention of pulling back. As the Lorax continues to reprimand him for shredding the forest, the Once-ler angrily reveals the essence of his business plan:

> I got terribly mad.
> I yelled at the Lorax, "Now listen here, Dad!
> All you do is yap-yap and say, 'Bad! Bad! Bad! Bad!'
> Well, I have my rights, sir, and I'm telling *you*
> I intend to go on doing just what I do!
> And for your information, you Lorax, I'm figgering
> on biggering
> and BIGGERING
> and BIGGERING
> and BIGGERING,
> turning MORE Truffula Trees into Thneeds
> which everyone, EVERYONE, *EVERYONE* needs!"[5]

Soon after, the last Truffula Tree falls, and the Once-ler's business goes bust, the result of economic "biggering" beyond the capacity of the ecosystem. Having exploited the last of the available resources, the formerly bright-eyed industrialist is forced to shutter the factory. His employees, the pesky Lorax, and the forest creatures have no choice but to move elsewhere.

Dr. Seuss's story of collapse is just that—a story. But such occurrences are not confined to the make-believe land of Truffula Trees and Swomee-Swans. The story strikes a chord because it resembles real-world events. The aftermath of the Anaconda Copper Mine in Butte, Montana, is a good example.

Miners began digging around Butte in the nineteenth century, but smaller mines gave way to large-scale strip mining when the Anaconda Copper Mining Company (later purchased by ARCO) opened the Berkeley Pit in 1955. Over twenty-seven years, the corporation removed 300 million cubic meters of rock and extracted over a billion tons of ore, mostly copper, but also lead, zinc, gold, and manganese.[6] It produced so much ore that it became known as the "Richest Hill on Earth."[7]

Interstates 15 and 90 overlap for a few miles where they take an east–west route across the south side of Butte. If you drive this highway, you won't see the "Richest Hill on Earth." You will, however, see one of the biggest messes on earth. There's no hill anymore. Instead, there's a massive hole, defined by yellow walls of bare rock, that looks as though it could hold the entire city standing next to it. At the bottom of the hole is a dark blue lake that appears implausibly cool and inviting in this ruptured landscape.

The lake is actually an acidic stew of toxic metals. After digging up the economically viable ore, ARCO stopped mining the site in 1995, and now it's part of America's largest complex of Superfund sites (Superfund is a program of the Environmental Protection Agency designed to clean up hazardous waste areas). In the year the mine was abandoned, 350 snow geese made the mistake of stopping to rest on the lake. Needing a break on their annual southward migration, they died from burns and sores.[8]

Not all businesses are involved in the inherently unsustainable practice of extracting nonrenewable resources like copper. And not all businesses that "mine" renewable resources, such as Truffula Trees, do so at a rate that wipes out the stock. But it's clear that something is wrong with business as usual.

The dominant form of business in the world today is the shareholder-owned corporation. A key feature of the corporation, which separates it from other forms of business organization such as privately owned companies, is that it is legally bound to maximize profits for its shareholders—an interest it must put above all others.[9] Henry Ford had a plan for improving social conditions that famously ran up against the profit mandate in 1918. Ford had declared that he wanted "to employ still more men; to spread the benefits of this industrial system to the greatest number of people, to help them build up their lives and their homes," instead of paying increased profits to shareholders. However, a court order forced the Ford Company to issue a special dividend to shareholders rather than reinvest the money as Henry Ford wanted.[10]

Shareholder-owned corporations have become so dominant that, if you rank nations (by GDP) and corporations (by revenues), then forty-eight of the top one hundred economies in the world are corporations (Table 11.1).[11] Walmart is a little smaller than Norway and a little bigger than Venezuela. The big oil companies, Royal Dutch Shell, Exxon Mobil, and BP, are all nestled together between Colombia and Finland. And Toyota has put Ireland in its rearview mirror while it races toward Israel. Without judging the prudence of allowing corporations to control wealth on the scale of a nation, we can say that these companies have been spectacularly successful at growing revenues and concentrating power.

Of course, not all businesses are shareholder-owned corporations. Other forms of business organization exist as well, such as privately owned companies and cooperatives, and these other forms are not explicitly mandated to pursue profits in the same way as publicly traded corporations. Nevertheless, most businesses chase profits to some extent. A key question, then, is whether the profit motive is compatible with a nongrowing economy.

On the one hand, profit and growth are two different things. Profit is the difference between the money a firm makes (revenue) and the money it spends (costs), whereas growth is an increase in total production. Thus a firm can grow without increasing profits, and increase profits without growing. Furthermore, when looking across a collection of firms, it's possible to imagine a situation in which some profitable companies grow and other unprofitable ones go out of business, such that the total size of the economy remains the same.

On the other hand, even though they're different things, there is certainly a connection between profit and growth. Companies must compete against one another for market share or simply to survive. The more goods a company produces, the cheaper its individual unit costs become, and the easier it can reach or surpass the financial break-even point. In addition, companies that earn profits are more likely to invest in equipment, research, and assets that spur growth and give them the potential to earn more profits. And within the current economic system, a company is more likely to attract funds from investors if it can demonstrate both profitability and the potential for growth.

Much like the debt-based system of money creation discussed in Chapter 8, the profit motive appears to be one of the factors that drives economic growth. Other factors include population growth, the use of GDP as a measure of progress, the fear of unemployment, and the culture of consumerism. Taken together, these factors constitute something of a "growth imperative." To achieve a steady-state economy, we need to find ways to diminish and eventually eliminate this growth imperative.

In Chapter 5, we proposed a number of policies to limit material and energy throughput. Implementation of these policies would significantly change the rules of the game for business. National caps on resource use and waste emissions would force businesses to be far more efficient with materials and energy. Enacting such policies and letting businesses adapt according to their own means has a certain hands-off appeal, but there are at least three reasons to take a more proactive approach. First, if we're serious about knocking the growth imperative out of businesses, it makes sense to set up business models and structures that work well in a nongrowing economy. Second, to give businesses a greater likelihood of achieving social and environmental goals, it's important to align their operations with these goals from the start. And third, given the power that corporations wield, it will be difficult to enact throughput limits without business reforms—these two things must happen together.

TABLE 11.1. NATIONS AND CORPORATIONS RANKED BY 2010 GDP AND REVENUE, RESPECTIVELY (*CORPORATIONS IN ITALICS*).

Rank	Country/ Company	GDP/ Revenue ($ millions)	Rank	Country/ Company	GDP/ Revenue ($ millions)
1	United States	14,582,400	26	Austria	376,162
2	China	5,878,629	27	Argentina	368,712
3	Japan	5,497,813	28	South Africa	363,704
4	Germany	3,309,669	29	Thailand	318,847
5	France	2,560,002	30	Denmark	310,405
6	United Kingdom	2,246,079	31	Greece	304,865
7	Brazil	2,087,890	32	Colombia	288,189
8	Italy	2,051,412	33	*Royal Dutch Shell*	*285,129*
9	India	1,729,010	34	*Exxon Mobil*	*284,650*
10	Canada	1,574,052	35	*BP*	*246,138*
11	Russia	1,479,819	36	Finland	238,801
12	Spain	1,407,405	37	Malaysia	237,804
13	Mexico	1,039,662	38	Portugal	228,538
14	South Korea	1,014,483	39	Hong Kong	224,458
15	Netherlands	783,413	40	Singapore	222,699
16	Turkey	735,264	41	Egypt	218,912
17	Indonesia	706,558	42	Israel	217,333
18	Switzerland	523,772	43	*Toyota*	*204,106*
19	Poland	468,585	44	Ireland	203,892
20	Belgium	467,472	45	Chile	203,443
21	Sweden	458,004	46	*Japan Post*	*202,196*
22	Saudi Arabia	434,666	47	Philippines	199,589
23	Norway	414,462	48	Nigeria	193,669
24	*Walmart*	*408,214*	49	Czech Republic	192,152
25	Venezuela	387,852	50	*Sinopec*	*187,518*

Source: see note 11.

Rank	Country/ Company	GDP/ Revenue ($ millions)	Rank	Country/ Company	GDP/ Revenue ($ millions)
51	State Grid	184,496	76	Hewlett-Packard	114,552
52	AXA	175,257	77	E.ON	113,849
53	Pakistan	174,799	78	Berkshire Hath.	112,493
54	CNPC	165,496	79	GDF Suez	111,069
55	Chevron	163,527	80	Daimler	109,700
56	ING Group	163,204	81	NTT	109,656
57	Romania	161,624	82	Samsung	108,927
58	Algeria	159,426	83	Citigroup	108,785
59	General Electric	156,779	84	McKesson	108,702
60	Total S.A.	155,887	85	Verizon	107,808
61	Peru	153,845	86	Crédit Agricole	106,538
62	Bank of America	150,450	87	Santander	106,345
63	Volkswagen	146,205	88	General Motors	104,589
64	Kazakhstan	142,987	89	HSBC	103,736
65	ConocoPhillips	139,515	90	Siemens	103,605
66	Ukraine	137,929	91	Vietnam	103,572
67	BNP Paribas	130,708	92	AIG	103,189
68	Hungary	130,419	93	Lloyds Bank	102,967
69	Generali	126,012	94	Bangladesh	100,076
70	Allianz	125,999	95	Cardinal Health	99,613
71	AT&T	123,018	96	Nestlé	99,114
72	Carrefour	121,452	97	CVS Caremark	98,729
73	Ford	118,308	98	Wells Fargo	98,636
74	ENI	117,235	99	Hitachi	96,593
75	JPMorgan Chase	115,632	100	IBM	95,758

WHAT COULD WE DO INSTEAD?

Businesses have a critical and positive role to play in the transition to a steady-state economy. They will need to continue generating employment, creating new technologies, and fostering innovation, but within a framework that respects ecological limits and promotes human well-being. Three ways to align business practices with the goals of a steady-state economy are: (1) promote new business models that generate *shared value*, (2) create business structures that are less prone to growth, and (3) adopt new measures of success for business.

Promote New Business Models
That Generate Shared Value

Businesses are organizations that create *value*, but that value does not need to be limited to producing consumer goods and services; it can (and must) also include generating social and environmental value. New business models will be needed to accomplish this shift.

A business model refers to the plan a company follows to generate revenue and earn a profit—it's about how the business creates, delivers, and captures value.[12] Today's most common business model involves selling physical products to customers. In a steady-state economy, however, more businesses would probably focus on providing "service solutions." Instead of trying to sell a product (such as a washing machine, car, or heating oil), businesses would aim to provide customers with a particular *result* or *function* (such as clean clothes, mobility, or warmth).[13]

Businesses following a service solution model generally maintain ownership of the equipment that provides the service, and take responsibility for supplying, maintaining, and recycling this equipment. This arrangement helps businesses deliver the desired result while economizing on material and energy use. The U.S. firm Interface is one of the best-known companies that uses this business model. Interface provides a "floor-covering service." Rather than buy a carpet from Interface, customers may lease the service of keeping a space carpeted. As individual carpet tiles wear out, they are collected, broken down, remanufactured, and replaced by the company, greatly reducing resource use.[14]

A business that provides a service solution may also reduce resource use by encouraging product sharing. For example, several companies supply transportation services through car sharing or bicycle pooling. These companies offer customers the convenience of vehicle ownership while eliminating the need to purchase a vehicle. Such sharing can reduce resource use in other ways, too. Researchers studying a local vehicle rental service in the Netherlands found that participants reduced their car mileage by a third on average. Besides reducing resource use, such schemes also share the cost and risk of introducing new technologies (such as electric cars), and thus provide a market for environmental innovations.[15]

It's encouraging that firms are already demonstrating the benefits of service-based business models, but the transition from selling products to selling service solutions is not enough. Businesses need to operate with a much broader understanding of *value*. In an influential article published in the *Harvard Business Review*, Michael Porter and Mark Kramer argue that companies have become trapped in an overly narrow approach to value creation that emphasizes the short-term and ignores people's real needs. They claim that "the solution lies in the principle of *shared value* [emphasis added], which involves creating economic value in a way that also creates value for society by addressing its needs and challenges." The purpose of the modern-day corporation, they go on, "must be redefined as creating shared value, not just profit per se."[16]

The idea of creating shared value goes beyond the conventional notion of "corporate social responsibility," in which a company might donate some of its profits to charity or adopt a fair-trade purchasing policy, but still pursue activities that are fundamentally damaging to the environment or society. Many companies now have social responsibility programs (and it's worth cheering genuine attempts), but such programs have been criticized for focusing mostly on reputation, and having only a limited influence on a company's core business.[17] As Brad Parrish, a business researcher and entrepreneur, explains, there is "an important distinction between those enterprises that are driven by a sense of *duty* to act responsibly towards society and the environment as they pursue their private interests, and those enterprises that are driven by a sense of *purpose* to contribute to the sustainable development of the social-ecological system of which they are a part."[18] In a steady-state economy, more businesses would be driven by purpose rather than duty.

Many firms, generally referred to as "social enterprises," embed social or environmental goals into their business model. An example is The Big Issue, a U.K. company that addresses the problem of homelessness by providing homeless people with the opportunity to earn an income selling newspapers.[19] Just as shareholder corporations have become the principal agents of the growth economy, social enterprises could become the principal agents of a steady-state economy. But to open space for the rise of social enterprises, alternative ways of organizing business need to be supported.

Create Business Structures That Are Less Prone to Growth

Certain business structures can de-prioritize the pursuit of profit and dampen the growth imperative found in shareholder corporations. One such structure, the cooperative, has been around for a long time. Another structure, the public interest company, has emerged recently. These legal structures permit, and even encourage, firms to pursue social and environmental goals ahead of financial returns.

Cooperatives, which were first formalized as legal entities in eighteenth-century Europe and North America, predate the modern corporation by about a hundred years. Significant early examples include the Rochdale Society of Equitable Pioneers (a food and consumer-goods cooperative in the United Kingdom) and the Philadelphia Contributionship (a fire insurance cooperative in the American colonies). A cooperative has two defining characteristics: (1) it works to achieve a goal that is beneficial for its members, and (2) it equitably distributes decision-making responsibilities and earnings to its members.[20]

Economic theory suggests that cooperatives are less expansionist than conventional businesses, and, although some cooperatives have grown quite large, they have shown themselves to be less growth-oriented than corporations in practice. The main reason for this difference is that the two types of organization have different markers of performance. The corporate indicator of performance is profitability. Corporations typically increase their size and number of employees in order to achieve targets for profitability. In contrast, cooperatives measure performance by tracking the flow of benefits to members. Since growth may or may not increase benefits, cooperatives have a weaker incentive to increase their size.[21] Furthermore, comparisons of cooperatives in several countries show that they tend to use inputs more efficiently than corporations.[22]

In recent years, cooperatives have seen a renaissance in economic life. In the United Kingdom, John Lewis, a cooperatively owned department store, recovered from the 2009 recession more quickly than many of its rivals.[23] Membership in The Co-operative, the United Kingdom's biggest farming operation, is increasing.[24] The Mondragon cooperatives in Spain, established in the mid-1950s, employ 83,000 people.[25] In Germany, cooperative laws were overhauled in 2007. And a new legal form, established in 2006 under the Latin name *Societas Cooperativa Europaea*, makes it easier to set up and administer cooperatives in multiple European countries.[26]

The second type of business structure that may be particularly well suited for a steady-state economy is the public interest company. In the past, social enterprises were stuck between the choice of forming as for-profit businesses (which limited their ability to achieve social or environmental objectives), or as nonprofit organizations (which limited their ability to achieve commercial objectives). But recently a number of new legal forms have emerged that combine features of both profit-seeking and not-for-profit organizations.[27] These include the:

- Low-profit limited-liability company, or L3C (United States)
- Benefit Corporation, or B-Corp (United States)
- *Gemeinnützige GmbH*, or public interest limited company (Germany)
- *Gemeinnützige Kapitalgesellschaft*, or public interest corporation (Germany)
- Community Interest Company, or CIC (United Kingdom)

These new legal forms allow social enterprises to prioritize social and environmental aims, while still pursuing profit as a secondary goal. CICs have been particularly successful. The legal structure has existed only since 2004, but more than six thousand CICs have opened for business in the United Kingdom.[28] Two important restrictions distinguish CICs from standard companies: (1) dividends to shareholders cannot exceed 35 percent of total company profits, and (2) a CIC must be able to demonstrate that "its purposes could be regarded by a reasonable person as being in the community or wider public interest."[29] These two requirements represent a radical departure from conventional corporations. And although CICs must still pay taxes, some countries grant tax breaks to public interest companies. In Germany, for example, public interest companies do not pay income tax, creating an additional incentive for social enterprise.[30]

Adopt New Measures of Success for Business

In Chapter 9, we proposed new measures of progress for the overall economy. Indicators such as the ecological footprint, income inequality, and happy life years would replace GDP as measures of progress. This change in the economic landscape would require new measures of progress for businesses, too. As businesses increasingly seek to create social and environmental value, they will need indicators to track their performance. New indicators would provide valuable information not only to managers but also to investors, who would be able to direct funds to firms that seek a balance between social, environmental, and financial returns.

A vast accounting infrastructure already exists to measure profitability within a firm. But there is no such infrastructure for measuring a firm's social and environmental impacts. Still, some standards are being used by companies, and others continue to emerge. For example, the Natural Step is a nonprofit organization that helps businesses assess their performance on sustainability objectives.[31] The International Organization for Standardization (ISO) has developed a standard that helps firms reduce pollution and protect the environment (ISO 14001).[32] This standard includes guidance on how to evaluate environmental performance, while another standard (ISO 26000) contains guidance for corporate social responsibility.[33]

These standards offer a starting point for businesses to measure their environmental and social performance. However, André Reichel, an economist and research fellow at Zeppelin University in Germany, proposes a radically different approach. He believes that instead of attempting to maximize and continually grow profits, firms should aim to achieve "right-size profits."[34] He argues that a firm's revenues should be large enough to allow it to be financially viable, but not so large as to cause environmental damage. In order for firms to determine whether they are achieving right-size profits, Reichel proposes establishing two new pieces of information for businesses: (1) a measure of each firm's total ecological impact, and (2) an ecological allowance to compare this impact to.[35]

However, neither the ISO standards nor Reichel's proposal address what could be the most important measurement challenge for businesses. As discussed above, firms in a steady-state economy would need to embrace a much broader concept of value creation and explicitly pursue social and environmental returns. For this to happen, both firms and their investors would require new indicators to measure the efficiency with which financial inputs were transformed into social and environmental outputs. Although there are currently no accepted standards for this sort of accounting, the SROI Network is developing and promoting a methodology for calculating "social return on investment."[36] Improved methods and accepted standards in this area would provide better guidance to investors, and in the process increase the amount of investment in businesses that create social and environmental value.[37]

WHERE DO WE GO FROM HERE?

It's a fitting coincidence that a chapter about rethinking business happens to be Chapter 11. Chapter 11 is a section of the U.S. bankruptcy code that provides protection and reorganization rules for a business that is unable to pay its debts. The phrase "filing for Chapter 11" has made its way into the vernacular as a synonym for "business failure." Some of the most prominent companies that have filed for Chapter 11 are Lehman Brothers, Enron, and WorldCom. These infamous corporate collapses represent the worst of the worst in traditional business, but as we've seen, there is a general problem with the way large shareholder corporations operate.

Taken together, corporate impacts are overwhelming the capacity of the world's ecological systems: the atmosphere can't take the emissions; the soil can't take the depletion; the forests can't take the felling. At the same time, by focusing narrowly on profits, many businesses are squandering opportunities to create social and environmental value. We need to declare a Chapter 11 on the way businesses are currently operating.

Confronting corporations and curtailing their power is a necessary step for new business models and structures to gain traction. But make no mistake: it's not going to be easy to wrest power away from entrenched corporate interests. This may be particularly true in the United States, where the courts have granted corporations the power to spend virtually unlimited sums of money on political campaigns.[38]

Fortunately, people are calling for measures to level the playing field. For example, David Cobb, a lawyer, politician, and activist, has initiated a movement to amend the U.S. Constitution to restrict the rights of corporations, particularly when it comes to campaign finance.[39]

But confronting corporations will only get us so far. As Buckminster Fuller, the famous designer and systems theorist, said: "You never change things by fighting the existing reality. To change something, build a new model that makes the existing model obsolete."[40] In the transition to a steady-state economy, entrepreneurs can follow Fuller's advice by nurturing business models that create shared value, applying alternative business structures, and tracking social and environmental performance.

Governments also have a role to play in the transformation of business. First, they can tax the excess profits captured by shareholder corporations. Second, they can provide incentives to set up (or change to) alternative business structures by streamlining administrative requirements or providing tax breaks. And third, they can mandate the use of measures of social and environmental performance to accompany measures of financial performance.

With leaders in both the public and private sectors working together to overhaul the way business is done, positive changes will emerge. Businesses will adapt to the development of steady-state policies and flourish in the new economic landscape. They will continue to generate employment, create new technologies, and foster innovation, but within a framework that respects ecological limits and promotes human well-being. Some inspiring businesses are already doing these things, even in resource-extracting industries.

Much like the Once-ler, T. D. Collins saw an opportunity to build an enterprise based on logging. But Collins's enterprise, which he started in 1855, couldn't be more different from the Once-ler's. To understand how, you need only read the core values championed by the Collins Companies today:

[W]e believe that third party, independent certification of our forestland is the best way to protect the legacy of the total forest ecosystem—now and into the future. To achieve this, we have had to listen, learn, and change. We have.

We also believe that integrating the principles of The Natural Step into our business operations will result in a sustainable society. Once more, it means we have had to listen, to learn, to change. And, again, we have.

In some ways change is simple, in some ways it's complex. But if your principles demand that you work to create a healthy, viable Earth, in addition to a healthy, viable business, then you must risk change. You must be change.[41]

The firm, which sells wood products certified by the Forest Stewardship Council, is neither beholden to absentee shareholder-owners, nor hamstrung by a short-term profit motive. Over five generations, the owners have maintained a successful business and served as conscientious caretakers of both land and water. Their business creates far more than just financial value; it creates social and environmental value as well, and serves as a model for business in a steady-state economy.

Business reforms, when combined with the other steady-state reforms introduced in Chapters 5 through 10, provide a pathway from the frantic and unsustainable quest for *more* to the desirable pursuit of *enough*. But putting these policy reforms in place will require additional work to change values, overcome entrenched interests, and get the word out. Part III of this book, *Advancing the Economy of Enough*, explores strategies to: (1) move past the culture of consumerism, (2) start a public dialogue about the downsides of growth and the upsides of a steady-state economy, and (3) expand cooperation among nations. Successful implementation of these strategies can help turn the steady-state economy from a hopeful vision into a hopeful reality.

[PART III]
ADVANCING THE ECONOMY OF ENOUGH

CHAPTER 12

ENOUGH MATERIALISM

Changing Consumer Behavior

In rich countries today, consumption consists of people spending money they don't have to buy goods they don't need to impress people they don't like.
CLIVE HAMILTON[1]

WHAT ARE WE DOING?

The stuff lying around in the workshop reveals that someone has been working on two distinct projects: building a wooden cabinet and re-pairing a bicycle. The warm smell of sawdust competes with the earthy odor of grease, and the tools of both the carpenter and the bike me-chanic stake their claims on the workbench. Cardboard boxes of scrap lumber fight with crates of old bike parts for territory on the floor. For both projects (or any other conceivable project), there's a bin contain-ing several rolls of duct tape. And keeping guard over this scene are sanders and saws, wrenches and routers, and pliers and planes arranged on the racks and shelves that line the walls.

Even though it's been decommissioned for years, I can still see my dad down there, thumbing through drawers of nuts, bolts, and spare parts to find just the right doohickey to solve some mechanical mishap. It's the workshop he kept in the basement of our house, and by any measure, it was overstocked. The tool usage rate was minuscule. Sure, he knew how to use (and even how to find) every item down there, but he had stuff you'd hardly ever need. He was clearly a tool addict. He'd buy an oscillating, pump-action, hot-glue demagnetizer if he could find a reason to justify the purchase.

It's both convenient and reassuring to have the right tool on hand for a job, and a well-provisioned workshop can be a source of creativity, fun, and empowerment. At the same time, it's disconcerting to have tools that spend most of their lives collecting dust. The same goes for clothes, knickknacks, electronics, toys, and all sorts of other material artifacts that clutter the closets of consumers. But it's beyond disconcerting—there's something rotten at the core of a culture that places so much emphasis on the purchase, ownership, and display of stuff.

The culture of consumerism, which values consuming over doing, being, or producing, dominates the modern economy in high-income nations.[2] This dominance is not helping people reach their potential or lead more fulfilling lives.[3] In the race for the latest and greatest, people are chasing iPods, iPads, iPhones, and plenty of other "I wants" instead of seeking true well-being. For many people, the accumulation of stuff, and always more and better stuff, has become the ultimate goal rather than a means to achieve a higher purpose. Where did this culture come from?

Consumerism was on the rise in America, but still in its infancy, when Thorstein Veblen coined the term "conspicuous consumption" in the late nineteenth century.[4] Wars and the Great Depression kept it in check, but it sprang into adolescence in the 1950s. That's when the economist and marketer Victor Lebow wrote his article "Price Competition in 1955" in the *Journal of Retailing*. With stunning frankness, Lebow laid out this vision for the shopper society:

> Our enormously productive economy demands that we make consumption our way of life, that we convert the buying and use of goods into rituals, that we seek our spiritual satisfactions, our ego satisfactions, in consumption. The measure of social status, of social acceptance, of prestige, is now to be found in our consumptive patterns. The very meaning and significance of our lives today [is] expressed in consumptive terms.[5]

Lebow pinpointed the emerging strategy of marketers, and since then consumerism has matured into a powerful force that rules over the economic household. The anecdotal evidence is everywhere. Terms like "Christmas creep," "big-box retail," and "mega-mall" have become commonplace. Phrases such as "When the going gets tough, the tough go shopping" adorn T-shirts and bumper stickers.

Statistical evidence of consumerism's maturity also abounds. U.S. citizens, on average, now consume twice as much as they did when Lebow published his article (and let's not forget that there are almost 150 million more Americans to do the consuming). In addition, Americans today are exposed to more advertisements in one year than Lebow and his contemporaries saw in a lifetime.[6] The story is similar in Europe. Sweden, for example, spends as much money on advertising each year as it does on education.[7]

With calculated efforts to "make consumption our way of life," it's predictable that businesses would embrace planned obsolescence, a strategy to design products not for durability, but for rapid disposal (but not so rapid that a consumer's "brand loyalty" might be affected). Stigma-based marketing is another objectionable, but unsurprising, hallmark of consumerism. According to business gurus Dan and Chip Heath, marketers deliberately cultivate insecurity and social stigma among consumers in the hope of selling a product that promises relief.[8] As an example of this practice, they cite Procter & Gamble's strategy to sell more shampoo in China. Dandruff is (or at least was) a nonissue in Chinese culture, but Procter & Gamble's ad campaigns paint dandruff as a social stigma—a stigma that can be overcome by purchasing the company's product.[9]

The unholy alliance between consumers' quest for novelty and the relentless (and sometimes dirty) tactics of marketers has put shopping and the rituals of consumption at the heart of today's economy. Lebow, again, makes this point openly. His take on the incoming tide of materialism seems almost clairvoyant:

We need things consumed, burned up, replaced, and discarded at an ever-accelerating rate. We need to have people eat, drink, dress, ride, live, with ever more complicated and, therefore, constantly more expensive consumption. The home power tools and the whole "do-it-yourself" movement are excellent examples of "expensive" consumption.[10]

Lebow even foresaw the state of affairs in my dad's workshop. Perhaps with the way the economy was developing in 1955, the materialistic program, complete with forlorn, under-utilized tools in the basement, was inevitable. But does it have to remain this way? The collection of steady-state policies detailed in Part II of this book, if enacted, would make for an entirely different sort of economy—one that favors sharing and sufficiency over shopping and insatiability. But the key phrase here is "if enacted." For without sweeping changes to the culture of consumerism, there is little hope of enacting these policies and replacing the mania of *more* with the wisdom of *enough*.

WHAT COULD WE DO INSTEAD?

My dad's basement workshop is very similar to another one. This other workshop has the same smells, the same collection of useful tools, and the same intense competition for shelf and floor space. It's housed in a garage instead of a basement, but the only significant difference is the cast of characters who use it. Instead of one owner who rarely employs his assortment of tools, the garage workshop belongs to a community of thirty-four households. Feeling fortunate to have access to such a well-stocked workshop, one of the owners told me, "Without it, I'd be trying to do every single project with a hammer and a screwdriver!"

I suspect that my dad would have been just as happy (and maybe even happier) using a community workshop. In the end, what was he really after? The feeling of usefulness in solving a problem, the feeling of pride in building something beautiful, and the feeling of satisfaction that can come from working with one's own hands. All of these feelings can be had in a community workshop, but there's something more, too. In a shared shop, he would have had other people to work with, people who could swap know-how, ideas, and friendly conversation. But to establish such a workshop, he and his neighbors would have had to favor community sharing over individual shopping.

A good number of people are finding ways to resist the culture of consumerism and establish vibrant cultures of their own. Many older people, for example, spend less of their income on things and more on experiences, which tend to have a lower material impact. In addition, increasing numbers of people, either as individuals or as groups, are selecting "downshifted" lifestyles, aiming for what sociologist Duane Elgin calls "outwardly simple, yet inwardly rich" lives.[11] These people are attempting to focus less on the things money can buy (stuff) and more on the things it can't (time, relationships, and community).

Such people are taking the idea of *enough* to heart, and they're living better lives because of it. Both social scientists and neuroscientists have been conducting research into what makes people happy—what makes fulfilling lives—and their findings point squarely away from consumer culture. The New Economics Foundation has summarized the evidence and describes five proven ways to achieve well-being:

1. **Connect.** Maintain close relationships with family, friends, neighbors, and colleagues.
2. **Be active.** Take part in enjoyable physical activities.
3. **Take notice.** Be curious, savor the moment, and be aware of what's happening in the world.
4. **Keep learning.** Try new things and set challenges that would be enjoyable to achieve.
5. **Give.** Express gratitude and do helpful things for others.[12]

At a presentation in late 2011, author and environmentalist Paul Gilding noted that the five ways to well-being have two things in common: (1) they all take time, and (2) they're all free. That's a cheerful thought because, as Gilding notes, "The future of the economy looks like less money, less stuff, less debt and more time, more fun, more happiness."[13] Science and common sense agree that consumerism is an ill-advised strategy for achieving good health and finding meaning in life. Once we've met our basic needs, we simply can't buy our way to happiness. The challenge now is to plan the obsolescence of consumer culture.

WHERE DO WE GO FROM HERE?

Given how deeply consumerism has become embedded in everyday life (despite the way it coaxes people to chase fulfillment in ineffective ways), it's going to take a revolutionary change in values to overcome the prevailing orthodoxy. The change is unlikely to happen quickly or easily because of the anxieties that will inevitably arise in response to such a transformation. In addition, plenty of powerful forces benefit from consumer spending, and they won't give up their positions of power without a fight. Advertisers, credit card companies, soft drink makers, banks, car companies, computer manufacturers, and government stimulus programs are but a few of the institutions aligned with consumerism.

Successfully fighting these forces will require a sustained and coordinated effort to curtail the power of large corporations and the media, both of which exercise substantial influence over people's lives. It is important not to underestimate these entities and the often subtle methods they use to influence consumers. But bankers, advertisers, and manufacturers are simply responding to consumer demand (although they're complicit in creating some of that demand). So perhaps the shift needs to originate from people's personal values, and a grassroots rejection of the "mass infantilization" program that promotes mindless consumption. A positive way forward is to support those people who choose nonmaterialistic lifestyles and encourage others to follow in their footsteps. There's a huge opportunity to foster the diffusion of sustainable values throughout society, but to be effective, such an exercise needs to be comprehensive and find multiple points of intervention.[14] Here are some ideas for getting the transition under way.

Turn marketing on its ear. Marketers have been honing their techniques for many years. These techniques could be used to "sell" sound cultural values instead of copious quantities of consumer goods. Imagine if Victor Lebow had said, "We need to make well-being our way of life." Now imagine if the full force of the Coca-Cola and McDonald's marketing teams went to work on this change instead of selling more fizzy drinks.

Harness the power of art. The arts, from music to dance to visual media, can feed the soul far more effectively than shopping trips and excessive consumption. Art inspires people and helps them imagine a better world than the one we live in today. By participating in the creative and often collaborative processes that produce art, people can play a direct role in bringing about that better world.

Be the change. Individuals who understand the downsides of consumerism can reject unnecessary consumer items and set a positive example by "living their values." They can participate in local initiatives and develop alternatives to mass consumption by buying less, producing locally, and boycotting mass consumer outlets. Much of the self-serving behavior inherent in consumerism derives from a trend away from community-based values and toward individualistic ones. People who set a nonmaterialist example can help reverse this trend.

Recruit influential individuals. Influential individuals occupy pivotal positions in social networks and are key figures in the processes by which new social norms emerge. Such individuals, if they understood the downsides of consumerism and the upsides of less materialistic lifestyles, could be potent agents of change toward sustainability.[15]

Juxtapose "zombie consumerism" with the nonmaterialistic good life. A materialistic lifestyle can be shallow, boring, and deadening. A nonmaterialistic, sustainable lifestyle, on the other hand, can be dynamic and refreshing, but people must be able to visualize it. The Transition Towns movement has captured many people's imaginations and begun the daunting process of demonstrating ways to live simpler and more purposeful lives.[16] If politicians see Transition Towns and similar movements emerging on a sufficient scale, they will feel pressure to get on board.

Eliminate planned obsolescence. Planned obsolescence has become a widespread strategy in products ranging from sweaters to semiconductors, and some marketing practitioners (who probably haven't been keeping up with certain environmental and social trends) even praise it as a positive development.[17] But in a world with 7 billion people, finite resources, and serious environmental problems, "durable" needs to become the watchword of consumers, not "disposable." Refusal to buy short-lived products is a sure way to influence companies to stop designing for the dump.

Limit advertising. Lawmakers have restricted advertising that promotes unhealthy behavior (e.g., tobacco and alcohol use), so there is a precedent for tempering the excesses of marketing departments. A ban on advertising aimed at children took effect in the Canadian province of Quebec in 1980, and it has helped children maintain healthier consumption habits.[18] When it comes to stigma-based advertising, Dan and Chip Heath suggest that the marketing community has a responsibility to self-regulate.[19] Whether through self-regulation or other means, it would be healthy to put a stop to stigma-based advertising and other toxic marketing practices.

Cultivate nonconsumerist institutions. Governments and communities can play an important role by creating and empowering organizations that de-emphasize consumerism. Such organizations would focus on meeting needs rather than selling stuff. They would manage assets for the purpose of delivering long-term well-being to asset owners, rather than delivering short-term financial returns to managers.[20] Examples include cooperatives, land trusts, and even community workshops.

The ideas described above offer some intriguing ways to abate the flood of materialism, but a true turning of the cultural tide will require people to accept a basic truth: the spoils of shopping provide little support for a long life of fulfillment. Some people easily grasp this wisdom; they seem naturally immune to the onslaught of marketers. Others take time to develop such immunity—they have to experience the emptiness of consumer culture, sometimes over the course of decades. It has become a cliché, at least in American consumer society, for people to turn over a new leaf after suffering through a midlife crisis. Following a fruitless attempt to quell such a crisis through conspicuous consumption (think of a forty-five-year-old man buying a bright red Ferrari or some other gas-guzzling sports car), they end up finding peace by refocusing their lives on relationships, well-being, and the search for deeper meaning. It's inspiring that pockets of people, no matter at what stage of life, are acting on their nonconsumerist instincts. Transition Towns, voluntary simplicity, economic localization, and ecovillages are all positive signs that people are striving to live happy, but less materially intensive lives.

People from all walks of life are establishing creative models of living well, but for such models to diffuse more broadly throughout society, communities will have to oppose the corporate forces that promote the consumer culture. These forces, which exert an undue influence on politicians and the media, ignore the finite nature of resources, entice people into chasing fulfillment in ineffective ways, and drive inequality. Through concerted and persistent action, we can overcome them. Then we can replace the culture of consumerism and the value of *more* with the culture of sustainability and the value of *enough*.

CHAPTER 13

ENOUGH SILENCE
Engaging Politicians and the Media

A voice is a human gift; it should be cherished
and used, to utter fully human speech as possible.
Powerlessness and silence go together.

MARGARET ATWOOD[1]

WHAT ARE WE DOING?

During the summer before my final year in college, I worked as an intern for America's largest labor union, the American Federation of Labor and Congress of Industrial Organizations. Ironically, the AFL-CIO hired my services for less than minimum wage. Despite the low pay, it turned out to be a great summer, especially after I learned which bars in downtown Washington, D.C., offered free tacos at happy hour. At my first day on the job, I learned (perhaps not too surprisingly) that the AFL-CIO cares a great deal about how members of Congress view a variety of labor issues. In fact, my boss told me that my top task each day was to comb through newspapers and collect articles about unions and the politics of labor. This was at a time just before the Internet held sway, so I would literally skim through a stack of newspapers and cut and paste the relevant articles onto sheets of paper. Then I would file the pasted articles in folders to be read by the union leaders.

Suppose I had a similar job collecting articles today, but the topic was economic growth instead of labor. I'd need gallons of glue to paste a week's worth of columns. The collection of columns advocating growth would make a thick file, filled with headlines like these:

- "Economic Growth Picks Up, So Why All the Gloom?"[2]
- "Bright Spot in Europe: Poland's Economy Grows 4.3 Percent in 2011 Despite Euro Troubles"[3]
- "Scotland Is Celebrating GDP Growth"[4]

This last headline is particularly interesting. Is Scotland really celebrating GDP growth? Has a holiday been declared in honor of robust GDP figures? The article makes no mention of dancing in the streets of Edinburgh. Oddly enough, it focuses mostly on how growth was slower in Scotland than in the United Kingdom at large.

I could also assemble an equally thick file with articles lamenting any slowdown or absence of economic growth. Some recent examples include:

- "Analysis: Asia's Economic Growth Slipping into Neutral"[5]
- "Fed Signals That a Full Recovery Is Years Away"[6]
- "World Stock Markets Fall as Improvement in US Economic Growth Falls Short of Investor Hopes"[7]

Headlines like these are predictable—economic slowdowns pose clear problems, because the current economic system only functions well when there is growth. Economic contraction results in unemployment and a tougher time making ends meet. But with the assumption of growth firmly entrenched, no ink is spent on how a nongrowing economy might work. The frequent publication of such articles in recent times demonstrates another important point: try as they might, businesses and national governments are struggling to achieve economic expansion.

The failure to get the economy growing has politicians feeling anxious. If, as at the AFL-CIO, my boss in this article-pasting venture wanted confirmation of such political viewpoints, it would be easy to put together yet another stack of news clippings:

- "An End to Cut, Cut, Cut? Merkel and Sarkozy Agree to Focus on Growth"[8]

- "Obama Says He Is 'Hopeful' for 2012, Greater Economic Growth"[9]
- "Bold Action Can Fuel European Growth, Says British Prime Minister"[10]

Cheerleading for economic growth has become the norm for the majority of journalists and politicians. But on topics like the limits to growth and the steady-state economy, the mainstream media remain conspicuously quiet. Alternative media sources do, from time to time, publish stories on these subjects, and every once in a while, a steady-state-themed article makes its way into bigger news sources. For example, Herman Daly wrote an article for *Scientific American* called "Economics in a Full World."[11] The *New York Times* published an editorial by Eric Zencey titled "Mr. Soddy's Ecological Economy."[12] *Harper's Magazine* has printed stories by Wendell Berry ("Faustian Economics: Hell Hath No Limits")[13] and Steven Stoll ("Fear of Fallowing: The Specter of a No-Growth World").[14] And *New Scientist* magazine published a special issue with multiple articles about "the folly of growth."[15] But these articles are a trickle compared to the flood of pro-growth commentaries.

Politicians seem even more unwilling than the media to discuss steady-state topics. To be fair, some of them have never encountered the steady-state economy in their academic or professional lives. Cecilia Rouse is a labor economist from Princeton University, and, as a political appointee of President Obama, she served on the U.S. Council of Economic Advisers from 2009 to 2011. When she was speaking at a public forum, she fielded a question about her views on steady-state economics. In her response, she talked about "sustainable growth," "steady-state growth," and "balanced growth."[16] It quickly became evident that she had not previously come across the concept of a nongrowing economy as a path to sustainability.

Other politicians seem to believe that championing a philosophy other than growth would cause the electorate to disown them (and they're probably right, given the media's portrayal of growth in an overwhelmingly positive light). At another public forum, Peter DeFazio, a member of the U.S. House of Representatives, was speaking about the future of Oregon's economy. When asked about the limits to growth, he answered by criticizing a speech Jimmy Carter had delivered decades before. In his so-called Malaise Speech, President Carter called for conservation of energy, sharing of resources, and pursuit of meaning through channels other than "owning things and consuming things."[17] Representative DeFazio explained that acknowledging the limits to growth would be like endorsing Carter's "pessimistic approach" (and look where it got him—booted out of the White House after only one term).

As with the occasional appearance of a steady-state story in the media, it's refreshing when a politician is bold enough to discuss alternatives to growth. Caroline Lucas, a U.K. Member of Parliament and a former member of the European Parliament, is one such politician. She has signed the CASSE Position on Economic Growth, which calls for the transition to a steady-state economy.[18] She is also the former leader of the Green Party of England and Wales, one of a small number of political parties that have endorsed the position statement.

Given what's at stake—the health of the biosphere and the well-being of humanity—politicians and the media need to address the limits to growth. To have a chance at implementing needed economic reforms, they will have to break their long-held silence on the alternative to perpetual economic growth. Overcoming this silence is a critical step toward igniting a movement aimed at the transition to a sustainable and fair economy.

Silence reigns because politicians, media moguls, and other people who influence public opinion share a common perception that economic growth equates to prosperity and serves as a proxy for progress. For several generations, political parties have been locked in a competition to see who can promise the fastest growth and highest standard of living. At the same time, the media's coverage of the economy has remained geared toward monitoring the amount of growth. The way economic growth is portrayed in the public sphere makes it seem as if we have no economic alternatives.

Steady-state options are also largely absent from discussions in schools and universities. Currently, academic training in economics, business, and politics offers inadequate coverage of sustainable development and environmental issues, let alone models of a nongrowing economy. Limited opportunities exist for students to become acquainted with steady-state economics, and there are even fewer opportunities to study the subject in depth. As a result, the topic has been neglected for decades, and too few theorists and practitioners have been working on how to achieve an orderly transition to a prosperous, nongrowing economy.

WHAT COULD WE DO INSTEAD?

To help end the silence, we propose a three-part strategy: (1) make the steady-state message more accessible, (2) engage with politicians, journalists, and academic institutions in new forums, and (3) build academic capacity for research, analysis, and teaching of steady-state concepts at colleges and universities.[19] Below we discuss each part of this strategy in more detail.

Make the Steady-State Message More Accessible

Franny Armstrong knows how to get a point across. As an environmental and social activist, she has successfully attracted attention and raised funds for just causes, and those skills have transferred to her filmmaking projects. Armstrong has created three documentaries that have been viewed by a total of 70 million people. Her movie *The Age of Stupid* rose to number one at the U.K. box office without formal advertising or major-studio funding.[20] Not content to sit back while her film delivered its message about the urgency of addressing climate change, she also founded the 10:10 campaign, which helped spur the United Kingdom and other nations to cut their carbon emissions.

To raise the profile of steady-state economics, Armstrong offers a simple piece of advice: "Change the name." She has a point. "Steady-state economics" sounds like a specialized subset of the broader field of economics (the same holds true for "ecological economics"). In reality, "economics" should embrace the idea that the economy is a subsystem of the biosphere, and steady-state principles should permeate the field of economics. Labeling these principles under an appealing banner could help them gain some traction.

Some people hear the words "steady-state" negatively. Even with a hopeful and promising goal—to enhance human well-being within the ecological capacity of the planet—the name conjures up stagnation in some people's minds. Finding a new and captivating name for the steady-state economy could help attract a critical mass of people committed to taking the concept forward.

What the name should be, though, remains an open question. As described in Chapter 4, scholars and activists have suggested a variety of labels, all of which have their particular flaws. Some, such as "green economics" and "new economics," seem too nebulous. Others, such as "biophysical economics," veer into the realm of scientific jargon. Ideally some top marketing talent would pause on the quest to sell sugary snacks and tooth whiteners, and instead apply their considerable know-how to solving this naming problem.

In the meantime, part of the rebranding process includes assembling a cast of campaigners who can tell a good story. Banging people over the head with data, figures, and rational arguments often fails to persuade them to take action, largely because it doesn't generate an emotional response. Delivering real stories of real families engaged in the transition to a steady-state economy could create an emotional impact and provide a more effective way to gain attention. The challenge is to create a message that is accessible without being trite. Taking a page out of Armstrong's script, a film could serve as a catalyst for a fundamental shift in how the public views economic growth. But regardless of the medium used, the most important skill of Armstrong's to emulate is her ability to tell a compelling story.

In addition, any attempts to deliver an effective message about the steady-state economy need to overcome what Dan Kahan, a legal scholar at Yale University, calls "protective cognition." Kahan has concluded that people tend to dismiss scientifically sound evidence if it poses a threat to their worldview. They don't want to believe that something they hold in esteem could be detrimental to society. Kahan writes, "Because accepting such a claim could drive a wedge between them and their peers, they have a strong emotional predisposition to reject it."[21]

Kahan's findings help explain why people resist messages about the limits to economic growth. Even though scientists are providing evidence that continued economic growth is having detrimental effects on both environmental and social systems, people tend to deny the evidence because it clashes with their preexisting worldview.

The key to bypassing protective cognition is to frame information about economic growth in a way that prevents people from feeling threatened. One possibility is to focus the conversation on needs that all people share (e.g., subsistence, security, and participation) and how the economy can help meet these needs without growth. Such framing could dampen denial and diminish the dangerous allure of economic growth.

Engage with People in New Forums

Innovative ways need to be found to engage decision makers and opinion influencers in a more active debate about the problems of growth and potential economic reforms to solve them. "Forums for exploration" with policy makers, politicians, and researchers could provide places to hold such debates. These forums could explore the tricky policy issues discussed in Part II of this book, such as population growth, material and energy throughput, and inequality. Development of such forums has already started in the form of conferences, including the international conferences on degrowth held in Paris, Barcelona, and Montreal; the Growth in Transition Conference held in Vienna; and the Steady State Economy Conference held in Leeds.[22] These and other similar conferences need to disperse their results more widely to governments, businesses, universities, and the general public.

One way to raise the profile of steady-state principles at conferences and other venues is through the use of a position statement, such as the CASSE Position on Economic Growth or the Declaration on Degrowth.[23] If such statements can gain significant numbers of endorsements from think tanks, businesses, professional societies, universities, and concerned citizens, then they can encourage mainstream institutions and public figures to "break ranks."[24] Once a few politicians become more willing to enter the debate on economic growth, the safety-in-numbers principle will create space for their colleagues to do the same. A small but dedicated group of politicians could significantly raise the profile of steady-state options for dealing with social and environmental problems.

In order to develop new forums for discussion, put pressure on politicians, and educate the public, steady-state activists will need to build strong centers of action. A few such centers, mostly underfunded nonprofit organizations, are scattered around the globe. Examples include CASSE, the New Economics Foundation, Feasta, SERI, Research & Degrowth, the Post Growth Institute, the Post Carbon Institute, Earth Economics, the New Economics Institute, the New Economy Network, the New Economy Working Group, Ethical Markets, and

Gaian Economics. These organizations need help to expand public awareness of alternative economic systems and to introduce politicians and members of the media to the concept of a prosperous but nongrowing economy.

Build Academic Capacity on Steady-State Concepts

Successful transformation of the economy will require a growing number of students, academics, and economists who understand the concepts of ecological economics and the steady-state economy. However, finding university economics departments that house research programs or offer courses on the steady-state economy is difficult. Many of the professors interested in teaching such courses have developed them as electives in other departments such as environmental studies and anthropology. This lack of a steady-state presence in economics departments has left a research gap—there's a need for more rigorous study of how a steady-state economy would work. If the brainpower currently dedicated to pursuing economic growth could be applied to pursuing economic sustainability, we'd have a lot more ideas about how to achieve a prosperous, nongrowing economy.

The good news is that the discipline of ecological economics has been making strides, thanks largely to the development of an academic society. Herman Daly, Robert Costanza, AnnMari Jansson, Joan Martínez-Alier, and other scholars established the International Society for Ecological Economics (ISEE) in 1990. The founding principles of the society are:

- The human economy is embedded in nature, and economic processes consist of biological, physical, and chemical processes and transformations.
- Ecological economics is a meeting place for researchers committed to environmental issues.
- Ecological economics requires trans-disciplinary work to describe economic processes in relation to physical reality.

Since its inception, the ISEE has grown in popularity and influence.[25] Through the momentum generated by the society, and the development of new books, journal articles, and other information sources, there is a solid base of material to expand teaching and research at academic institutions. But more work is needed, especially to satisfy the demands of students who are fed up with the current economics curriculum (see Chapter 4). Like the news stories dedicated to steady-state principles and the underfunded nonprofit organizations that promote steady-state ideas, the ISEE is a minor player compared to its pro-growth counterparts.

WHERE DO WE GO FROM HERE?

At this point in history, when humanity faces widespread economic and environmental turmoil, most people can agree that some amount of change is needed to manage the problems caused by economic growth. Everyone, including the most steadfast skeptics of steady-state concepts, would benefit from a wider, more inclusive conversation about economic growth. The three recommendations for initiating this conversation—making the steady-state message more accessible, engaging with people in new forums, and building academic capacity on steady-state concepts—are mutually reinforcing measures for breaking the disconcerting silence surrounding the steady-state economy. The time to implement these strategies is at hand. The longer politicians and journalists remain in their cone of silence, the more ecological limits will exert their influence, and the more urgent our social and environmental problems will become.

At a public discussion on alternative economics in Leeds, Sheryl Odlum—a vocal member of the Occupy Movement—was asked how to make the transition to a sustainable and fair economy. Her answer was simple: "We rise." Movements and protests offer an opportunity to raise the profile of steady-state ideas. Protestors have been demanding secure jobs, equitable distribution of income, more restraints on banking practices, reduced corporate influence in politics, and more scrupulous use of public funds (e.g., money for education instead of bank bailouts).[26] In a nutshell, people around the world are seeking social and environmental justice—the same motivation for establishing a steady-state economy. Steady-state principles, therefore, could provide a unifying economic agenda for Occupiers and other people in search of positive change. The more protestors realize the potential of this agenda, the more they can provide a powerful voice to overcome the silence on the alternative to perpetual economic growth.

As the silence subsides, perhaps instead of headlines colored by the assumptions of growth-mania, we'll see columns with headlines like these:

- Council of Economic Advisers Raises Questions about Growth
- Full-Reserve Banking Proposed to End Debt Crisis
- How the "Steady Staters" Are Saving the Economy and the Environment

The arrival of such hopeful headlines would signal a profound shift—one that coincides with two other shifts required for the transition to a steady-state economy: the cultural shift away from consumerism (see Chapter 12), and a shift in national goals to enhance international cooperation (to be discussed in Chapter 14). But none of these changes will happen without pushing politicians, the media, and academic institutions to engage in a wider discussion—the changes will only happen when we rise.

CHAPTER 14

ENOUGH UNILATERALISM

Changing National Goals and
Improving International Cooperation

> On a visit to Leningrad some years ago, I consulted a map to find out where
> I was, but I could not make it out. From where I stood, I could see several
> enormous churches, yet there was no trace of them on my map. When finally an
> interpreter came to help me, he said: "We don't show churches on our maps." . . .
> It then occurred to me that this was not the first time I had been given a map
> which failed to show many things I could see right in front of my eyes. All through
> school and university I had been given maps of life and knowledge on which there
> was hardly a trace of many of the things that I most cared about and that seemed
> to me to be of the greatest possible importance to the conduct of my life.
>
> E. F. SCHUMACHER (1977)[1]

WHAT ARE WE DOING?

The United States, with less than 5 percent of the world's population, emits about 18 percent of the world's total output of greenhouse gases.[2] The five largest coal users, China, the United States, India, Russia, and Japan, consume 77 percent of the world's coal production.[3] In the twenty-first century, when a single nation's consumption habits can produce global consequences, unilateral economic decisions can be downright dangerous. Aggressive competition, especially among the wealthiest nations, for control of critical resources like land, water, and oil could prove disastrous. The last thing we need is a race to wring the final fragments of growth out of an already overgrown global economy.

On the flip side, suppose a nation faced the facts, acknowledged the

179

limits to growth, and wanted to make the transition to a steady-state economy. Such virtuous behavior could put the nation in a tight spot if all of its global neighbors were to continue aiming for growth. Nations that seek to improve their own economic footing with little regard for broader social and environmental consequences are following a strategy more suited to the nineteenth century than the twenty-first.

In 1884, German Chancellor Otto von Bismarck was becoming increasingly concerned about the colonial aspirations of Britain and Portugal in Africa, because they were interfering with his plans for control of the Congo. He viewed international diplomacy as the path of least resistance for protecting his nation's interests in Africa. Toward this end, he invited representatives of Britain, France, Portugal, the Netherlands, Belgium, Spain, the United States, Austria-Hungary, Sweden-Norway, Denmark, Italy, Turkey, and Russia to a conference. The representatives convened in Berlin to map out their vision for commerce in Africa.

Bismarck proposed three main topics for the agenda: (1) freedom of trade in the Congo basin, (2) freedom of navigation on the Congo and Niger Rivers, and (3) rules to follow when taking possession of new territory.[4] Conferences in those days tended to last longer than the three-day affairs of modern times, but even so, the Berlin Conference stretched on for an exceedingly long time. It started on November 15, 1884, and by the time it concluded on February 26, 1885, the colonial powers had laid the foundation for the "scramble for Africa" that took place over the next six years.[5]

Both Bismarck and the British ambassador, Edward Malet, expressed humanitarian goals in their speeches at the conference. To be sure, they emphasized commercial operations, but each stressed the importance of maintaining the welfare of the native population.[6] Their notions of native welfare were blatantly paternalistic, but even worse, they remained mostly notions. The colonial powers commenced a race to grow their realm of commerce and expand their power and prestige. The land grab was perpetrated without consent, and colonial cultures and external economic institutions were "superimposed upon an already vigorous people with a long history."[7]

Today a more eclectic and less coordinated club is seeking riches in Ethiopia, Tanzania, Sudan, Ghana, Madagascar, and other African nations. Its unusual roster of members includes American universities such as Harvard and Vanderbilt, the king of Saudi Arabia, the Korean corporate conglomerate Daewoo, British financiers, Chinese agribusinesses, and other deep-pocketed investors.[8] Big money is scooping up lands all over the continent for crop production. This twenty-first-century group is exercising more subtlety than its nineteenth-century counterpart, but the win-win rhetoric still abounds. Promises of 25 percent returns on investment intermingle with announcements about sustainable farming practices, job creation, and feeding hungry local populations—all of this despite cases of poor land management, importation of workers, and ongoing focus on the export market and the conversion of crops to biofuels.[9] Whether these land deals result in more food for locals remains to be seen, but foreign investors are definitely feeding their own appetites. According to the World Bank, they have gobbled up an area of farmland larger than France over the last few years.[10]

The parties involved in the current African land deals are prospecting for economic returns. Wealthy foreign nations are looking for investment opportunities, and cash-strapped African nations are hoping to kick-start the agricultural sector, create jobs, and improve food security. But the scene is playing out more like a modern-day Berlin Conference. Investor nations, such as water-starved Saudi Arabia and overpopulated China, have their own food security in mind. And there have been reports of evictions of people from traditional farming and grazing lands.[11]

Even if the investor nations had honorable intentions in executing these land deals, they would still be following the wrong map. It didn't work in 1884, and it won't work now. To get a handle on what nations can do differently—to figure out the details of a new map to sustainable well-being for all—it's important to understand the broad historical pattern of economic growth and international trade.

Over the past two hundred years, only a handful of countries have experienced high and continuous rates of economic growth, and they have done so largely at the expense of the rest of the world, which has remained almost stagnant in economic terms.[12] In the last sixty to seventy years, however, more and more nations have begun to follow suit, emulating the development paths taken by the industrialized nations, but at different rates and with different outcomes. Differences in rates of industrialization explain, to some degree, the enormous disparities between rich and poor—or North and South—around the globe. Only 16 percent of people live in the so-called developed nations, yet these nations account for about 78 percent of global consumption expenditures.[13] Meanwhile, 40 percent of the world's population struggles to subsist on less than $2 per day.[14]

This disparity is a problem of global proportions. The poor people of the world must be able to meet their needs within an economic framework that accepts the limits of a finite planet. But mainstream economics offers only the "solution" of growth. Economists used to believe that an increase in income per capita would lead to increased equality across society (the "Kuznets curve" hypothesis), but that belief was based on an overly simplified set of assumptions about how economies develop and grow.[15] Some economists have also argued that higher incomes reduce environmental degradation (the "environmental Kuznets curve" hypothesis).[16] The theory is that wealthy countries tend to have better environmental performance because they can spend surplus resources on pollution prevention and remediation (although wealthy countries also tend to purchase more products, and the manufacture and transport of these products is often linked to resource use and pollution elsewhere).

According to mainstream economic theory, then, becoming rich not only takes care of poverty and social problems, but also provides a remedy for environmental troubles. But the theory, in this case, fails to match the reality. Empirical evidence casts serious doubts on both types of Kuznets curve.[17] Moreover, as described in Chapter 2, it is not possible to solve problems of poverty and inequality by continuing to grow the global economy, because of the biophysical limits imposed by the planet.

Unfortunately, the mainstream view of growth and development has blocked other ideas from materializing on the global policy agenda. The Millennium Development Goals, the result of an enormous United Nations effort, present objectives for reducing poverty and ensuring that all people have the ability to meet basic needs.[18] From the time the Goals were published in 2000, most of the discourse about attaining them has focused on economic growth as the policy tool to employ. Consequently, discussions about development generally revolve around stimulating and expanding trade. Governments and international organizations seldom consider alternative strategies for improving social, technological, or environmental conditions among all nations.[19]

The result is that both rich and poor countries have become tangled in a convoluted web of international trade. The ongoing African land grab is one egregious example. Another is provided by Charles Wheelan in his book *Naked Economics* (even though he is attempting to praise the unscripted effectiveness of the market). In considering the question "Who feeds Paris?" he writes:

> Somehow the right amount of fresh tuna makes its way from a fishing fleet in the South Pacific to a restaurant on the Rue de Rivoli. A neighborhood fruit vendor has exactly what his customers want every morning—from coffee to fresh papayas— even though those products may come from ten or fifteen different countries. In short, a complex economy involves billions of transactions every day, the vast majority of which happen without any direct government involvement.[20]

Wheelan's "right amount" of fresh tuna may correspond to the demand for tuna sandwiches in Parisian bistros, but it also corresponds to a disappearing population of tuna. An Australian newspaper reported in 2008 that tuna fishing was being banned in two vast areas of the South Pacific "in an attempt to halt the chronic over-exploitation of the highly prized fish."[21] The plight of tuna reflects how global trade can deplete stocks of natural resources, but other impacts are also troubling. The transport of products around the world (e.g., shipments of papayas to Paris) involves elaborate, energy-intensive processes. For example, in manufacturing and marketing a product, raw materials are typically sourced from numerous nations. After these materials have been assembled in some other far-flung location (or locations), the finished products are distributed to yet other regions for consumption. Sometimes nonsensical trade is the result, as nearly identical products are traded back and forth.[22]

Stuck in this web of trade, nations in the North have come to depend on the South for raw materials, cheap labor, and markets for their products. In turn, nations in the South depend on the North for manufactured goods, direct investments, and revenues from exports. Such dependencies, although beneficial to some parties, come with risks and the potential for problems.[23] This potential was realized in the aftermath of the financial crisis of 2008 when the effects of irresponsible financial decisions and reduced consumption in wealthy countries cascaded to relatively poor, trade-dependent countries and plunged many of them into economic hardship.[24] According to the United Nations, the financial meltdown in the wealthy countries drew almost 100 million more residents of low-income countries into extreme poverty.[25]

We need to avoid such systemic failures and find alternatives to the labyrinth of international trade. Much as a traveler needs a roadmap to find the best route and avoid getting lost, we need a map for economic development that properly accounts for the environmental, social, and economic challenges of modern times.

WHAT COULD WE DO INSTEAD?

If the current development map (i.e., pursuit of continuous economic growth through increasing international trade) is leading us to degraded environmental conditions and resource-grabbing behavior like the land deals in Africa, then it's time to consult a better map. This new map must be able to guide not only high-income nations that need to reduce consumption, but also low-income nations that need to increase well-being while maintaining a sustainable ecological footprint. In other words, the map must be able to direct any nation from its current economic starting point to the destination of an optimal steady state.

Such a map, therefore, must be able to show which countries should pursue degrowth, which countries should still aim for economic growth, and which countries are closing in on a steady-state economy. It seems likely that wealthy countries in Western Europe and North America need to degrow their economies before establishing a steady state. It seems equally likely that poor countries in sub-Saharan Africa can still benefit substantially from economic growth (provided that the benefits of growth are distributed equitably). But what about China? Should it continue to pursue rapid growth, or has resource use already reached an unsustainable level? What about India, or countries in South America and Eastern Europe?

Figure 14.1 provides a conceptual map (really it's a chart) that can be used to help answer these questions. We can plot each country's position on the chart based on two factors: the size of its economy with respect to the capacity of ecosystems, and the change in its amount of resource use from one year to the next. The first of these factors corresponds to the idea of "economic scale" introduced in Chapter 3.

The second measures whether the country's economy is growing in biophysical terms. The combination of these two factors places an economy into one of four categories, or quadrants, on the chart: (1) Undesirable Growth, (2) Desirable Degrowth, (3) Undesirable Degrowth, and (4) Desirable Growth.[26]

Once a country identifies its position on the chart, its pathway to a steady-state economy becomes clear. A nation in Quadrant 1 (Undesirable Growth) has an economy that is consuming too many resources, and its resource use is still increasing. Degrowth is necessary before this nation can achieve a steady state. A nation that finds itself in Quadrant 2 (Desirable Degrowth) is still consuming too many resources, even though its resource use is falling. It will need to continue with degrowth until resource use reaches a sustainable level, at which point it can maintain a steady state. A nation in Quadrant 3 (Undesirable De-

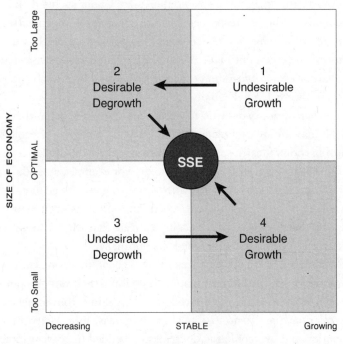

FIG. 14.1. To achieve a steady-state economy (SSE), a nation must stabilize its resource use at a scale that does not exceed the capacity of ecosystems. Each nation's path to a steady-state economy will differ depending on its starting point. SOURCE: see note 26.

growth) is experiencing something quite different. The resource use of its economy is below the optimal level and decreasing, so growth is necessary before it can achieve a steady state. Finally, a nation in Quadrant 4 (Desirable Growth) is consuming resources below the optimal level, but its resource use is increasing. This nation's economy can continue growing until it reaches the optimal size and achieves a steady state.

Figure 14.1 provides a map for nations to follow toward a sustainable and fair economy, but to make this map useful in the real world, we need rigorous and reliable indicators of both economic scale and resource use over time. These indicators should adopt a consumption-based approach that accounts for international trade. In such an approach, the environmental impact of goods produced in China, but consumed in the United States, would be attributed to U.S. citizens.

We also need to define the optimal scale of an economy. "Optimal" could mean the "maximum sustainable" size. Under such a definition, an economy could use resources at a rate equal to the regenerative capacity of ecosystems. If the ecological footprint were used as the indicator of size, then optimal scale might be defined as a *fair earthshare* (the share of global ecosystem capacity that would be available to each person if it were divided equally).

Another option would be to define optimal scale somewhere below the maximum sustainable level to provide a degree of ecological breathing room. Ideally, social indicators would also be used to help determine the optimal scale of the economy. For example, a nation could have excess ecological capacity with room to grow its economy. But if that nation achieved sufficient scores on indicators of human well-being without using its excess ecological capacity, then it might conclude that its economy had reached the optimal scale.[27]

Recognizing the path to a steady-state economy is one thing, but setting out on it is a different matter. A country that wants to put one foot in front of the other has to begin disengaging from unnecessary trade relationships. To do so, it must both increase its capacity for local production and overcome the doctrines embedded in current international trade agreements.

Nations can work independently to encourage local production, but they must cooperate to restructure international trade agreements. Consider a scenario in which producers in one country incorporate environmental and social costs in the prices of their products (a move in line with the transition to a steady-state economy). Their products would likely become more expensive than those produced in a second country pursuing growth through the externalization of such costs. In the absence of any remedy, the first nation would be penalized for its sustainability-seeking behavior. One solution would be for this nation to introduce compensating tariffs on cheap imports to protect its industries from unfair competition with countries where environmental and social costs were not being internalized.[28] But a better solution would be for all nations to agree to internalize costs.

Now consider another potential disincentive to pursuing a steady-state economy: capital flight. If a nation began to internalize environmental and social costs, investment capital might flee that nation because of fears of lower profits. Such capital flight could be deterred by employing capital controls and minimum residency times for foreign investment. Not surprisingly, current trade agreements, which were developed with an eye toward economic expansion, fail to make provisions for tariffs or capital controls aimed at sustainability.

We need to maintain the benefits of trade, but we can't continue to disregard the shortcomings in the current trade framework. Trade should be encouraged among nations that internalize the environmental and social costs of production, but discouraged among nations that do not. Four major benefits would result from efforts to restructure trade agreements and increase local production capacity:

1. Nations that have lost domestic industries would regain the security and resilience derived from being able to produce more goods and services locally.
2. Nations that are currently "offshoring pollution" by relying on imported products would be forced to develop clean manufacturing processes at home.
3. Low-income nations would be able to fight poverty by creating local jobs and economic opportunities.
4. All nations would be able reduce the energy used to transport products back and forth over long-distance trade routes.

A strategy to increase local production capacity could benefit a nation like Tanzania, where the proportion of undernourished people has reached the crisis stage. Development of organic agriculture on small farms could increase food production, raise incomes with locally available technologies, and prevent environmental damage.[29] In fact, some Tanzanians are already making it happen. In the Mkuranga District south of Dar es Salaam, farmers have been collaborating since 2004 on organic cashew and vegetable production. The agricultural practices have improved soil and water conservation efforts, the cooperative practices have built community trust, and, best of all, the farmers have been able to provide more (and more nutritious) food for the children of the community.[30] These homegrown farmers in Tanzania are laying the foundation for a better future, certainly more so than the people involved in a sell-off of lands to foreign investors.

WHERE DO WE GO FROM HERE?

We've suggested that nations need to recognize the limits to growth and help one another develop steady-state economies by reconfiguring international trade and focusing more on local production capacity. It sounds appealing, but there's a big catch—doing so will require unprecedented cooperation. Given that global resource use is already at an unsustainable level, the world cannot wait until all developing economies reach a certain size and level of industrialization before they begin the shift to a steady state. Developing nations need to identify alternative paths to increase the well-being of their citizens, and these paths must be less materially intensive than those of today's industrialized nations.[31] At the same time, high-consuming nations need to take greater responsibility for the impacts of their consumption.

All nations, therefore, need to incorporate a robust development discourse in the global policy agenda and intensify their efforts to cooperate with one another. To make an orderly transition from the era of growth to the era of sustainability, people will have to stop seeing the world as a collection of individual countries, competing against one another for dominance. Instead we need to view ourselves as heterogeneous societies and cultures whose fates are intertwined. Wealthy economies that have reached the end of growth and those economies still in need of growth must work together on the mechanisms that will allow them to co-exist and co-develop so that all people can flourish. As a first step, international organizations such as the United Nations,

World Bank, International Monetary Fund, and World Trade Organization should be democratized. These organizations should represent all people on the planet, not just the interests of a few nations.[32]

Once some basic agreements about the limits to growth have been reached, the wealthy nations, where the costs of further economic growth outweigh the benefits, will need to take the lead on the transition to a steady-state economy. Stabilization and even degrowth of these economies will free up ecological space to allow poor countries to expand their economies and realize the benefits of growth.[33] These wealthy nations also need to demonstrate leadership on technology transfer. The transfer of technology from nations where it is abundant to those where it is scarce can help localize production and improve well-being around the globe. As this transition gets under way, trade with low-income countries will likely fall, with the potential to exacerbate the North–South divide. To manage this scenario, South–South trade should be encouraged.[34] In fact, such trade is already growing, with almost 40 percent of exports from low-income countries destined for other low-income countries (although the majority of these exports originate from China, India, and five other countries).[35]

At the same time, the global North must learn to follow the lead of the global South. On measures of well-being and ecological stewardship, many low- and middle-income countries outperform their high-income counterparts. Grassroots movements centered in the South have also brought about significant positive social changes. For example, the fair-trade movement has worked to ensure that the benefits of trade accrue more equitably to low-income producers.

In 1776, the economist and philosopher Adam Smith published *The Wealth of Nations*. A little less than two hundred years later, another economist and philosopher, Leopold Kohr, published *The Breakdown of Nations*. Whereas Smith's thesis is about national adoption of free-market strategies to concentrate wealth and power, Kohr's thesis is about how bigness (achieved through unchecked economic growth and too much concentration of wealth and power) begets big wars, big social ills, and an assortment of other big breakdowns.[36]

For more than two centuries, free-market economies have been diligently practicing Smith's prescriptions, such as the pursuit of enlightened self-interest and the division of labor to boost productivity. But Smith developed his ideas at a time when the world was very different, with fewer people, less human-built capital, and smaller environmental impacts. Some of his designs for growing national wealth seem antiquated, even immoral, when viewed through a modern lens. For example, in *The Wealth of Nations*, Smith wrote:

> The colony of a civilized nation which takes possession either of a waste country, or of one so thinly inhabited that the natives easily give place to the new settlers, advances more rapidly to wealth and greatness than any other human society. The colonies carry out with them a knowledge of agriculture and of other useful arts superior to what can grow up of its own accord, in the course of many centuries, among savage and barbarous nations.[37]

The nations that followed Smith's prescriptions may have used violent or unfair means (as in the "scramble for Africa"), but these nations have certainly accumulated wealth. Along the way, however, they've arrived at a precipitous point on the edge of breakdown. Kohr linked the massive brutality of World War II and other conflicts throughout history to the over-accumulation of wealth and power. His theme, that smallness is the basis of sustainability, resonates more with each passing day. He wrote, "Below a certain size, everything fuses, joins, or accumulates. But beyond a certain size, everything collapses or explodes."[38] This insight cries out for the transition from *more* to *enough*. Nations need to find the political will to maintain checks and balances on economic scale and power. Now is the time to cultivate national temperance, intensify international cooperation, and achieve an economic scale that provides for the wealth, but not the breakdown, of nations.

[CHAPTER 15]
ENOUGH WAITING
Taking Action to Start the Transition

*[H]ere's the deal: forget that this task of planet-saving is
not possible in the time required. Don't be put off by people
who know what is not possible. Do what needs to be done,
and check to see if it was impossible only after you are done.*

PAUL HAWKEN[1]

THE BLUEPRINT

According to Greek mythology, Helios, the sun god, lights the earth
each day by driving his fiery chariot across the sky. He has made the
trip from sunrise to sunset nearly nine hundred thousand times while
the Parthenon has stood atop the Athenian Acropolis. This ancient
temple has survived for more than two thousand years because it was
conceived and constructed with durability in mind. The architects developed a timeless design, and the builders delivered a strong foundation and support structure. The same principles apply to creating a
lasting economy: start with a good blueprint, construct a strong economic foundation, and build well-crafted policy pillars on top of it.

As described in Part I of this book, the social and environmental challenges of our times call for a new economic blueprint. The
business-as-usual approach of chasing perpetual growth is failing. It is
not sustainable on a finite planet, and it is damaging the natural systems upon which the economy depends. It is also not solving the problems of unemployment, poverty, and inequality. Nor is it improving
the well-being of those who already have enough material wealth. To

193

address these issues, we need a new economic structure designed for stability instead of growth.

More than 250 people attended the Steady State Economy Conference held in Leeds, U.K., in 2010. They provided a wealth of ideas that we have incorporated into the blueprint for a steady-state economy. More work remains to be done, but the basics of the building are clear (Figure 15.1). The foundation consists of the defining features of the economy—the ideals that guide our choices. The support structure consists of policy pillars designed to fulfill these economic ideals over the long term. And the roof that is held up by this support structure represents the ultimate goal of the economy: sustainable and equitable human well-being.

ROOF
THE GOAL OF AN SSE
Sustainable and equitable human well-being.

PILLARS
POLICIES TO SUPPORT AN SSE AND STRATEGIES FOR THE TRANSITION
Limit resource use, stabilize population, distribute income and wealth equitably, reform monetary and financial systems, change the way we measure progress, secure full employment, rethink commerce, change consumer behavior, engage politicians and the media, and improve international cooperation.

FOUNDATION
FEATURES OF AN SSE
Sustainable scale, fair distribution, efficient allocation, high quality of life, improved investment, optimal labor productivity, innovative models of ownership, and environmental values.

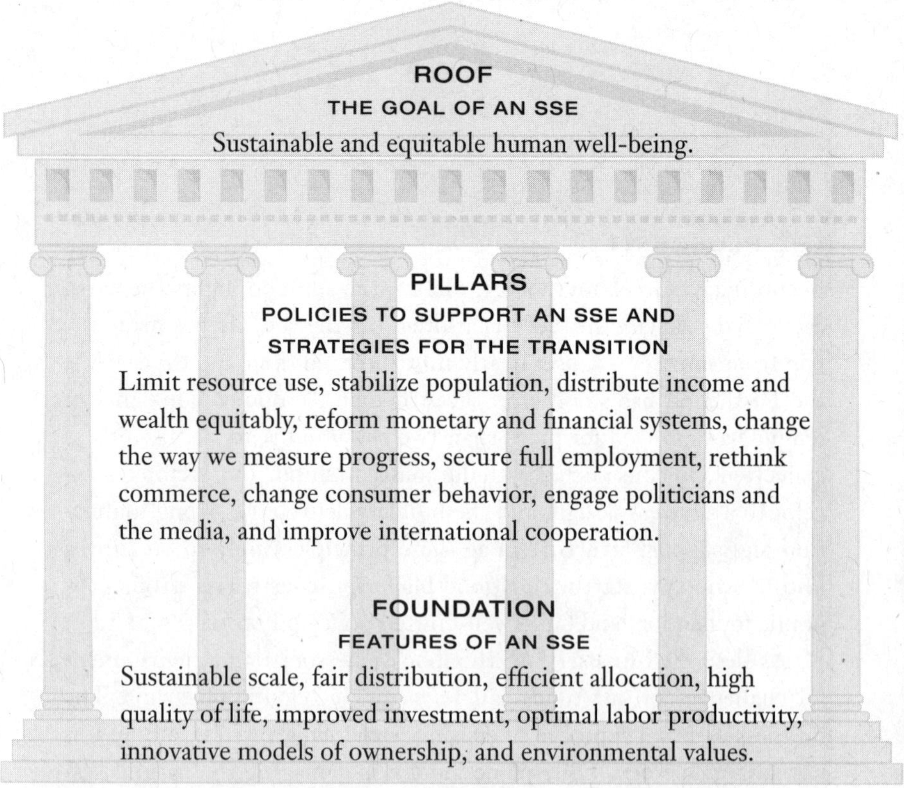

FIG. 15.1. The blueprint for a steady-state economy (SSE) includes a foundation (defining features of the economy), pillars (economic policies and transitional strategies), and roof (the ultimate goal of sustainable and equitable human well-being).

The Foundation

The foundation of a steady-state economy includes the four key features discussed in the first part of this book:

1. **Sustainable scale.** Material and energy use are stabilized and kept within ecological limits. This means stabilizing both population and the stock of built capital. In some economies, degrowth may be required before sustainable scale can be achieved.
2. **Fair distribution.** People have equal opportunities to obtain wealth and income, and limits to inequality prevent excessive gaps between the rich and the poor.
3. **Efficient allocation.** Societies harness the power of markets to allocate resources among competing interests, taking account of where markets work and where they don't.
4. **High quality of life.** GDP growth takes a backseat to the things that really matter to people, such as health, happiness, secure employment, leisure time, strong communities, and economic stability.

A society with these four features embedded in its economic institutions stands to achieve a lasting prosperity.

But building this foundation from scratch is not an option. We are saddled with the current economic system, an unstable foundation that is in need of substantial repairs. The repair work requires us to re-envision four keystones of the economy:

1. **Investment.** We need to embrace a deeper view of investment that encompasses more than using money to make money. Our investments should generate environmental and social returns, not just financial returns.
2. **Productivity.** The way firms regard productivity needs to change as well. In the relentless pursuit of profits, firms currently seek to maximize productivity, a practice that causes job losses and overexploitation of natural resources. Optimization, not maximization, must become the watchword when pursuing labor productivity.
3. **Ownership.** It's long past time to acknowledge that we have

many options besides the extremes of state socialism and private capitalism. A steady-state economy would contain a variety of ownership arrangements, especially ones founded on democratic principles.

4. **Environmental values.** We need to reacquaint ourselves with a fundamental truth that seems to have been lost, at least where the economy is concerned—that humanity is part of a living planet. We depend on the natural world for our survival, and this fact needs to be reflected in our economic decisions.

It's difficult to conceive of a more worthwhile project than building the foundation for a steady-state economy, but widespread public support is still needed. Once that support emerges (and it surely will as the limits to growth continue to assert themselves), we must be prepared to build a cohesive set of policies and strategies atop the foundation.

The Pillars

Part II of this book, *Strategies of Enough*, describes seven policy directions that serve as pillars of a steady-state economy:

1. Limit resource use and waste production.
2. Stabilize population.
3. Distribute income and wealth equitably.
4. Reform monetary and financial systems.
5. Change the way we measure progress.
6. Secure full employment.
7. Rethink how businesses create value.

In addition to these, three more pillars (introduced in the third part of this book) are needed to energize the transition to a steady-state economy:

1. Replace the culture of consumerism with a culture of sustainability.
2. Stimulate political debate and media coverage of the limits to growth and the steady-state alternative.
3. Change national goals regarding growth and improve international cooperation.

Although we have presented these ten ideas in separate chapters, they cannot work in isolation. Just like the pillars in an architectural structure, the economic policies and transitional strategies must work in parallel to support a sound economy. For example, throughput-limiting policies must be accompanied by policies that distribute income and wealth equitably to ensure everyone has access to a fair share of material and energy flows. And throughput-limiting policies are likely to be ineffective in a world where population continues to rise, so policies to stabilize population are also essential.

In Chapter 7, we proposed democratizing the institutions where people work. This process of democratization would require a fundamental change in the way businesses operate, perhaps along the lines discussed in Chapter 11. A shift toward more democratic forms of business organization (such as cooperatives) would likely dampen the growth imperative found in current business practices, and thus reduce resource use as well.

In Chapter 10, we proposed reducing working hours in order to achieve full employment. A reduction in working hours would likely lead to a decrease in resource use and an increase in well-being. However, to reduce their working hours, people would need to embrace the notion of *enough* when it comes to consumption. Thus, behavioral change away from consumerism would go hand-in-hand with policies to reshape employment practices. Some policies, such as adoption of new measures of progress, can probably gain traction on their own. But in most cases, it is difficult to imagine advancement on one policy without concurrent advancement on others.

In general, the policy and strategy pillars recommended in this book are mutually reinforcing, which is good news. It suggests that a steady-state economy would be a stable economy, with checks and balances that restore it to equilibrium in the face of economic or environmental shocks. This stability is in contrast to the current growth-based system, which exists far from equilibrium. Shocks such as oil price rises and debt defaults have pushed growth-based economies to the brink of collapse.

Deployment of any of the policies discussed in this book requires a shift from the culture of consumerism to a culture of sustainability. Neither the policies nor the shift will be forthcoming without broadening the society-wide discussion on economic goals and the limits to growth, or without stepping up international cooperation. In short, we need to build all of the pillars, perhaps not simultaneously, but with a view toward completing the entire economic structure.

The Roof

The purpose of laying a foundation and raising pillars is to support a roof. After all, the roof is the part of the building that provides shelter. The roof, or ultimate goal, for the economy is *sustainable and equitable human well-being*. Each part of this phrase plays a critical role:

- **Sustainable.** There is little point in attaining well-being for one generation at the expense of future generations. Careless consumption of tomorrow's resources for today's enjoyment is no basis for a lasting prosperity.
- **Equitable.** Failure to provide equitable opportunities has derailed economic systems through the ages. Well-being for certain individuals without regard for others undermines the basis for community and societal health.
- **Well-being.** Human well-being, as measured by subjective indicators such as happiness and life satisfaction, needs to become the unifying theme of the economy. If people are unable to lead happy and satisfying lives, they will not accept their situation for long.

The foundation and pillars described in this book offer hope for achieving sustainable and equitable well-being. Herman Daly's definition of a steady-state economy is one with "constant stocks of people and artifacts, maintained at some desired, sufficient levels by low rates of maintenance 'throughput,' that is, by the lowest feasible flows of matter and energy from the first stage of production to the last stage of consumption."[2] Such an economy maximizes its ends (sustainable and equitable well-being), while economizing on the ultimate sources of that well-being (flows of materials and energy). It is a true economy of *enough*.

THE WHOLE BUILDING

Many people, as they begin to consider the problems with pursuing perpetual growth, ask with some trepidation what a nongrowing economy would look like. We hope our descriptions of the institutions and policies needed for a steady state have provided some idea. A nongrowing economy certainly doesn't have to resemble the recessions and depressions of a failed growth economy. Daly has joked that some people mistakenly believe a steady-state economy would mean "freezing in the dark under communist tyranny."[3] But a steady-state economy is not about deprivation, and it doesn't require the heavy hand of a Politburo. It's not even about a return to the "good old days." It is, in fact, a progression to the "good new days." As Peter Victor's model of the Canadian economy has shown, we can achieve important goals for society in an economy with a stable size.[4]

We began writing this book because we wanted to know how a steady-state economy would work in practice, and how the world might make the transition to one. We wanted to better understand how future generations could flourish within the capacity of the planet. Along the way, we have become increasingly hopeful about the possibilities. We don't want to sugarcoat the difficulty of shifting to a steady-state economy—it's likely to be a tough transition—but the destination is well worth the journey. Once society can put aside its obsession with economic growth, the stage will be set for achieving prosperity over the long run. To provide a glimpse of what the days ahead might look like, we've sketched out ten encouraging scenes from a steady-state economy:

1. **Consumption.** People consume enough to meet their needs and lead meaningful, joyful lives without undermining the life-support systems of the planet. They choose to consume energy and materials responsibly, conserving, economizing, and recycling where possible. Conspicuous consumption becomes a thing of the past. Citizens (yes, citizens, not consumers) recognize the culture of materialism as a bankrupt ideology and a poor path to happiness. They forget about trying to accumulate ever-more stuff and focus on more worthwhile pursuits.

2. **Population.** As population stabilizes (and decreases in some places), streets become less crowded. Frenzied competition subsides as each person is able to obtain sufficient resources for a high quality of life. Overcrowded slums become a curiosity for historians to study.

3. **Families.** In their households, families emphasize healthy lifestyles and relationships. With a shorter workweek, family members can spend more quality time with one another and explore personal development. Maybe they pick up a musical instrument every once in a while, learn a new language, or watch a sunset. Children receive more attention, and the lament "I wish I'd spent more time with my family" is rarely heard.

4. **Community.** As we change our economic focus from the global to the local, communities become more connected, more resilient, and more neighborly. A vibrant local economy supports local businesses and keeps wealth circulating within the community. The layout of the community is designed (or redesigned) for the human scale, allowing people to more easily navigate from one location to another and develop a strong sense of place.

5. **Business.** Entrepreneurial businesses provide valuable services not just to earn a profit, but to improve social and environmental conditions. As workplaces adopt democratic structures, employees find that they have more opportunities to use their creativity and explore innovative ideas. With a greater sense of purpose driving them, workers feel more content and more energized in their jobs.

6. **Cities.** Redesigned cities have smaller populations working and living in more compact land areas. Buildings and transportation networks are much more efficient and require less energy. Natural areas and gardens are reintegrated into city landscapes. At the same time, local cooperative enterprises, businesses, and regional trade activities generate good prospects for employment. Revamped urban landscapes provide both improved livability and a smaller ecological footprint.

7. **Agriculture.** Elimination of the need for constantly increasing food production lightens the impacts people have on the landscape, with less land devoted to crop production. The agricultural sector decentralizes into local systems of production, distribution, and consumption, resulting in fewer large-scale agribusiness operations, lower fuel inputs, less application of chemicals, less reliance on long-distance

transportation, and less unnecessary packaging. Consumers of food (all of us!) can expect increased food security, healthier foods, and a stronger connection to farmers and other people who produce and sell food.

8. **Nature.** Without a continuously growing economy crowding out nature, our lands and waters enter a new era of healing. People enjoy more opportunities for outdoor recreation. Wildlife becomes more abundant, and restored ecosystems are more capable of providing vital services such as climate regulation, food production, and water purification.

9. **Energy.** Energy conservation becomes a high priority as people seek ways to accomplish their goals while minimizing energy inputs. Societies phase out fossil fuels, and instead favor energy sources that use solar income, such as photovoltaic cells, wind turbines, biofuels, and hydroelectric generators. Businesses and households retrofit existing structures to be more energy-efficient and eliminate machines that consume wasteful amounts of energy, especially items consumed for status.

10. **Money.** Expectations about money and investing are adjusted to match reality. Ponzi schemes and get-rich-quick dreams blink out of existence, replaced by investments in real wealth that earn modest returns. Investments are used to build low-carbon infrastructure, restore ecosystems, improve social conditions, and develop innovative and useful technologies. We climb out from under the enormous heap of debt as we learn to restrain borrowing within the bounds of savings. As gaps in income and wealth shrink, no one is left behind, and no one becomes obscenely affluent.

These scenes from a steady-state economy depict a society in which people are more attuned to where they live and what they are doing. Living in such an economy would encourage a sort of mindfulness that would increase appreciation for the available bounty of resources. We would participate in the economy not just for a paycheck or because we were *supposed to*, but because we were striving to achieve positive outcomes for ourselves, our families, our communities, our societies, and the biosphere.

The Case for Starting Construction

The steady-state economy is an idea whose time has come, but even though it has gained a solid core of supporters, it has failed to grab the imagination of the broader public. The consequences of too much economic growth have been recorded in a host of sources, ranging from books to peer-reviewed articles to blogs to videos (although growth isn't always identified as the culprit). Reams and reams of pages are covered with statistics about biodiversity loss, ecosystem declines, income gaps, unemployment, resource shortages, poverty, and so on. It's clear that economic growth is no longer an appropriate goal in many countries, and it's time to try something else.

We've attempted to compile a comprehensive set of ideas and policies to clarify how a steady-state economy would work, but we know the job isn't complete. Even though some parts of the blueprint remain faint, societies should resist the temptation to wait for more details. The current draft contains enough carefully designed features to start construction. Besides, we face a choice between acting now to build a steady-state economy through sensible reforms, or delaying action until our addiction to growth relegates us to a world of depleted resources and reduced ecosystem capacity. The first choice offers the benefits of preventing suffering, preserving ecosystem capacity, and moving toward sustainable and equitable human well-being. Is the second choice really even a choice?

Now is the moment to get started on the economy of enough, and *it's about time!* The concept of a steady-state economy has been developing for centuries. Economists have long considered a transition from a growing economy to a stable one. In the eighteenth century Adam Smith anticipated such a transition. He believed that in the long run, population growth would push wages down, natural resources would become increasingly scarce, and division of labor would approach the limits of effectiveness. He even estimated that the period of growth would last for about two hundred years.[5]

In the nineteenth century John Stuart Mill, a pioneer of economics and a gifted philosopher, developed his idea of the "stationary state." He believed that after a phase of growth, the economy would reach a constant population and constant stock of capital, and he viewed this scenario as a positive development:

It is scarcely necessary to remark that a stationary condition of capital and population implies no stationary state of human improvement. There would be as much scope as ever for all kinds of mental culture, and moral and social progress; as much room for improving the Art of Living and much more likelihood of its being improved, when minds cease to be engrossed by the art of getting on.[6]

One of the twentieth century's foremost economists, John Maynard Keynes, looked with anticipation toward the day when society could focus on ends (happiness and well-being, for example) rather than means (economic growth and individual pursuit of profit). His essay "Economic Possibilities for Our Grandchildren" strikes a steady-state chord and hints at the transition to a nongrowing economy:

I see us free, therefore, to return to some of the most sure and certain principles of religion and traditional virtue—that avarice is a vice, that the exaction of usury is a misdemeanour, and the love of money is detestable. . . . We shall once more value ends above means and prefer the good to the useful.[7]

These leading thinkers from the last three centuries were onto something. Today in the twenty-first century, increasing numbers of ecological economists, sustainability scientists, well-being researchers, and concerned citizens are recognizing the urgent need to make the transition away from growth and focus instead on sustainable and equitable well-being. The blueprint continues to develop, but the steady-state design has yet to be put into practice. To be sure, the blueprint can be improved (especially as societies gain experience with the policies), but enough ideas exist today to break ground on the new economy.

The Grand Construction Project

Crises tend to have a cascading effect, with one crisis paving the way for the next. It's precisely because of this effect that we face a frightening combination of economic and environmental crises, including a debt-riddled financial system, widespread unemployment, inequities between the haves and the have-nots, climate change, species extinctions, and dwindling supplies of natural resources. But solutions can also have a cascading effect.[8] Once we decide to get on with the process of building a steady-state economy, the policies and strategies can reinforce and feed off one another.

When the cascading effect has been set in motion, the steady-state economy will advance from a rough sketch to a reality. It's a lot to take in—this process of building a whole new economy—but remember that the economy is a human construct. Economic "laws" are not like the law of gravity. They can be changed. In the end, economic institutions and the policies that support them are dependent on culture. With culture serving as the source for what happens in the economy, it follows that an economic paradigm shift will occur only in response to a cultural shift. People have to grasp that consumption is only a small fraction of the complete picture when it comes to well-being and life satisfaction. Citizens everywhere, but especially those living in high-consuming nations, need to work toward this cultural shift—a process that will require effective activism.

Bill McKibben, the author of *Deep Economy*, understands the arguments in favor of this cultural shift, and he also has a feel for effective activism. As the founder of 350.org, he has successfully organized grassroots campaigns and global public actions aimed at solving the climate crisis. Despite his successes, McKibben retains a down-to-earth demeanor. When prompted to discuss his experience as an activist, he almost seems surprised that someone would seek his advice on the subject. Even so, his advice is helpful for anyone interested in working on the cultural shift needed to build a steady-state economy. Some of his principles are:

- **Get people interested and trust them to do good things.**
  His metaphor for this principle is a potluck dinner; if you set a date and time, people will bring food, and things generally work out.
- **Combine science and art.** The scientific facts provide the starting point, but art and imagery provide the inspiration.
- **Have fun.** One of the best ways to motivate people to join a cause is to create opportunities for them to enjoy themselves.
- **Consider options besides attack and escalation.** In many circumstances, creative and artistic actions can be more effective than aggressive ones.

- **Use different currencies.** Entrenched interests mostly use money as their currency, and while activists can also use money, they may find power in other currencies, such as shared goals or close community ties.

Achieving a monumental shift in culture and the way people behave may sound daunting, but there's hope that it can be done. All we need to do is look at the numerous ways in which culture and behavioral norms have shifted over time. And in today's hyper-connected world, changes can happen faster than at any point in history.

As the cultural shift gets under way, as researchers continue to advance the thinking on how to manage a nongrowing economy, and as publicity for the concept of an economic transition builds, it will be time to start the earnest work of putting the policy pillars in place. Policies such as democratization of economic institutions, ecological tax reform, and work-time reduction are positive responses to systems that aren't working. However, implementation will require us to overcome ingrained ways of doing things. Plenty of opportunities and challenges will arise during this process. We should begin with the most politically feasible policies (taking advantage of the opportunities), and use these to spur complementary changes (to overcome the challenges). Since there is already strong support for adopting new indicators of progress, it makes sense to push for this change to start the cascade of other changes that are needed.

Walking in a different direction from the rest of society is a challenging thing to do. Belief in an unpopular idea, even if it's true, can be an isolating experience (just ask Galileo!). It can also be disquieting to support policies that—because they are counter to the conventional wisdom of economic growth—are viewed by many as harmful. In considering the transition to a steady-state economy, it's tempting to give in to the mainstream fear that without growth there will be unemployment, but remember that the mainstream has generally not considered the hopeful blueprint for a steady-state economy. Many jobs will be available in the transition to a steady-state economy, and these jobs will have more meaning than much of the busywork involved in making a bigger economy. As Thoreau wrote, "It is not enough to be industrious; so are the ants. What are you industrious about?"[9]

At the same time, the transition will offer opportunities for improving quality of life. It may be true that improving quality of life and economic growth once went hand in hand, but the diminishing returns of growth and the negative consequences of too much growth have changed that. As McKibben colorfully describes:

> For most of human history, the two birds More and Better roosted on the same branch. You could toss one stone and hope to hit them both. That's why the centuries since Adam Smith have been devoted to the dogged pursuit of maximum economic production. . . . But the distinguishing feature of our moment is this: Better has flown a few trees over to make her nest. That changes everything. Now, if you've got the stone of your own life, or your own society, gripped in your hand, you have to choose between them. It's More *or* Better.[10]

This is a heartening assessment of our future prospects, and it's a good thing, too, because it will take boldness to adjust our aim and throw the stone at Better. It will take boldness to open our minds to what science and our own senses are telling us. And it will take boldness to break out of old economic patterns, unseat entrenched elites, and reconcile our actions with the capacity of the planet.

Real action to achieve a prosperous and sustainable economy does not include bailouts and futile attempts to squeeze more growth out of an already overgrown economy. It certainly does not involve throwing more and more debt-based "stimulus" money into an unstable system of finance, or cutting valuable public services. Real action requires us to recognize the limits to growth, and embrace the viable and desirable alternative: a steady-state economy. But we must act now, for time is the ultimate limit that we face, and it's the one commodity that we can never have enough of.

NOTES

CHAPTER I: HAVE YOU HAD ENOUGH?

1. E. F. Schumacher, *A Guide for the Perplexed* (New York: Harper & Row, 1977), 122.
2. Wendell Berry, "Three Ways of Farming in the Southwest (1979)," in *The Gift of Good Land* (New York: North Point Press, 1982), 47–76.
3. Herman Daly and Joshua Farley, *Ecological Economics: Principles and Applications* (Washington, D.C.: Island Press, 2003).
4. Dan O'Neill, Rob Dietz, and Nigel Jones, eds., "Enough Is Enough: Ideas for a Sustainable Economy in a World of Finite Resources. The Report of the Steady State Economy Conference" (Center for the Advancement of the Steady State Economy and Economic Justice For All, Leeds, U.K., 2010), http://steadystate.org/enough-is-enough/ (accessed October 12, 2011).
5. Tim Jackson, *Prosperity without Growth: Economics for a Finite Planet* (London: Earthscan, 2009).
6. Tim Jackson, "Investment, Productivity, and Ownership" (Steady State Economy Conference, Leeds, U.K., June 19, 2010), http://steadystate.org/learn/leeds2010/videos/ (accessed October 12, 2011).

CHAPTER 2: WHY SHOULD ENOUGH BE THE GOAL?

1. Telephone conversation between Kenneth Boulding and Lindsey Grant, March 1988.
2. Jack Santa-Barbara, interview with Rob Dietz, November 14, 2011.
3. Herman Daly and John Cobb, Jr., *For the Common Good: Redirecting the Economy toward Community, the Environment, and a Sustainable Future*, 2nd ed. (Boston: Beacon Press, 1994).
4. Angus Maddison, "Statistics on World Population, GDP and Per Capita GDP, 1–2008 AD" (Groningen Growth and Development Centre, University of Groningen, 2010), http://www.ggdc.net/MADDISON/Historical_Statistics/horizontal-file_02-2010.xls (accessed November 22, 2011).
5. Fridolin Krausmann et al., "Growth in Global Materials Use, GDP and Population during the 20th Century," *Ecological Economics* 68, no. 10 (August 2009): 2696–2705.
6. Johan Rockström et al., "Planetary Boundaries: Exploring the Safe Operating Space for Humanity," *Ecology and Society* 14, no. 2 (2009): 32.
7. Ibid.
8. Brad Ewing et al., *Ecological Footprint Atlas 2009* (Oakland, Calif.: Global Footprint

Network, 2009), http://www.footprintnetwork.org/images/uploads/Ecological_ Footprint_Atlas_2009.pdf (accessed December 5, 2011).

9. Global Footprint Network, "National Footprint Accounts: 2010 Edition" (Global Footprint Network, 2010), http://www.footprintnetwork.org (accessed December 5, 2011).

10. Quoted in Steven Stoll, "Fear of Fallowing: The Specter of a No-Growth World," *Harper's Magazine*, March 2008.

11. Thomas Friedman, "The Inflection Is Near?" *New York Times*, March 7, 2009, http://www.nytimes.com/2009/03/08/opinion/08friedman.html (accessed December 5, 2011).

12. Richard Heinberg, *The End of Growth: Adapting to Our New Economic Reality* (Gabriola Island, Canada: New Society Publishers, 2011), 2–3.

13. David Murphy and Charles Hall, "Year in Review—EROI or Energy Return on (Energy) Invested," *Annals of the New York Academy of Sciences* 1185 (January 2010): 102–118.

14. Ibid.

15. Ibid.

16. Energy data represent total primary energy consumption and are from the U.S. Energy Information Administration, "International Energy Statistics" (2011), http://www.eia.gov/countries/data.cfm (accessed November 28, 2011). GDP data are from the World Bank, "World Development Indicators, September 2011 Edition" (University of Manchester: ESDS International, 2011), http://dx.doi.org/ 10.5257/wb/wdi/2011-04 (accessed November 24, 2011).

17. Andrew Simms, Victoria Johnson, and Peter Chowla, *Growth Isn't Possible* (London: New Economics Foundation, 2010).

18. Ibid., 24.

19. James Hansen et al., "Target Atmospheric CO_2: Where Should Humanity Aim?" *The Open Atmospheric Science Journal* 2 (2008): 217.

20. Jeremy Grantham, "Time to Wake Up: Days of Abundant Resources and Falling Prices Are Over Forever," *GMO Quarterly Newsletter*, April 2011, reprinted in *The Oil Drum*, http://www.theoildrum.com/node/7853 (accessed November 14, 2011).

21. Leslie Christian and Carsten Henningsen, *Portfolio 21 Annual Report*, June 30, 2011.

22. Happiness data are calculated based on the method used by Richard Layard, *Happiness: Lessons from a New Science* (New York: Penguin Press, 2005), 30. Happiness data for 1946–1971 are from the American Institute of Public Opinion, as reported in Tom Smith, "Happiness: Time Trends, Seasonal Variations, Intersurvey Differences, and Other Mysteries," *Social Psychology Quarterly* 42, no. 1 (1979): 18–30. Happiness data for 1972–2010 are from the National Opinion Research Center, "General Social Survey 1972–2010, Cumulative Datafile" (Chicago: National Opinion Research Center, 2012), http://www3.norc.org/GSS+Website (accessed February 14, 2012). GDP data are from the U.S. Bureau of Economic Analysis, "Current-Dollar and Real GDP" (Washington, D.C.: U.S. Department of Commerce, 2012), http://www .bea.gov/national/index.htm (accessed February 14, 2012).

23. Life satisfaction data are from Ruut Veenhoven, "World Database of Happiness" (Erasmus University Rotterdam, 2011), http://worlddatabaseofhappiness.eur.nl (accessed November 12, 2011). GDP data are from the World Bank, "World Development Indicators, September 2011 Edition."

24. Anne Krueger, "Letting the Future In: India's Continuing Reform Agenda" (key-

note speech, Stanford India Conference, Stanford University, Stanford, Calif., June 4, 2004), http://www.imf.org/external/np/speeches/2004/060404.htm (accessed November 30, 2011).

25. United Nations Millennium Project, "Fast Facts: The Faces of Poverty" (United Nations Millennium Project, U.N. Development Group, 2006), http://www.un millenniumproject.org/resources/fastfacts_e.htm (accessed August 3, 2010).

26. World Bank, "Macroeconomics and Growth" (2008), http://go.worldbank.org/ E5RR830FI1 (accessed September 19, 2010).

27. David Woodward and Andrew Simms, *Growth Isn't Working: The Unbalanced Distribution of Benefits and Costs from Economic Growth* (London: New Economics Foundation, 2006).

28. Richard Wilkinson and Kate Pickett, *The Spirit Level: Why Greater Equality Makes Societies Stronger* (London: Bloomsbury Press, 2009), 235.

29. United Nations Development Programme, *Human Development Report 2009: Overcoming Barriers: Human Mobility and Development* (New York: Palgrave Macmillan, 2009), http://hdr.undp.org/en/reports/global/hdr2009/ (accessed November 30, 2011).

30. Wilkinson and Pickett, *The Spirit Level*.

31. OECD.Stat, "Key Short-Term Economic Indicators: Harmonised Unemployment Rate" (Organisation for Economic Co-operation and Development, 2012), http://stats.oecd.org/index.aspx (accessed February 12, 2012).

32. John Maynard Keynes, *First Annual Report of the Arts Council (1945–1946)* (London: U.K. Arts Council, 1946).

CHAPTER 3: HOW MUCH IS ENOUGH?

1. Jackson, *Prosperity without Growth*, 13 (cited in chap. 1, n. 5).

2. National Park Service, *Chesapeake and Ohio Canal: A Guide to Chesapeake and Ohio Canal National Historical Park, Maryland, District of Columbia, and West Virginia* (Washington, D.C.: Bernan Assoc., 1991), 24.

3. Joel Cohen, *How Many People Can the Earth Support?* (New York: W. W. Norton & Company, 1995), 369.

4. Ibid., 368–369.

5. Erik Assadourian, "The Rise and Fall of Consumer Cultures," in *State of the World 2010: Transforming Cultures*, edited by Linda Starke and Lisa Mastny, 3–20 (Washington, D.C.: Worldwatch Institute, 2010), 6.

6. Richard Horan, Erwin Bulte, and Jason Shogren, "How Trade Saved Humanity from Biological Exclusion: An Economic Theory of Neanderthal Extinction," *Journal of Economic Behavior and Organization* 58, no. 1 (September 2005): 1–29.

7. Paul Ehrlich, *The Population Bomb* (San Francisco: Sierra Club/Ballantine Books, 1968).

8. Daly and Farley, *Ecological Economics* (cited in chap. 1, n. 3), 63.

9. Gregg Easterbrook, "The Man Who Defused the 'Population Bomb,'" *Wall Street Journal*, September 16, 2009, http://online.wsj.com/article/SB10001424052970203 9173045744113826769924044.html (accessed December 8, 2011).

10. Paul Ehrlich, "Homage to Norman Borlaug," *International Journal of Environmental Studies* 66, no. 6 (2009): 673–677.

11. Jackson, *Prosperity without Growth*, 68.

12. Material extraction data are from the Sustainable Europe Research Institute,

"Global Material Flows Database" (Vienna: Sustainable Europe Research Institute, 2010), http://www.materialflows.net (accessed November 24, 2010). GDP data are from the World Bank, "World Development Indicators, September 2011 Edition" (cited in chap. 2, n. 16).

13. Energy use data are from the U.S. Energy Information Administration, "International Energy Statistics" (cited in chap. 2, n. 16). GDP data are from the World Bank, "World Development Indicators, September 2011 Edition" (cited in chap. 2, n. 16).

14. Peter Victor, *Managing without Growth: Slower by Design, Not Disaster* (Cheltenham, U.K.: Edward Elgar Publishing, 2008), 125.

15. Jackson, *Prosperity without Growth*, 80–81.

16. Ibid., 81.

17. Ibid., 81–82.

18. Chris Goodall, "Peak Stuff: Did the U.K. Reach a Maximum Use of Material Resources in the Early Part of the Last Decade?" (Oxford: Carbon Commentary Research Paper, October 13, 2011), http://www.carboncommentary.com/wp-content/uploads/2011/10/Peak_Stuff_17.10.11.pdf (accessed November 29, 2011).

19. Glen Peters et al., "Growth in Emission Transfers Via International Trade from 1990 to 2008," *Proceedings of the National Academy of Sciences* 108, no. 21 (2011): 8903–8908.

20. William Stanley Jevons, *The Coal Question: An Enquiry Concerning the Progress of the Nation, and the Probable Exhaustion of Our Coal-Mines*, 3rd ed. (New York: Augustus M. Kelley, 1905), 140.

21. Steve Sorrell, *The Rebound Effect: An Assessment of the Evidence for Economy-Wide Energy Savings from Improved Energy Efficiency* (London: Sussex Energy Group and U.K. Energy Research Centre, October 2007), http://www.ukerc.ac.uk/Downloads/PDF/07/0710ReboundEffect/0710ReboundEffectReport.pdf (accessed December 7, 2011).

22. Peter Victor, "Managing without Growth" (keynote presentation, Steady State Economy Conference, Leeds, U.K., June 19, 2010), http://steadystate.org/learn/leeds2010/videos/ (accessed October 20, 2010).

23. N. Gregory Mankiw, *Principles of Economics*, 4th ed. (Mason, Ohio: Thomson Higher Education, 2007), 557–558.

CHAPTER 4: WHAT SORT OF ECONOMY PROVIDES ENOUGH?

1. Herman Daly, *Steady-State Economics: Second Edition with New Essays* (Washington, D.C.: Island Press, 1991), xv.

2. Jose Delreal, "Students Walk out of Ec 10 in Solidarity with 'Occupy,'" *Harvard Crimson*, November 2, 2011, http://www.thecrimson.com/article/2011/11/2/mankiw-walkout-economics-10/ (accessed December 1, 2011).

3. Post-Autistic Economics Network, "A Brief History of the Post-Autistic Economics Movement," http://www.paecon.net/HistoryPAE.htm (accessed December 1, 2011).

4. Daly, *Steady-State Economics*, 16–18.

5. Herman Daly, "The Steady-State Economy: Toward a Political Economy of Biophysical Equilibrium and Moral Growth," in *Valuing the Earth: Economics, Ecology, Ethics*, edited by Herman Daly and K. N. Townsend, 325–364 (Cambridge, Mass.: MIT Press, 1993), 325–326.

6. Daly, *Steady-State Economics*, 182.

7. Herman Daly, "Two Meanings of 'Economic Growth,'" *Daly News*, March 1, 2010, http://steadystate.org/two-meanings/ (accessed October 12, 2011).

8. Krueger, "Letting the Future In" (cited in chap. 2, n. 24).

9. Wilkinson and Pickett, *The Spirit Level* (cited in chap. 2, n. 28).

10. Victor, *Managing without Growth*, 171–173 (cited in chap. 3, n. 14).

11. Figure 4.1 is based on Victor, *Managing without Growth*, 174. Note that Victor completed his model prior to the financial crisis of 2008; some extrapolations would change based on what has happened in the economy since the crisis.

12. Ibid., 173–176.

13. Hansen et al., "Target Atmospheric CO_2: Where Should Humanity Aim?" (cited in chap. 2, n. 19).

14. Larry Elliott, "Can a Dose of Recession Solve Climate Change?," *The Guardian*, August 24, 2008.

15. Victor, *Managing without Growth*, 178.

16. Ibid., 181.

17. Jackson, "Investment, Productivity, and Ownership" (cited in chap. 1, n. 6).

18. Ibid.

19. Ibid.

20. E. F. Schumacher, *Small Is Beautiful: Economics as If People Mattered* (1973), First Harper Perennial Edition with a new foreword by Bill McKibben (New York: Harper Perennial, 2010), 59.

21. Jackson, "Investment, Productivity, and Ownership."

22. James Famiglietti et al., "Satellites Measure Recent Rates of Groundwater Depletion in California's Central Valley," *Geophysical Research Letters* 38 (2011).

23. "BP Leak the World's Worst Accidental Spill," *The Telegraph*, August 3, 2010, http://www.telegraph.co.uk/finance/newsbysector/energy/oilandgas/7924009/BP-leak-the-worlds-worst-accidental-oil-spill.html (accessed February 4, 2012).

24. Serge Latouche, *Farewell to Growth* (Cambridge, U.K.: Polity Press, 2009); François Schneider, Giorgos Kallis, and Joan Martínez-Alier, "Crisis or Opportunity? Economic Degrowth for Social Equity and Ecological Sustainability. Introduction to This Special Issue," *Journal of Cleaner Production* 18, no. 6 (2010): 511–518; and Joan Martínez-Alier, "Socially Sustainable Economic De-Growth," *Development and Change* 40, no. 6 (2009): 1099–1119.

25. Giorgos Kallis, "In Defence of Degrowth," *Ecological Economics* 70, no. 5 (March 2011): 873–880.

26. Research & Degrowth, "Degrowth Declaration of the Paris 2008 Conference," *Journal of Cleaner Production* 18, no. 6 (April 2010): 523–524.

27. Victor, *Managing without Growth*, 193 (cited in chap. 3, n. 14).

28. Center for the Advancement of the Steady State Economy, "CASSE Position on Economic Growth" (May 2004), http://steadystate.org/act/sign-the-position/ (accessed December 10, 2011).

CHAPTER 5: ENOUGH THROUGHPUT

1. Donella Meadows, "Earth Day Plus Thirty, as Seen by the Earth," Donella Meadows Institute, April 20, 2000, http://www.donellameadows.org/archives/earth-day-plus-thirty-as-seen-by-the-earth/ (accessed February 7, 2012).

2. Peter Menzel, *Material World: A Global Family Portrait* (San Francisco: Sierra Club Books, 1994), 28–34 (Getu family), 136–143 (Skeen family).

3. U.S. Census Bureau, "Median and Average Square Feet of Floor Area in New

Single-Family Houses Completed by Location" (2011), http://www.census.gov/const/C25Ann/sftotalmedavgsqft.pdf (accessed December 12, 2011).

4. Sean Cole, "An Average Family? Meet the Simpsons," *Marketplace*, November 9, 2007, http://www.marketplace.org/topics/sustainability/consumed/average -family-meet-simpsons (accessed December 12, 2011).

5. Self Storage Association, "2011 Self Storage Industry Fact Sheet" (June 30, 2011), http://www.selfstorage.org/ssa/Content/NavigationMenu/AboutSSA/FactSheet/2011SSAFACTSHEETrevised6-30-11.doc (accessed December 12, 2011).

6. Ibid.

7. Jon Mooallem, "The Self-Storage Self," *New York Times Magazine*, September 2, 2009.

8. Paul Brunner and Helmut Rechberger, *Practical Handbook of Material Flow Analysis* (Boca Raton, Fla.: CRC Press, 2004), 3.

9. Fridolin Krausmann et al., "Growth in Global Materials Use, GDP and Population during the 20th Century" (cited in chap. 2, n. 5).

10. Paul Brunner and Helmut Rechberger, "Anthropogenic Metabolism and Environmental Legacies," in *Encyclopedia of Global Environmental Change*, vol. 3, edited by T. Munn (West Sussex, U.K.: John Wiley & Sons, 2001): 54–72.

11. Herman Daly, "Economics in a Full World," *Scientific American* 293, no. 3 (September 2005): 100–107.

12. Henry George, *Progress and Poverty: An Inquiry into the Cause of Industrial Depressions, and of Increase of Want with Increase of Wealth* (London: Reeves, 1884), 173–174.

13. Lee Hannah et al., "A Preliminary Inventory of Human Disturbance of World Ecosystems," *Ambio* 23, no. 4/5 (July 1994): 246–250.

14. David Trauger et al., *The Relationship of Economic Growth to Wildlife Conservation*, Technical Review 03-1 (Bethesda, Md.: The Wildlife Society, 2003).

15. Herman Daly, "Toward Some Operational Principles of Sustainable Development," *Ecological Economics* 2, no. 1 (1990): 1–6.

16. Victoria Johnson, "Workshop 1: Limiting Resource Use and Waste Production" (Steady State Economy Conference, Leeds, U.K., June 19, 2010), http://steadystate .org/wp-content/uploads/WS1_Proposal_ResourceUse.pdf (accessed February 7, 2012).

17. Daly, *Steady-State Economics* (cited in chap. 4, n. 1), 61–68.

18. Feasta, *Cap and Share: A Fair Way to Cut Greenhouse Gas Emissions* (Dublin, Ireland: Feasta, May, 2008), http://www.feasta.org/documents/energy/Cap-and-Share -May08.pdf (accessed December 16, 2011).

19. Herman Daly, *Ecological Economics and Sustainable Development: Selected Essays of Herman Daly* (Northampton, Mass.: Edward Elgar Publishing, 2007), 111.

20. Robert Dietz and Brian Czech, "Conservation Deficits for the Continental United States: An Ecosystem Gap Analysis," *Conservation Biology* 19, no. 5 (October 2005): 1478–1487.

21. J. Michael Scott, Robbyn Abbitt, and Craig Groves, "What Are We Protecting?" *Conservation Biology in Practice* 2 (2001): 18–19.

22. Ana Rodrigues et al., "Effectiveness of the Global Protected-Area Network in Representing Species Diversity," *Nature* 428 (April 8, 2004): 640–643.

23. Ana Rodrigues et al., "Global Gap Analysis: Priority Regions for Expanding the Global Protected-Area Network," *BioScience* 54, no. 12 (December 2004): 1092–1100.

24. Aldo Leopold, *A Sand County Almanac and Sketches Here and There* (London: Oxford University Press, 1949), 221.

25. United Nations, European Commission, International Monetary Fund, Organisation for Economic Co-operation and Development, and World Bank, *Handbook of National Accounting: Integrated Environmental and Economic Accounting 2003* (New York: United Nations, 2003).

26. Ezra Markowitz and Tom Bowerman, "How Much Is Enough? Examining the Public's Beliefs about Consumption," *Analyses of Social Issues and Public Policy* 11, no. 1 (2011).

CHAPTER 6: ENOUGH PEOPLE

1. "Sir David Attenborough Calls for UK Baby Limit to Stop 'Frightening' Population Growth," *Daily Mail*, April 14, 2009, http://www.dailymail.co.uk/news/article-1169707/Sir-David-Attenborough-calls-UK-baby-limit-stop-frightening-population-growth.html (accessed October 12, 2011).

2. U.K. Office for National Statistics, "National Population Projections, 2010-Based Projections" (October 26, 2011), http://www.ons.gov.uk/ons/rel/npp/national-population-projections/2010-based-projections/index.html (accessed November 15, 2011).

3. Ewing et al., *Ecological Footprint Atlas 2009* (cited in chap. 2, n. 8).

4. Maddison, "Statistics on World Population, GDP and Per Capita GDP, 1–2008 AD" (cited in chap. 2, n. 4).

5. National Geographic, *7 Billion Is a Big Number*, video (Washington, D.C.: National Geographic Society, 2011), http://video.nationalgeographic.com/video/player/specials/sitewide-redesign/ngm-7billion.html (accessed October 12, 2011).

6. United Nations, *World Population Prospects: The 2010 Revision* (New York: Population Division, Department of Economic and Social Affairs, United Nations, 2011).

7. Data from 1900 to 1950 are from Maddison, "Statistics on World Population, GDP and Per Capita GDP, 1–2008 AD." Data from 1950 onward are from the United Nations, *World Population Prospects: The 2010 Revision*.

8. Population Reference Bureau, *World Population Data Sheet 2007* (Washington, D.C.: Population Reference Bureau, 2007), http://www.prb.org/pdf07/07wpds_eng.pdf (accessed October 12, 2011).

9. U.S. Central Intelligence Agency, "Country Comparison: Total Fertility Rate," in *The World Factbook* (U.S. Central Intelligence Agency, 2012), https://www.cia.gov/library/publications/the-world-factbook/rankorder/2127rank.html (accessed February 8, 2012).

10. Dan Glaister, "Number of Babies Born in the US Reaches Record Levels," *The Guardian*, March 18, 2009, http://www.guardian.co.uk/world/2009/mar/18/birth-rate-us-baby-boomers (accessed October 13, 2011).

11. Fred Weir, "A Second Baby? Russia's Mothers Aren't Persuaded," *The Christian Science Monitor*, May 19, 2006, http://www.csmonitor.com/2006/0519/p01s04-woeu.html (accessed February 8, 2012).

12. U.S. Central Intelligence Agency, "Country Comparison: Total Fertility Rate," in *The World Factbook*.

13. Gretchen Daily and Paul Ehrlich, "Population, Sustainability, and Earth's Carrying Capacity," *BioScience* 42 (1992): 761–771.

14. John Polimeni et al., *The Jevons Paradox and the Myth of Resource Efficiency Im-*

provements (London: Earthscan, 2008); and Brian Czech, "Prospects for Reconciling the Conflict between Economic Growth and Biodiversity Conservation with Technological Progress," *Conservation Biology* 22 (2008): 1389–1398.

15. Christian Kerschner, "Economic De-growth vs. Steady-state Economy," *Journal of Cleaner Production* 18 (2010): 544–551.

16. Latouche, *Farewell to Growth*, 25–29 (cited in chap. 4, n. 24); and George Monbiot, "The Population Myth," *The Guardian*, September 29, 2009, http://www.monbiot .com/2009/09/29/the-population-myth/ (accessed October 21, 2010).

17. Anthony LoBaido, "The Overpopulation Lie," *WorldNet Daily*, May 2, 2000, http://www.wnd.com/?pageId=5695 (accessed October 21, 2010); and "How to Deal with a Falling Population," *The Economist*, July 26, 2007, http://www .economist.com/node/9545933 (accessed October 21, 2010).

18. Melanie Phillips, "The Deep Green Fear of the Human Race," February 2, 2009, http://www.melaniephillips.com/the-dep-green-fear-of-the-human-race (accessed September 13, 2010).

19. Marq de Villiers, *Our Way Out: Principles for a Post-Apocalyptic World* (Toronto, Canada: McClelland & Stewart, 2011), 188.

20. John Guillebaud, *Youthquake: Population, Fertility and Environment in the 21st Century* (London: Optimum Population Trust, 2007), http://populationmatters.org/ wp-content/uploads/youthquake.pdf (accessed October 21, 2010).

21. U.S. Central Intelligence Agency, "Country Comparison," in *The World Factbook* (U.S. Central Intelligence Agency, 2012), https://www.cia.gov/library/ publications/the-world-factbook/index.html (accessed February 8, 2012).

22. De Villiers, *Our Way Out*, 199–200.

23. Wolfgang Lutz and Samir KC, "Global Human Capital: Integrating Education and Population," *Science* 333, no. 6042 (July 29, 2011): 587–592.

24. Jeffrey Sachs, *Common Wealth: Economics for a Crowded Planet* (New York: The Penguin Press, 2008), 187–188.

25. Emma Lazarus, "The New Colossus," in Lloyd Douglas, *The Statue of Liberty* (New York: Rosen Book Works, 2003), 19.

26. U.S. Congressional Budget Office, "Immigration Policy in the United States" (Washington, D.C.: U.S. Congressional Budget Office, February 2006), http:// www.cbo.gov/ftpdocs/70xx/doc7051/02-28-Immigration.pdf (accessed February 8, 2012).

27. Victor, *Managing without Growth*, 197 (cited in chap. 3, n. 14).

28. Ibid., 198–201.

29. Albert Bandura, *Social Foundations of Thought and Action: A Social-Cognitive Theory* (Englewood Cliffs, N.J.: Prentice-Hall, 1986).

30. Population Media Center, "What We Do," http://www.populationmedia.org/ what/ (accessed October 18, 2011).

31. William Ryerson, "The Effectiveness of Entertainment Mass Media in Changing Behavior" (Population Media Center), http://www.populationmedia.org/ wp-content/uploads/2007/08/EFFECTIVENESS-OF-ENTERTAINMENT -EDUCATION-012609.pdf (accessed October 18, 2011).

32. Global Population Speak Out, "The Global Population Speak Out," http://www .populationspeakout.org (accessed October 18, 2011).

33. Jonathan Tilove, "Time to Move Over, Mr. 200 Millionth," *San Diego Union-Tribune*, September 20, 2006, http://www.signonsandiego.com/uniontrib/2006 0920/news_1n20woo.html (accessed October 14, 2011).

CHAPTER 7: ENOUGH INEQUALITY

1. Alexis de Tocqueville, *Democracy in America* (1835; Indianapolis, Ind.: Hackett Publishing Company, 2000), 1.

2. Samuel Charters, *The Complete Blind Willie Johnson*, compact disc booklet (Columbia/Legacy, April 20, 1993); and Francis Davis, *The History of the Blues* (New York: Hyperion, 1995), 119.

3. Charters, *The Complete Blind Willie Johnson.*

4. Davis, *The History of the Blues*, 119.

5. Nobel Prize Committee, "The Nobel Prize in Literature 1949," http://www .nobelprize.org/nobel_prizes/literature/laureates/1949/ (accessed December 29, 2011).

6. University of Mississippi, "The Mississippi Writers Page: William Faulkner," November 11, 2008, http://www.olemiss.edu/mwp/dir/faulkner_william/ (accessed December 29, 2011).

7. Quoted in Daniel Singal, *William Faulkner: The Making of a Modernist* (Chapel Hill: University of North Carolina Press, 1999), 268.

8. Robert Reich, "Foreword," in Wilkinson and Pickett, *The Spirit Level* (cited in chap. 2, n. 28), vi.

9. Data are an average of the 20:20 income inequality data published by the United Nations Development Programme in its *Human Development Reports* for the years 2003, 2004, 2005, and 2006. The data are the same as those used by Wilkinson and Pickett in *The Spirit Level.*

10. Wilkinson and Pickett, *The Spirit Level*, 20.

11. Ibid., 1–45.

12. Gerald Marwell and Ruth Ames, "Economists Free Ride, Does Anyone Else?: Experiments on the Provision of Public Goods, IV," *Journal of Public Economics* 15, no. 3 (1981).

13. Raj Patel, *The Value of Nothing: How to Reshape Market Society and Redefine Democracy* (New York: Picador, 2009), 29–30.

14. Henry Wallich, "Zero Growth," *Newsweek*, January 24, 1972.

15. Wilkinson and Pickett, *The Spirit Level.*

16. Equality Trust, "Why Equality: Frequently Asked Questions," http://www .equalitytrust.org.uk/why/evidence/frequently-asked-questions (accessed January 3, 2012).

17. Daniel Pink, *Drive: The Surprising Truth about What Motivates Us* (New York: Riverhead Books, 2009), 85–146.

18. Wilkinson and Pickett, *The Spirit Level*, 5–10.

19. Robert Putnam, *Bowling Alone: The Collapse and Revival of American Community* (New York: Simon & Schuster, 2000).

20. Wilkinson and Pickett, *The Spirit Level*, 236–237.

21. Stephen Bezruchka, Tsukasa Namekata, and Maria Gilson Sistrom, "Improving Economic Equality and Health: The Case of Postwar Japan," *American Journal of Public Health* 98, no. 4 (April 2008): 589–594.

22. Citizen's Income Trust, "Citizen's Income Online," http://www.citizensincome .org/ (accessed July 30, 2010).

23. Michael Marmot et al., *Fair Society, Healthy Lives: The Marmot Review* (London: The Marmot Review, February 2010), http://www.instituteofhealthequity.org/ projects/fair-society-healthy-lives-the-marmot-review (accessed January 3, 2011).

24. Sylvia Allegretto, "The Few, the Proud, the Very Rich," *The Berkeley Blog*, University of California at Berkeley, December 5, 2011, http://blogs.berkeley.edu/2011/12/05/the-few-the-proud-the-very-rich/ (accessed January 3, 2012).

25. Kate Pickett, "Workshop 3: Distribution of Income and Wealth" (Steady State Economy Conference, Leeds, U.K., June 19, 2010), http://steadystate.org/wp-content/uploads/WS3_Proposal_Distribution.pdf (accessed August 20, 2010).

26. David Herrera, "Mondragon: A For-Profit Organization That Embodies Catholic Social Thought," *Entrepreneur*, 2004, http://www.entrepreneur.com/tradejournals/article/116926710_1.html (accessed August 20, 2010).

27. Will Hutton, "Hutton Review of Fair Pay in the Public Sector: Terms of Reference" (HM Treasury, 2010), http://www.hm-treasury.gov.uk/indreview_will hutton_fairpay_tor.htm (accessed August 20, 2010).

28. UK Co-operatives, "About Co-operatives," http://www.uk.coop/co-operatives (accessed July 30, 2010).

29. Gar Alperovitz, Thad Williamson, and Ted Howard, "The Cleveland Model," *The Nation*, March 1, 2010, http://www.thenation.com/article/cleveland-model (accessed January 3, 2012).

CHAPTER 8: ENOUGH DEBT

1. Bill McKibben, *Deep Economy: The Wealth of Communities and the Durable Future* (New York: Times Books, 2007), 162.

2. John Fullerton, interview with Rob Dietz, January 17, 2012.

3. Daly and Farley, *Ecological Economics* (cited in chap. 1, n. 3), 245.

4. Neva Goodwin, Julie Nelson, and Jonathan Harris, *Macroeconomics in Context* (Armonk, N.Y.: M. E. Sharpe, 2009).

5. Frederick Soddy, *Wealth, Virtual Wealth, and Debt* (London: George Allen & Unwin, 1926).

6. Philip Lawn, "Facilitating the Transition to a Steady-State Economy: Some Macroeconomic Fundamentals," *Ecological Economics* 69, no. 5 (March 15, 2010): 931–936.

7. GDP data are in current prices and are from the World Bank, "World Development Indicators, September 2011 Edition" (cited in chap. 2, n. 16). Money supply data are from the Bank of England series "LPQAUYN: Quarterly amounts outstanding of M4 (monetary financial institutions' sterling M4 liabilities to private sector) (in sterling millions) seasonally adjusted" (Bank of England, November 25, 2009). M4 is a broad measure of the money supply that includes sterling notes and coin, sterling deposits (including certificates of deposit), commercial paper, bonds, floating-rate notes, and several other types of assets.

8. Josh Ryan-Collins et al., *Where Does Money Come From? A Guide to the UK Monetary and Banking System* (London: New Economics Foundation, 2011), 15–16.

9. Ibid., 55–56.

10. Board of Governors of the Federal Reserve System, "Reserve Requirements" (October 26, 2011), http://www.federalreserve.gov/monetarypolicy/reservereq .htm (accessed January 19, 2012).

11. Joshua Feinman, "Reserve Requirements: History, Current Practice, and Potential Reform," *Federal Reserve Bulletin* (June 1993), http://www.federalreserve.gov/monetarypolicy/0693lead.pdf (accessed January 19, 2012).

12. Board of Governors of the Federal Reserve System, "Reserve Requirements."

13. James Robertson and John Bunzl, *Monetary Reform—Making It Happen!* (London: International Simultaneous Policy Organisation, 2003).

14. Mary Mellor, *The Future of Money: From Financial Crisis to Public Resource* (London: Pluto Press, 2010).

15. David Korten, *Agenda for a New Economy: From Phantom Wealth to Real Wealth* (San Francisco: Berrett-Koehler, 2009).

16. U.S. Bureau of Economic Analysis, "Industry Economic Accounts Information Guide" (Washington, D.C.: U.S. Department of Commerce, February 2, 2012), http://www.bea.gov/industry/iedguide.htm#gdpia_ad (accessed February 29, 2012).

17. Molly Scott Cato and Mary Mellor, "Workshop 4: Money and the Financial System" (Steady State Economy Conference, Leeds, U.K., June 19, 2010), http://steadystate.org/wp-content/uploads/WS4_Proposal_Money.pdf (accessed August 5, 2010).

18. Daly and Farley, *Ecological Economics* (cited in chap. 1, n. 3), 252–254.

19. Joseph Huber and James Robertson, *Creating New Money: A Monetary Reform for the Information Age* (London: New Economics Foundation, 2000).

20. BerkShares, Inc., "BerkShares Web Directory," http://www.berkshares.org/directory/index.htm (accessed January 24, 2012); and BerkShares, Inc., "BerkShares Exchange Banks," http://www.berkshares.org/banks.htm (accessed January 24, 2012).

21. B£ Group, "B£ e-Currency," http://brixtonpound.org/b-e-currency/ (accessed February 12, 2012).

22. Dave Harvey, "'Bristol Pound' Currency to Boost Independent Traders," *BBC News*, February 5, 2012, http://www.bbc.co.uk/news/uk-england-bristol-16852326 (accessed February 12, 2012).

23. Richard Douthwaite, *The Ecology of Money, Online Edition* (Dublin: Feasta, 2006), http://www.feasta.org/documents/moneyecology/contents.htm (accessed September 19, 2010).

24. Pietro Alessandrini and Michele Fratianni, "Resurrecting Keynes to Stabilize the International Monetary System," *Open Economies Review* 20 (January 10, 2009): 339–358.

25. Douthwaite, *The Ecology of Money*; and Molly Scott Cato, "Sustainable Economics: A New Financial Architecture Based on a Global Carbon Standard," in *The Transition to Sustainable Living and Practice*, Advances in Ecopolitics, vol. 4, edited by L. Leonard and J. Barry, 55–76 (Bingley, U.K.: Emerald Group Publishing, 2009).

26. Rupert Neate, "France Plans Tobin Tax on Financial Transactions," *The Guardian*, January 30, 2012, http://www.guardian.co.uk/business/2012/jan/30/france-tobin-tax-nicolas-sarkozy?newsfeed=true (accessed February 12, 2012).

27. Binyamin Appelbaum, "Bailed-Out Banks Raking in Big Profits," *Washington Post*, October 16, 2009, http://www.washingtonpost.com/wp-dyn/content/article/2009/10/15/AR2009101504007.html (accessed January 25, 2012).

28. David Korten et al., "How to Liberate America from Wall Street Rule" (New Economy Working Group, July 2011), http://www.yesmagazine.org/pdf/liberateamericadownload.pdf.

29. Milton Friedman, *Capitalism and Freedom* (Chicago: University of Chicago Press, 1982), 2.

CHAPTER 9: ENOUGH MISCALCULATION

1. Robert F. Kennedy, "Excerpt of a Speech," 1968, in Robert Costanza et al., "Estimates of the Genuine Progress Indicator (GPI) for Vermont, Chittenden County and Burlington, from 1950 to 2000," *Ecological Economics* 51 (2004): 139–155.

2. Nadia Mustafa, "What about Gross National Happiness?" *Time*, January 10, 2005, http://www.time.com/time/health/article/0,8599,1016266,00.html (accessed October 3, 2011).

3. Gross National Happiness USA, "What Is GNH?" http://www.gnhusa.org/what -is-gnh/ (accessed August 17, 2011).

4. John de Graaf, "The Landlocked Heart of Gross National Happiness," *Utne Reader*, December 4, 2009, http://www.utne.com/mind-body/Bhuton-Heart-of -Gross-National-Happiness.aspx (accessed October 3, 2011).

5. Allegra Stratton, "Happiness Index to Gauge Britain's National Mood," *The Guardian*, November 14, 2010, http://www.guardian.co.uk/lifeandstyle/2010/nov/ 14/happiness-index-britain-national-mood (accessed October 3, 2011).

6. Australian Bureau of Statistics, "Measures of Australia's Progress: Is Life in Australia Getting Better?" http://abs.gov.au/about/progress (accessed October 3, 2011).

7. United Nations, "Happiness Should Have Greater Role in Development Policy," UN News Centre, July 19, 2011, http://www.un.org/apps/news/story.asp? NewsID=39084 (accessed August 17, 2011).

8. "Government Drafts 'Happiness Indicators' to Supplement Economic Data," *The Japan Times*, December 6, 2011, http://www.japantimes.co.jp/text/nn20111206a7 .html (accessed February 13, 2012).

9. Saamah Abdallah, "Workshop 5: Measuring Progress/Quality of Life" (Steady State Economy Conference, Leeds, U.K., June 19, 2010), http://steadystate.org/ wp-content/uploads/WS5_Proposal_MeasuringProgress.pdf (accessed October 3, 2011).

10. U.S. Bureau of Economic Analysis, "Current-Dollar and Real GDP" (cited in chap. 2, n. 22).

11. Layard, *Happiness*, 32–33 (cited in chap. 2, n. 22).

12. Juliet Michaelson et al., *National Accounts of Well-Being: Bringing Real Wealth onto the Balance Sheet* (London: New Economics Foundation, 2009).

13. European Commission, "Beyond GDP: Measuring Progress, True Wealth, and the Well-Being of Nations," http://www.beyond-gdp.eu/ (accessed October 12, 2011); Organisation for Economic Co-operation and Development, "Better Life Initiative: Measuring Well-Being and Progress" (Paris: Organisation for Economic Co-operation and Development), http://www.oecd.org/betterlifeinitiative (accessed October 12, 2011); and Joseph Stiglitz, Amartya Sen, and Jean-Paul Fitoussi, *Report by the Commission on the Measurement of Economic Performance and Social Progress* (Paris: Commission on the Measurement of Economic Performance and Social Progress, 2009), http://www.stiglitz-sen-fitoussi.fr (accessed October 12, 2011).

14. Abdallah, "Workshop 5: Measuring Progress/Quality of Life."

15. Mark Easton, "Britain's Happiness in Decline," *BBC News*, May 2, 2006, http:// news.bbc.co.uk/1/hi/programmes/happiness_formula/4771908.stm (accessed October 12, 2011).

16. Chris Coulter and Hazel Henderson, "Worldwide Support for True Wealth Measures: Three-Quarters Say Governments Should Look beyond Economics and

Measure Social and Environmental Progress," press release (London: GlobeScan and Ethical Markets Media, November 12, 2007), http://www.globescan.com/news_archives/emm_beyondgdp.htm (accessed October 12, 2011).

17. Daniel O'Neill, "Measuring Progress in the Degrowth Transition to a Steady State Economy," *Ecological Economics* (in press), doi: 10.1016/j.ecolecon.2011.05.020.

18. Research & Degrowth, "Degrowth Declaration of the Paris 2008 Conference" (cited in chap. 4, n. 26).

19. David Leonhardt, "How Obama Reconciles Dueling Views on Economy," *New York Times Magazine*, August 20, 2008, http://www.nytimes.com/2008/08/20/world/americas/20iht-24obamanomicst.15470639.html (accessed October 13, 2011).

20. For the Index of Sustainable Economic Welfare, see Herman Daly and John Cobb, Jr., *For the Common Good* (cited in chap. 2, n. 3), 443–507; for the Genuine Progress Indicator, see John Talberth, Clifford Cobb, and Noah Slattery, *The Genuine Progress Indicator 2006: A Tool for Sustainable Development* (Oakland, Calif.: Redefining Progress, 2007).

21. GPI data are from John Talberth, Clifford Cobb, and Noah Slattery, *The Genuine Progress Indicator 2006*. GDP data are from the U.S. Bureau of Economic Analysis, "National Economic Accounts" (Washington, D.C.: U.S. Department of Commerce), http://www.bea.gov/national/index.htm (accessed June 7, 2009).

22. Saamah Abdallah et al., *The Happy Planet Index 2.0: Why Good Lives Don't Have to Cost the Earth* (London: New Economics Foundation, 2010).

23. International Monetary Fund, "World Economic Outlook Database" (International Monetary Fund, September 2011), http://www.imf.org/external/pubs/ft/weo/2011/02/weodata/download.aspx (accessed October 3, 2011).

24. Abdallah et al., *The Happy Planet Index 2.0*.

25. U.K. Department for Environment, Food and Rural Affairs, "National Indicators" (London: U.K. Department for Environment, Food and Rural Affairs, 2011), http://sd.defra.gov.uk/progress/national/ (accessed August 25, 2011).

26. Abdallah, "Workshop 5: Measuring Progress/Quality of Life."

27. Ewing et al., *Ecological Footprint Atlas 2009* (cited in chap. 2, n. 8).

28. O'Neill, "Measuring Progress in the Degrowth Transition to a Steady State Economy."

29. Donella Meadows, *Indicators and Information Systems for Sustainable Development: A Report to the Balaton Group* (Hartland, Vt.: The Sustainability Institute, 1998), viii, 5, http://www.biomimicryguild.com/alumni/documents/download/Indicators_and_information_systems_for_sustainable_develoment.pdf (accessed February 13, 2012).

CHAPTER IO: ENOUGH UNEMPLOYMENT

1. From a discussion during "Workshop 8: Employment" at the Steady State Economy Conference (Leeds, U.K., June 19, 2010).

2. Deb Wren, interview by Rob Dietz, December 17, 2011.

3. Victor, *Managing without Growth*, 12–13 (cited in chap. 3, n. 14).

4. "Consumer-Product Diversity Now Exceeds Biodiversity," *The Onion* 34, no. 12, October 21, 1998, http://www.theonion.com/articles/consumerproduct-diversity-now-exceeds-biodiversity,1535/ (accessed February 14, 2012).

5. Martin Pullinger and Blake Alcott, "Workshop 8: Employment" (Steady State

Economy Conference, Leeds, U.K., June 19, 2010), http://steadystate.org/wp
-content/uploads/WS8_Proposal_Employment.pdf (accessed August 9, 2010).

6. Christer Sanne, "A Steady State of Leisure?" (Steady State Economy Conference, Leeds, U.K., June 19, 2010), http://steadystate.org/wp-content/uploads/WS8_ DiscussionPaper_ChristerSanne.pdf (accessed August 9, 2010).

7. Jackson, Prosperity without Growth, 130–133 (cited in chap. 1, n. 5).

8. Juliet Schor, The Overworked American: The Unexpected Decline of Leisure (New York: Basic Books, 1993), 129.

9. Andrew Clark, "Work, Jobs, and Well-Being across the Millennium," in International Differences in Well-Being, edited by Ed Diener, Daniel Kahneman, and John Helliwell, 436–468 (Oxford, U.K.: Oxford University Press, 2010), 449.

10. Jonathan Grossman, "Fair Labor Standards Act of 1938: Maximum Struggle for a Minimum Wage" (Washington, D.C.: U.S. Department of Labor), http://www .dol.gov/oasam/programs/history/flsa1938.htm#1 (accessed December 19, 2011).

11. Juliet Schor, Plenitude: The New Economics of True Wealth (New York: Penguin Press, 2010), 105; and Tim Robinson, Work, Leisure and the Environment: The Vicious Circle of Overwork and Overconsumption (Cheltenham, U.K.: Edward Elgar, 2007).

12. Mathieu Gorse, "Italy Quietly Raises Retirement Age," The Sydney Morning Herald, July 30, 2010, http://news.smh.com.au/breaking-news-world/italy-quietly -raises-retirement-age-20100730-10ya1.html (accessed December 19, 2011).

13. Juliet Schor, "Sustainable Consumption and Worktime Reduction," Journal of Industrial Ecology 9, no. 1–2 (January 2005): 37–50.

14. Pullinger and Alcott, "Workshop 8: Employment."

15. Robert Maier, Willibrord de Graaf, and Patricia Frericks, "Policy for the 'Peak Hour' of Life: Lessons from the New Dutch Life Course Saving Scheme," European Societies 9, no. 3 (2007): 339–358.

16. International Labour Organization, "Key Indicators of the Labour Market (KILM), Seventh Edition" (2011), http://kilm.ilo.org/kilmnet/ (accessed October 27, 2011).

17. Eurostat, "Eurostat Statistics Database: Labour Force Survey" (2010), http:// epp.eurostat.ec.europa.eu/portal/page/portal/statistics/search_database (accessed August 9, 2010).

18. Robert Costanza et al., "Scaling Back Our Energy-Hungry Lifestyles Means More of What Matters, Not Less," Grist, December 9, 2007, http://grist.org/?p=20707 (accessed December 21, 2010).

19. Pullinger and Alcott, "Workshop 8: Employment."

20. Ibid.

21. Robert Drake, "A Prideful Recollection of the Old CCC," The Minnesota Volunteer (July–August 1983): 3–9, http://webapps8.dnr.state.mn.us/mcv_pdf/articles/ 83_Prideful_Recollection_of_the_Old_CCC__A.pdf (accessed December 21, 2011).

22. Joy Stiles, "Interview with Isaac Louderback" (Shenandoah National Park, September 30, 1995), http://www.nps.gov/shen/historyculture/upload/ccc_oral_ history_isaac_louderback.pdf (accessed December 21, 2011), 2.

23. Ibid.; and Drake, "A Prideful Recollection of the Old CCC."

24. Stiles, "Interview with Isaac Louderback."

25. Drake, "A Prideful Recollection of the Old CCC."

26. Ibid.

27. Stiles, "Interview with Isaac Louderback."

28. Drake, "A Prideful Recollection of the Old CCC."

29. Stiles, "Interview with Isaac Louderback."

CHAPTER 11: ENOUGH BUSINESS AS USUAL

1. Karl-Henrik Robèrt, "Foreword," in Brian Nattrass and Mary Altomare, *The Natural Step for Business: Wealth, Ecology, and the Evolutionary Corporation*, 2nd ed. (Gabriola Island, Canada: New Society Publishers, 2001), xiv.

2. Dr. Seuss, *The Lorax* (New York: Random House, 1971).

3. Ibid., 24.

4. Ibid., 40.

5. Ibid., 49.

6. Johnnie Moore and Samuel Luoma, "Hazardous Wastes from Large-Scale Metal Extraction: A Case Study," *Environmental Science and Technology* 24 (1990): 1278–1285.

7. Colorado State University Department of Biology, "Berkeley Pit History" (2003), http://rydberg.biology.colostate.edu/Phytoremediation/2003/Boczon/Berkeley_Pit_History.html (accessed October 20, 2011).

8. Edwin Dobb, "New Life in a Death Trap," *Discover* (December 2000), http://discovermagazine.com/2000/dec/featnewlife (accessed October 20, 2011).

9. Joel Bakan, *The Corporation: The Pathological Pursuit of Profit and Power* (London: Constable, 2005).

10. Matthew Doeringer, "Fostering Social Enterprise: A Historical and International Analysis," *Duke Journal of Comparative & International Law* 20, no. 2 (2010): 304.

11. Corporate revenue data are from "Global 500: Our Annual Ranking of the World's Largest Corporations," *Fortune*, July 26, 2010, http://money.cnn.com/magazines/fortune/global500/2010/full_list/ (accessed October 20, 2011); GDP data are from the World Bank, "World Development Indicators & Global Development Finance" (2011), http://databank.worldbank.org/ddp/home.do (accessed October 20, 2011).

12. Alexander Osterwalder and Yves Pigneur, *Business Model Generation: A Handbook for Visionaries, Game Changers, and Challengers* (Hoboken, N.J.: John Wiley & Sons, 2010).

13. Robin Roy, "Sustainable Product-Service Systems," *Futures* 32, no. 3–4 (2000): 293.

14. Paul Hawken, Amory Lovins, and Hunter Lovins, *Natural Capitalism*, rev. ed. (London: Earthscan, 2010), 139–141.

15. Roy, "Sustainable Product-Service Systems," 295.

16. Michael Porter and Mark Kramer, "The Big Idea: Creating Shared Value," *Harvard Business Review* (January–February 2011): 64.

17. Ibid., 76.

18. Bradley Parrish, *Sustainability Entrepreneurship: Design Principles, Processes, and Paradigms* (Ph.D. diss., University of Leeds, 2007), 51.

19. The Big Issue, "About Us," http://www.bigissue.com/about-us (accessed March 3, 2012).

20. International Co-operative Alliance, "Statement on the Co-operative Identity" (May 26, 2007), http://www.ica.coop/coop/principles.html (accessed March 5, 2012).

21. Douglas Booth, "The Macroeconomics of a Steady State," *Review of Social Economy* 52, no. 2 (1994): 2–21.

22. Douglas Booth, *Regional Long Waves, Uneven Growth, and the Cooperative Alternative* (New York: Praeger Publishers, 1987), 67–78.
23. James Hall, "John Lewis Has Come out of the Recession Fighting," *The Telegraph*, December 19, 2009, http://www.telegraph.co.uk/finance/newsbysector/retailand consumer/6844453/John-Lewis-has-come-out-of-the-recession-fighting.html (accessed October 20, 2011).
24. Co-Operative Group Limited, "The Co-operative Membership," http://www.co -operative.coop/membership/ (accessed October 20, 2011).
25. Mondragon Corporation, "Mondragon," http://www.mondragon-corporation .com/language/en-US/ENG.aspx (accessed February 16, 2012).
26. André Reichel, "Workshop 9: Business and Production" (Steady State Economy Conference, Leeds, U.K., June 19, 2010), http://steadystate.org/wp-content/ uploads/WS9_Proposal_Business.pdf (accessed October 20, 2011).
27. Doeringer, "Fostering Social Enterprise," 295.
28. As of March 2, 2012, there were 6,217 registered CICs in the United Kingdom. Source: The Regulator of Community Interest Companies, "Community Interest Company Register," http://www.bis.gov.uk/cicregulator/cic-register (accessed March 2, 2012).
29. The Regulator of Community Interest Companies, "Community Interest Companies: Frequently Asked Questions" (2009): 10, http://www.bis.gov.uk/cicregulator/ leaflets (accessed March 2, 2012).
30. Reichel, "Workshop 9: Business and Production."
31. The Natural Step Network, "Solutions for Business," http://www.naturalstep.org/ en/usa/solutions-business (accessed March 5, 2012).
32. Praxiom Research Group Limited, "ISO 14001 2004 Translated into Plain English" (December 22, 2011), http://www.praxiom.com/iso-14001-2004.htm (accessed March 5, 2012).
33. International Organization for Standardization, "ISO 26000:2010" (2011), http:// www.iso.org/iso/catalogue_detail?csnumber=42546 (accessed March 5, 2012).
34. Reichel, "Workshop 9: Business and Production."
35. Ibid.
36. SROI Network, "What Is Social Return on Investment?" http://www.thesroi network.org/what-is-sroi (accessed March 3, 2012).
37. Doeringer, "Fostering Social Enterprise," 323.
38. Adam Liptak, "Justices, 5–4, Reject Corporate Spending Limit," *New York Times*, January 21, 2010, http://www.nytimes.com/2010/01/22/us/politics/22scotus.html? pagewanted=all (accessed March 5, 2012).
39. Tiffany Ray, "Riverside: Lawyer Advocates Rescinding Corporate Rights," *The Press-Enterprise*, March 1, 2012, http://www.pe.com/business/business-head lines/20120301-riverside-lawyer-advocates-rescinding-corporate-rights.ece (accessed March 5, 2012).
40. Buckminster Fuller Institute, "Buckminster Fuller Challenge," http://challenge .bfi.org/movie (accessed February 16, 2012).
41. The Collins Companies, "The Company—Commitment," http://www.collinsco .com/commitment/ (accessed November 7, 2011).

CHAPTER 12: ENOUGH MATERIALISM

1. Clive Hamilton and Richard Denniss, *Affluenza: When Too Much Is Never Enough* (Crows Nest, Australia: Allen and Unwin, 2005), 24.
2. David Fell, "Workshop 7: Changing Behaviour (The Psychology of Consumer-

ism)" (Steady State Economy Conference, Leeds, U.K., June 19, 2010), http://steadystate.org/wp-content/uploads/WS7_Proposal_ChangingBehaviour.pdf (accessed November 21, 2011).

3. See Oliver James, *Affluenza* (London: Vermillion, 2007); Neal Lawson, *All Consuming* (London: Penguin Books, 2009); Tim Kasser, *The High Price of Materialism* (Cambridge, Mass.: MIT Press, 2002); and John de Graaf, David Wann, and Thomas Naylor, *Affluenza: The All-Consuming Epidemic* (San Francisco: Berrett-Koehler, 2001).

4. Thorstein Veblen, *The Theory of the Leisure Class* (New York: MacMillan, 1899).

5. Victor Lebow, "Price Competition in 1955," *Journal of Retailing* (Spring 1955), http://classroom.sdmesa.edu/pjacoby/journal-of-retailing.pdf (accessed January 6, 2012).

6. Annie Leonard, "The Story of Stuff" (December 4, 2007), http://www.storyofstuff.org/movies-all/story-of-stuff/ (accessed January 6, 2012).

7. Christer Sanne, *Keynes Barnbarn: En Bättre Framtid med Arbete och Välfärd* [Keynes' Grandchildren: Looking for a Better Future with Work and Welfare] (Stockholm: Formas, 2007).

8. Dan Heath and Chip Heath, *The Myth of the Garage and Other Minor Surprises* (New York: Crown Publishing Group, 2011), 21.

9. Ibid., 22.

10. Lebow, "Price Competition in 1955."

11. Duane Elgin, *Voluntary Simplicity: Toward a Way of Life That Is Outwardly Simple, Inwardly Rich* (New York: William Morrow and Company, 1993).

12. Jody Aked et al., *Five Ways to Well-Being* (London: New Economics Foundation, 2008).

13. Paul Gilding, "The Mother of All Conflicts: Infinite Economic Growth vs. a Finite Planet" (Cressman Lecture in the Humanities, University of Oregon, Eugene, November 15, 2011), http://media.uoregon.edu/channel/2011/11/15/the-mother-of-all-conflicts-infinite-economic-growth-vs-a-finite-planet/ (accessed November 22, 2011).

14. Fell, "Workshop 7: Changing Behaviour (The Psychology of Consumerism)."

15. Ibid.

16. Rob Hopkins, *The Transition Handbook: From Oil Dependency to Local Resilience* (White River Junction, Vt.: Chelsea Green Publishing, 2008).

17. "Idea: Planned Obsolescence," *The Economist*, May 23, 2009, http://www.economist.com/node/13354332 (accessed January 9, 2012).

18. Tirtha Dhar and Kathy Baylis, "Fast Food Consumption and the Ban on Advertising Targeting Children: The Quebec Experience," *Journal of Marketing Research* 48, no. 5 (October 2011): 799–813.

19. Heath and Heath, *The Myth of the Garage and Other Minor Surprises*, 22.

20. Fell, "Workshop 7: Changing Behaviour (The Psychology of Consumerism)."

CHAPTER 13: ENOUGH SILENCE

1. Tim Adams, "Margaret Atwood on a Voyage to the World's End," *The Observer*, August 29, 2009, http://www.guardian.co.uk/theobserver/2009/aug/30/margaret-atwood-novel-ecology (accessed January 30, 2012).

2. Patti Domm, "Economic Growth Picks Up, So Why All the Gloom?" *CNBC Executive News*, January 27, 2012, http://www.cnbc.com/id/46163831 (accessed January 27, 2012).

3. Associated Press, "Bright Spot in Europe: Poland's Economy Grows 4.3 Percent in

2011 Despite Euro Troubles," *The Washington Post*, January 27, 2012, http://www .washingtonpost.com/business/economy/polands-economic-growth-accelerated -to-43-percent-in-2011-despite-euro-troubles/2012/01/27/gIQAbJEtUQ_story .html (accessed January 27, 2012).

4. Iain Laing, "Scotland Is Celebrating GDP Growth," *The Journal*, January 19, 2012, http://www.nebusiness.co.uk/business-news/latest-business-news/2012/01/19/ scotland-is-celebrating-gdp-growth-51140-30153271/ (accessed January 26, 2012).

5. Emily Kaiser, "Analysis: Asia's Economic Growth Slipping into Neutral," *Reuters*, January 19, 2012, http://www.reuters.com/article/2012/01/19/us-asia-economy -idUSTRE80I0E420120119 (accessed January 27, 2012).

6. Binyamin Appelbaum, "Fed Signals That a Full Recovery Is Years Away," *New York Times*, January 26, 2012, http://www.nytimes.com/2012/01/26/business/economy/ fed-to-maintain-rates-near-zero-through-late-2014.html (accessed January 26, 2012).

7. Pamela Sampson, "World Stock Markets Fall as Improvement in US Economic Growth Falls Short of Investor Hopes," *The Washington Post*, January 27, 2012, http://www.washingtonpost.com/business/markets/world-stock-markets-muted -ahead-of-us-economic-growth-figures-for-fourth-quarter/2012/01/27/gIQAB pWAVQ_story.html (accessed January 27, 2012).

8. Michael Steininger, "An End to Cut, Cut, Cut? Merkel and Sarkozy Agree to Focus on Growth," *Christian Science Monitor*, January 9, 2012, http://www.csmonitor .com/World/Europe/2012/0109/An-end-to-cut-cut-cut-Merkel-and-Sarkozy -agree-to-focus-on-growth (accessed January 27, 2012).

9. Hans Nichols, "Obama Says He Is 'Hopeful' for 2012, Greater Economic Growth," *Bloomberg Businessweek*, January 11, 2012, http://www.businessweek .com/news/2012-01-11/obama-says-he-is-hopeful-for-2012-greater-economic -growth.html (accessed January 26, 2012).

10. Nicholas Winning, "Bold Action Can Fuel European Growth, Says British Prime Minister," *The Wall Street Journal*, January 27, 2012, http://www.theaustralian .com.au/business/wall-street-journal/bold-action-can-fuel-european-growth -says-british-prime-minister/story-fnay3ubk-1226254991572 (accessed January 27, 2012).

11. Daly, "Economics in a Full World" (cited in chap. 5, n. 11).

12. Eric Zencey, "Mr. Soddy's Ecological Economy," *New York Times*, April 11, 2009, http://www.nytimes.com/2009/04/12/opinion/12zencey.html (accessed January 27, 2012).

13. Wendell Berry, "Faustian Economics: Hell Hath No Limits," *Harper's Magazine*, May 2008, 35–42.

14. Stoll, "Fear of Fallowing" (cited in chap. 2, n. 10).

15. "The Folly of Growth," Special Issue, *New Scientist* 200, no. 2678 (October 18, 2008).

16. Cecilia Rouse, question-and-answer session following "Closing Discussion: Progress of the Obama Administration in Moving toward a Green Economy" (10th National Conference on Science, Policy and the Environment, National Council for Science and the Environment, Washington, D.C., January 22, 2010).

17. Jimmy Carter, "'Crisis of Confidence' Speech (July 15, 1979)" (Miller Center, University of Virginia), http://millercenter.org/scripps/archive/speeches/detail/3402 (accessed January 27, 2012).

18. Center for the Advancement of the Steady State Economy, "CASSE Position on Economic Growth" (cited in chap. 4, n. 28).

19. Ian Christie, "Workshop 6: Engaging Politicians and the Media" (Steady State Economy Conference, Leeds, U.K., June 19, 2010), http://steadystate.org/wp-content/uploads/WS6_Proposal_Engagement1.pdf (accessed February 18, 2011).

20. Spanner Films, "Franny Armstrong," http://www.spannerfilms.net/people/franny_armstrong (accessed January 29, 2012).

21. Dan Kahan, "Fixing the Communications Failure," *Nature* 463 (January 21, 2010): 296–297.

22. Paris: "First International Conference on Economic De-growth for Ecological Sustainability and Social Equity" (April 2008), http://events.it-sudparis.eu/degrowthconference/en/; Barcelona: "Second International Conference on Economic Degrowth for Ecological Sustainability and Social Equity" (March 2010), http://barcelona.degrowth.org/; Montreal: "International Conference on Degrowth in the Americas" (May 2012), http://montreal.degrowth.org/; Vienna: "Growth in Transition" (January 2010), http://www.growthintransition.eu/engagement/conference/; and Leeds: "The Steady State Economy Conference: Working towards an Alternative to Economic Growth" (June 2010), http://steadystate.org/leeds2010/ (all conference webpages accessed January 30, 2012).

23. Research & Degrowth, "Degrowth Declaration of the Paris 2008 Conference" (cited in chap. 4, n. 26).

24. Brian Czech, "The Foundation of a New Conservation Movement: Professional Society Positions on Economic Growth," *BioScience* 57, no. 1 (2007): 6.

25. Inge Røpke, "Trends in the Development of Ecological Economics from the Late 1980s to the Early 2000s," *Ecological Economics* 55, no. 2 (2005): 262–290.

26. Roger Lowenstein, "Occupy Wall Street: It's Not a Hippie Thing," *Bloomberg Businessweek*, October 27, 2011, http://www.businessweek.com/magazine/occupy-wall-street-its-not-a-hippie-thing-10272011.html (accessed February 18, 2012).

CHAPTER 14: ENOUGH UNILATERALISM

1. Schumacher, *A Guide for the Perplexed* (cited in chap. 1, n. 1), 1.

2. Tom Boden, Gregg Marland, and Bob Andres, "Fossil-Fuel CO_2 Emissions" (Carbon Dioxide Information Analysis Center, Oak Ridge National Laboratory), http://cdiac.ornl.gov/trends/emis/meth_reg.html (accessed January 14, 2012).

3. World Coal Association, "Uses of Coal" (2012), http://www.worldcoal.org/coal/uses-of-coal/ (accessed January 14, 2012).

4. H.L. Wesseling, *Divide and Rule: The Partition of Africa, 1880–1914*, translated by Arnold Pomerans (Westport, Conn.: Praeger Publishers, 1996), 113–114.

5. M.E. Chamberlain, *The Scramble for Africa* (London: Longman Group, 1974), 55.

6. Wesseling, *Divide and Rule*, 114–115.

7. Chamberlain, *The Scramble for Africa*, 99.

8. For Harvard and Vanderbilt, see John Vidal and Claire Provost, "US Universities in Africa 'Land Grab,'" *The Guardian*, June 8, 2011, http://www.guardian.co.uk/world/2011/jun/08/us-universities-africa-land-grab (accessed January 11, 2012); for Saudi Arabia, Daewoo, and Britain, see John Vidal, "How Food and Water Are Driving a 21st-Century African Land Grab," *The Observer*, March 6, 2010, http://www.guardian.co.uk/environment/2010/mar/07/food-water-africa-land-grab (accessed January 11, 2012); and for Chinese businesses, see Jin Zhu, "China, Africa Forge Farming Ties," *China Daily*, August 12, 2010, http://www.chinadaily.com.cn/china/2010-08/12/content_11141295.htm (accessed January 11, 2012).

9. "Buying Farmland Abroad: Outsourcing's Third Wave," *The Economist*, May 21, 2009, http://www.economist.com/node/13692889 (accessed January 11, 2012).

10. Vidal and Provost, "US Universities in Africa 'Land Grab.'"

11. Shepard Daniel and Anuradha Mittal, *The Great Land Grab: Rush for the World's Farmland Threatens Food Security for the Poor* (Oakland, Calif.: The Oakland Institute, 2009).

12. Angus Maddison, *The World Economy: Historical Statistics* (Paris: Development Centre of the OECD, 2003).

13. Assadourian, "The Rise and Fall of Consumer Cultures" (cited in chap. 3, n. 5).

14. United Nations Development Programme, *Human Development Report 2007/2008: Fighting Climate Change: Human Solidarity in a Divided World* (New York: Palgrave Macmillan, 2007), 25, http://hdr.undp.org/en/reports/global/hdr2007-8/ (accessed November 30, 2011).

15. Simon Kuznets, "Economic Growth and Income Inequality," *American Economic Review* 45, no. 1 (March 1955): 1–28.

16. Amy Richmond and Eric Zencey, "Environmental Kuznets Curve," in *Encyclopedia of Earth*, edited by Cutler Cleveland (Washington, D.C.: National Council for Science and the Environment, 2006), http://www.eoearth.org/article/Environmental _kuznets_curve (accessed August 25, 2010).

17. Ha Joon Chang, *Kicking Away the Ladder: Development Strategy in Historical Perspective* (London: Anthem Press, 2002); Graham Dunkley, *Free Trade: Myth, Reality and Alternatives* (London: Zed Books, 2004); David Stern, "The Rise and Fall of the Environmental Kuznets Curve," *World Development* 32, no. 8 (2004): 1419–1439; and Julianne Mills and Thomas Waite, "Economic Prosperity, Biodiversity Conservation, and the Environmental Kuznets Curve," *Ecological Economics* 68 (2009): 2087–2095.

18. Ha Joon Chang, "Hamlet without the Prince of Denmark: How Development Has Disappeared from Today's Development Discourse," in *Towards New Developmentalism: Market as Means Rather than Master*, edited by Shahrukh Rafi Khan and Jens Christiansen, 47–58 (Abingdon, Canada: Routledge, 2010).

19. Marco Sakai, "Workshop 10: Global Issues" (Steady State Economy Conference, Leeds, U.K., June 19, 2010), http://steadystate.org/wp-content/uploads/WS10_ Proposal_GlobalIssues.pdf (accessed October 3, 2011).

20. Charles Wheelan, *Naked Economics: Undressing the Dismal Science* (New York: W. W. Norton, 2010), 4.

21. Nick Squires, "Tuna Fishing Ban for South Pacific Zones," *The Telegraph*, May 30, 2008, http://www.telegraph.co.uk/earth/earthnews/3343197/Tuna-fishing-ban -for-South-Pacific-zones.html (accessed January 16, 2012).

22. Andrew Simms, Dan Moran, and Peter Chowla, *The UK Interdependence Report: How the World Sustains the Nation's Lifestyles and the Price It Pays* (London: New Economics Foundation, 2006).

23. Pinelopi Goldberg and Nina Pavcnik, "Trade, Inequality, and Poverty: What Do We Know? Evidence from Recent Trade Liberalization Episodes in Developing Countries," in *Globalization, Poverty, and Inequality*, edited by Carol Graham and Susan Collins, 223–269 (Washington, D.C.: Brookings Institution Press, 2004).

24. Massoud Karshenas, *The Impact of the Global Financial and Economic Crisis on LDC Economies* (New York: United Nations–OHRLLS, 2009), http://eprints.soas.ac .uk/8021/1/Financial_crisis_and_LDCs.pdf (accessed June 14, 2010).

25. United Nations, *The Millennium Development Goals Report 2009* (New York: United Nations), http://www.endpoverty2015.org/files/MDG%20Report%202009%20 ENG%2014-06-23.pdf (accessed June 13, 2010).

26. O'Neill, "Measuring Progress in the Degrowth Transition to a Steady State Economy" (cited in chap. 9, n. 17).
27. Ibid.
28. Booth, "The Macroeconomics of a Steady State" (cited in chap. 11, n. 21).
29. United Nations Environment Programme, *Organic Agriculture and Food Security in Africa* (New York: United Nations, 2008), http://www.unctad.org/en/docs/ditcted200715_en.pdf (accessed January 21, 2012).
30. Ibid.
31. Sakai, "Workshop 10: Global Issues."
32. Ibid.
33. Peter Victor and Gideon Rosenbluth, "Managing without Growth," *Ecological Economics* 61 (2007): 492–504.
34. Sakai, "Workshop 10: Global Issues."
35. United Nations Development Programme, *Human Development Report 2005: International Cooperation at a Crossroads: Aid, Trade and Security in an Unequal World* (New York: United Nations Development Programme, 2005), http://hdr.undp.org/en/reports/global/hdr2005/ (accessed June 14, 2010).
36. Adam Smith, *An Inquiry into the Nature and Causes of the Wealth of Nations* (1776; London: T. Nelson and Sons, 1865); and Leopold Kohr, *The Breakdown of Nations* (1957; New York: E.P. Dutton, 1978).
37. Smith, *An Inquiry into the Nature and Causes of the Wealth of Nations*, 231.
38. Kohr, *The Breakdown of Nations*, 82.

CHAPTER 15: ENOUGH WAITING

1. Paul Hawken, "Commencement: Healing or Stealing" (University of Portland, May 3, 2009), http://www.up.edu/commencement/default.aspx?cid=9456 (accessed February 20, 2012).
2. Daly, *Steady-State Economics* (cited in chap. 4, n. 1), 17.
3. Herman Daly, "A Steady-State Economy: A Failed Growth Economy and a Steady-State Economy Are Not the Same Thing; They Are the Very Different Alternatives We Face" (U.K. Sustainable Development Commission, London, April 24, 2008), 2, http://www.sd-commission.org.uk/publications.php?id=775 (accessed October 12, 2011).
4. Victor, *Managing without Growth*, 181 (cited in chap. 3, n. 14).
5. Joseph Spengler, "Adam Smith on Population Growth and Economic Development," *Population and Development Review* 2, no. 2 (June 1976): 167–180.
6. John Stuart Mill, *Principles of Political Economy with Some of Their Applications to Social Philosophy*, rev. ed., vol. 2 (New York: P.F. Collier & Son, 1900), 264.
7. John Maynard Keynes, "Economic Possibilities for Our Grandchildren," in Keynes, *Essays in Persuasion* (New York: Harcourt, Brace and Company, 1932), 371–372.
8. De Villiers, *Our Way Out* (cited in chap. 6, n. 19), 7–8.
9. Henry David Thoreau, *The Quotable Thoreau*, edited by Jeffrey S. Cramer (Princeton, N.J.: Princeton University Press, 2011), 466.
10. McKibben, *Deep Economy* (cited in chap. 8, n. 1), 1.

ACKNOWLEDGMENTS

We could not have written *Enough Is Enough* without the support and contributions of many wonderful people. In particular, we would like to thank everyone who was involved in the organization and running of the Steady State Economy Conference. We are grateful to David Adshead, Lorna Arblaster, Claire Bastin, and Nigel Jones, who undertook the challenge of organizing the conference, and who were instrumental in drafting the conference report. Very special thanks also go to the conference's speakers and proposal writers, who provided many of the ideas described in this book. We thank Saamah Abdallah, Blake Alcott, Franny Armstrong, Molly Scott Cato, Ian Christie, David Fell, Tim Jackson, Victoria Johnson, Roger Martin, Mary Mellor, Kate Pickett, Martin Pullinger, André Reichel, Marco Sakai, Andrew Simms, and Peter Victor for their inspired contributions. And of course we would also like to thank the conference's numerous facilitators, rapporteurs, and attendees, who contributed considerable expertise that we have tried our best to incorporate. The conference was made possible by a generous contribution from an anonymous donor and sponsorship from the Ecology Building Society.

Rob would like to thank Jen Yang for offering love, support, and logistical help throughout the writing process, which she did with grace, despite all the complaints she endured. Skya Dietz provided a major motivation for writing this book—her generation will face the profound environmental and economic challenges described in these pages.

Dan would like to thank his housemates (past and present) for accommodating endless hours of writing in the dining room, and his parents (Nancy and Michael O'Neill) for their love and support. A special thank you also goes to Mireia Pecurul and John Davis for their friendship, advice, and many late-night discussions.

It's unusual to think of an economist as a hero, but this is how we see Herman Daly. His lifelong effort to develop the concept of a steady-state economy inspired us to write this book and to promote the goal of a sustainable and fair economy. Brian Czech (the founder of the Center for the Advancement of the Steady State Economy) provided encouragement for this project, and set the example of persistence needed to see such a project through to the end.

We would also like to thank Polyp for his cartoons, which provide much-needed art and humor throughout the book (see polyp.org.uk for many more). We are grateful to Dave Abson, Tim Foxon, Austin Bruce Hallock, and Jessica Osorio for reading the manuscript and for providing keen editorial advice that helped us say what we wanted to say more clearly. We also thank Aashish Khullar for helping with the early research.

Publishing a book, especially for the first time, can be a trying process. We are grateful to everyone who offered advice on how to navigate the publishing world, and we want to recognize Neal Maillet and his colleagues at Berrett-Koehler for their spirit of collaboration, for shepherding our book through to completion, and for believing in us and our ideas. Finally, we thank all of our family members, friends, and colleagues who have supported our efforts over the years to explore and promote the idea of a steady-state economy.

ROB DIETZ, *Corvallis, Oregon, United States*
DAN O'NEILL, *Leeds, United Kingdom*

INDEX

Page numbers in **bold** indicate figures or tables.

Tanzania, 187–188
taxation: and community interest
companies (CICs), 150; economic
equality achieved by, 93–94, 95; as
throughput-limiting strategy, 66;
and reform of business, 152; and
restructuring of financial institutions, 110
technology: and limits to growth,
36–40; transfer of, 189
Thoreau, Henry David, 139, 205
throughput, economic, 45, 59–70;
limitation of, 63–70, 143, 197, 198
Tocqueville, Alexis de, 87
Toyota, 142, **144**
trade. *See* international trade
Transition Towns, 163, 165
tuna fishing, 183

Uganda, 79, **80**
unemployment, 48, **48**, 49, **49**, 50,
50, 129, 136, 143
United Kingdom: CO$_2$ emissions in,
39; cooperatives in, 95, 148, 149;
economic inequality in, 89, **89**;
fertility rate in, **80**; gross domestic
product (GDP) ranking of, 120,
144; happiness indicators in, **26**,
115, 117, **121**; homelessness in,
148; immigration policy in, 82;
local currency in, 108; material
use in, 39; money supply in, 102,
102, 103; population density of,
75, **76**; population growth in, 74,
81–82; progress indicators in, 120;
work-time reduction in, 132
United Nations: democratization
of, 188–189; happiness indicators
sought by, 115; Human Poverty
Index of, 48; impact of financial
crisis reported by, 184; Millennium Development Goals of,
182; Monetary and Financial
Conference of, 109; population
growth estimates of, 75, **75**; Sys-

tem of Environmental-Economic
Accounts (SEEA) of, 69
United States: banking policy in,
103; coal used in, 179; and dollar's role in international finance,
108–109; economic inequality in,
88–89, **89**, 93; fertility rate in, **80**;
greenhouse gases emitted in, 179;
gross domestic product (GDP) in,
118, **119**, 120, **144**; happiness indicators in, **121**; household throughput in, 60–61; immigration policy
in, 82–83; overconsumption in, 60;
paid vacation time in, 132; population growth in, 74, 75, 76–77, 159;
progress indicators in, 118–119,
119; public debt in, ix; self-storage
units in, 60–61; working hours in,
133
Universal Declaration of Human
Rights, 134
Ura, Dasho Karma, 115

Venezuela, 142, **144**
Vermont, 93
Victor, Peter, 37, 47–50, **48**, **49**, **50**,
53, 54, 129, 199
Vietnam, 120, **121**, **145**

Wallich, Henry, 91–92
Walmart, 94, 142, **144**
Walton brothers, 94
wealth: accumulation of, 94, 100,
189–190; fair distribution of, 46;
redistribution of, 26–27, 78, 91, 94
Wharton School of Business, 43–44
Wheelan, Charles, 183
Wilkinson, Richard, 28, 90, 92
women: education of, 80–81;
empowerment of, 80–81, 95
work. *See* employment
World War II, 190
Wren, Deb, 127–129, 130, 137

Zencey, Eric, 169

ABOUT THE AUTHORS

ROB DIETZ unwittingly discovered the recipe for understanding the limits to growth.

Start with a suspicion that there's something rotten at the core of consumer culture. Simmer that suspicion in four years of formal education in environmental science. Add a bachelor degree's worth of study in economics, and stir in just a dash of doubt about the validity of the mainstream economic viewpoint.

Set aside those initial ingredients for the time being, and get to work combining a series of career moves. Begin with several years as an economic analyst at consulting firms in Washington, D.C., culminating in an overwhelming desire to get back to the basics of science. Add in a graduate degree in environmental science and engineering, including studies in geography and biology. Stir vigorously with a governmental stint (starting as a Presidential Management Fellow) at the U.S. Fish and Wildlife Service and U.S. Geological Survey. While stirring, be sure to add plenty of influential readings from authors like David Orr, Donella Meadows, and Herman Daly. Don't forget to sprinkle in facts about species extinctions, climate change, and other environmental calamities as documented in countless articles from peer-reviewed scientific journals. Slow-cook all these ingredients in one brain, especially a brain that craves a strong balance between work and play, and you'll see why the pursuit of infinite economic growth on a finite planet is a bad idea.

What to do once you've followed such a recipe? Rob's first response was to freak out. He got a little grouchy. Then he got a lot sarcastic. Then when people stopped wanting to be around him, he took some more constructive steps.

First, he took a couple of deep breaths. Then, with his wife and young daughter, he moved to an aspiring ecovillage in Corvallis, Oregon. The idea was to try to live the good life in a community that strives to leave light footprints. Next, he became the first executive director of the Center for the Advancement of the Steady State Economy, a nonprofit organization that promotes a prosperous, yet nongrowing economy. He served in that role for four years, before taking a crack at making it as a writer. *Enough Is Enough* is his first book.

Author photo: Phil Faulks

DAN O'NEILL has always been interested in the "big picture." He spent his childhood exploring the wide-open spaces of western Canada, often gazing up at the night sky and dreaming of becoming an astronomer. As an undergraduate student at the University of Victoria, he pursued a big-picture path, earning a degree in physics and receiving the Jubilee Medal for Science. While designing systems for large companies to manage their energy use, he felt the pull of another expansive topic—the state of the environment. It drew him across the country to Halifax, Nova Scotia, where he earned a master's degree in environmental studies from Dalhousie University. There, he took a course in ecological economics that dramatically changed his perspective. He realized that many of the toughest environmental and social problems facing humanity have a common cause—our economic system and its pursuit of growth at all costs.

After completing his master's degree, Dan moved back to Victoria and worked as a planning analyst for the Capital Regional District. His main responsibility was measuring the city's progress toward the goals of its Regional Growth Strategy.

Although the Growth Strategy achieved many benefits, Dan sensed the need for an entirely different economic model to reconcile the conflicts among economic, social, and environmental objectives. Consequently, he moved to England to begin doctoral studies in ecological economics at the University of Leeds. While on a plane over the Atlantic, he read Herman Daly's book *Steady-State Economics*, which turned his world upside down. He realized that a steady-state economy was the economic model of the future, but more research was needed to make it work in practice.

Since finishing his doctoral studies and writing this book, Dan has taken a position as lecturer in ecological economics at the University of Leeds, and chief economist at the Center for the Advancement of the Steady State Economy. His research continues to focus on the changes needed to achieve a successful nongrowing economy. Toward this end, he has designed a new system of national accounts to measure how close specific economies are to a steady-state economy, and what proximity to this goal means for their social performance. When he isn't involved in research or teaching, Dan enjoys hiking in the Yorkshire Dales and singing songs about the misguided pursuit of economic growth.

Berrett–Koehler
Publishers

Berrett-Koehler is an independent publisher dedicated to an ambitious mission: *Creating a World That Works for All*.

We believe that to truly create a better world, action is needed at all levels—individual, organizational, and societal. At the individual level, our publications help people align their lives with their values and with their aspirations for a better world. At the organizational level, our publications promote progressive leadership and management practices, socially responsible approaches to business, and humane and effective organizations. At the societal level, our publications advance social and economic justice, shared prosperity, sustainability, and new solutions to national and global issues.

A major theme of our publications is "Opening Up New Space." Berrett-Koehler titles challenge conventional thinking, introduce new ideas, and foster positive change. Their common quest is changing the underlying beliefs, mindsets, institutions, and structures that keep generating the same cycles of problems, no matter who our leaders are or what improvement programs we adopt.

We strive to practice what we preach—to operate our publishing company in line with the ideas in our books. At the core of our approach is stewardship, which we define as a deep sense of responsibility to administer the company for the benefit of all of our "stakeholder" groups: authors, customers, employees, investors, service providers, and the communities and environment around us.

We are grateful to the thousands of readers, authors, and other friends of the company who consider themselves to be part of the "BK Community." We hope that you, too, will join us in our mission.

A BK Currents Book

This book is part of our BK Currents series. BK Currents books advance social and economic justice by exploring the critical intersections between business and society. Offering a unique combination of thoughtful analysis and progressive alternatives, BK Currents books promote positive change at the national and global levels. To find out more, visit **www.bkconnection .com**.

Berrett–Koehler
Publishers

A community dedicated to creating
a world that works for all

Visit Our Website: www.bkconnection.com

Read book excerpts, see author videos and Internet movies, read our
authors' blogs, join discussion groups, download book apps, find out about
the BK Affiliate Network, browse subject-area libraries of books, get special
discounts, and more!

Subscribe to Our Free E-Newsletter, the *BK Communiqué*

Be the first to hear about new publications, special discount offers, exclu-
sive articles, news about bestsellers, and more! Get on the list for our free
e-newsletter by going to **www.bkconnection.com**.

Get Quantity Discounts

Berrett-Koehler books are available at quantity discounts for orders of ten or
more copies. Please call us toll-free at (800) 929-2929 or email us at **bkp
.orders@aidcvt.com**.

Join the BK Community

BKcommunity.com is a virtual meeting place where people from around
the world can engage with kindred spirits to create a world that works for
all. **BKcommunity.com** members may create their own profiles, blog, start
and participate in forums and discussion groups, post photos and videos,
answer surveys, announce and register for upcoming events, and chat with
others online in real time. Please join the conversation!